DAVID FELLMAN
Vilas Professor of Political Science
University of Wisconsin
ADVISORY EDITOR TO DODD, MEAD & COMPANY

THE DEVELOPING NATIONS:
What Path to Modernization?

THE DEVELOPING NATIONS:
WHAT PATH TO MODERNIZATION?

Readings Selected and Edited by

FRANK TACHAU
University of Illinois at Chicago Circle

Dodd, Mead & Company
NEW YORK   1972   TORONTO

ACKNOWLEDGMENTS

1. From *Economic Development: Past and Present*, 2nd ed., by Richard T. Gill.
© 1967. Reprinted by permission of Prentice-Hall, Inc., Englewood Cliffs, New Jersey.
2. From *The Dynamics of Modernization* by C. E. Black. Copyright © by C. E.
Black. Reprinted by permission of Harper & Row, Publishers, New York.
3. From *The Modernity of Tradition: Political Development in India* by L. I.
Rudolph and S. H. Rudolph. Copyright © 1967 by the University of Chicago Press.
Reprinted by permission of the authors and publisher.
4. Abridged from *Three Worlds of Development* by Irving Louis Horowitz. Copyright © 1966 by Irving Louis Horowitz. Reprinted by permission of Oxford University Press, Inc. Footnotes have been omitted.
5. From "Political Integration and Political Development" by Myron Weiner in
New Nations: The Problem of Political Development edited by Karl von Vorys. *The
Annals of the American Academy of Political and Social Science*, Vol. 358 (March
1965). Copyright © 1965. Reprinted by permission of the publisher and author. Most
footnotes have been omitted.
6. From *From Empire to Nation* by Rupert Emerson. Harvard University Press,
Cambridge, Massachusetts. Copyright 1960 by the President and Fellows of Harvard
College and reprinted by permission of the publishers. Footnotes have been omitted.
7. From *Communications and Political Development* edited by Lucian W. Pye for
Social Science Research Council. Copyright © 1963 by the Princeton University
Press. Reprinted by permission of the publisher. Most footnotes have been omitted.
8. From *Education and Political Development* edited by James S. Coleman for
Social Science Research Council. Copyright © 1965 by Princeton University Press.
Reprinted by permission of the publisher. Most footnotes have been omitted.
9. From "Non-Western Intelligentsias as Political Elites" by H. J. Benda. *The
Australian Journal of Politics and History*, Vol. VI, No. 2 (November 1960). Reprinted
by permission of the author and publisher.
10. From "Bureaucrats and Political Development: A Paradoxical View" by Fred
W. Riggs in *Bureaucracy and Political Development* edited by J. LaPalombara for
Social Science Research Council. Copyright © 1963 by Princeton University Press.
Reprinted by permission of the publisher. Footnotes have been omitted.
11. From *The Politics of Social Change in the Middle East and North Africa* by
Manfred Halpern. Copyright © 1963 by the RAND Corporation. Published by
Princeton University Press. Reprinted by permission of the publisher. Most footnotes
have been omitted.
12. From the Kapadia Memorial volume. Reprinted by permission of Wolfram
Eberhard. Most footnotes have been omitted.
13. Abridged from *The Springtime of Freedom* by William McCord. Copyright ©

1965 by Oxford University Press, Inc. Reprinted by permission of the publisher. Footnotes have been omitted.

14. From *The Challenge of Modernisation* by I. R. Sinai. Copyright © 1964 by I. R. Sinai. Reprinted by permission of W. W. Norton & Company, Inc.

15. Excerpts from two pieces by John H. Kautsky originally published in 1962 and reprinted from his *Communism and the Politics of Development*. Copyright © 1968 by John Wiley and Sons. Reprinted by permission of the publisher. Most footnotes have been omitted.

16. From "Government in the Developing Countries" by Richard Lowenthal in *Democracy in a Changing Society* edited by Henry W. Ehrmann. Copyright © 1964 by Frederick A. Praeger, Inc. Reprinted by permission of the publisher. Footnotes have been omitted.

17. "Democratic Collectivism" from *The Discovery of India* by Jawaharlal Nehru. Copyright © 1946 by The John Day Company, Inc. Reprinted by permission of the publisher. "Indian Socialism" from *Towards a Socialistic State*. All-India Congress Committee, New Delhi, 1956; this text taken from Paul Sigmund, ed., *The Ideologies of the Developing Nations*, revised edition. Frederick A. Praeger, Inc., publishers, 1968.

18. From a pamphlet published by *The Tanganyika Standard*, Dar-es-Salaam, 1962. This text taken from Paul Sigmund, ed., *The Ideologies of the Developing Nations*, revised edition. Frederick A. Praeger, Inc., publishers, 1968.

19. From an article published in Chinese newspapers on September 3, 1965. This text taken from Paul Sigmund, ed., *The Ideologies of the Developing Nations*, revised edition. Frederick A. Praeger, Inc., publishers, 1968.

20. Translated from the French by Constance Farrington. Copyright © 1963 by Presence Africaine. Reprinted by permission of Grove Press, Inc. Footnotes have been omitted.

21. From "How One Pleasant, Scholarly Young Man from Brazil Became a Kidnapping, Gun-Toting, Bombing Revolutionary," *The New York Times Magazine*, November 15, 1970. © 1970 by The New York Times Company. Reprinted by permission.

22. From "Counterrevolutionary America" by Robert Heilbroner. *Commentary*, April 1967. Copyright © 1967 by the American Jewish Committee. Reprinted by permission of *Commentary* and the author.

23. From "A Redefinition of the Revolutionary Situation" by Manfred Halpern in *National Liberation* edited by Norman Miller and Roderick Aya. Copyright © 1971 The Free Press, a Division of the Macmillan Company, and used by permission of the publisher. Most footnotes have been omitted.

IN MEMORY OF MY FATHER
Who suffered much from politics

FOR MY CHILDREN
In the hope that they may
benefit from modernization

Preface

THIS anthology is the product of some years of teaching, reading, and discussion about the politics of developing nations. It reflects the conviction that the problems of these societies are part and parcel of a widely ramified intellectual, moral, social, and political crisis. As with many crises, there are grounds both for hope and despair: hope that a recognition of the sources of the crisis may enable us to preserve the essential values of civilization; despair that the insecurity, frustration, hatred, and disorder produced by the crisis may destroy that civilization. Careful study of the politics of the developing nations and their relations with the wealthier states of the world, especially the United States, can contribute to a favorable outcome.

At the risk of presumptuousness, I should like to record here the personal and intellectual indebtedness that was incurred in the preparation of this volume. Students at both Rutgers University and the University of Illinois at Chicago Circle are probably unaware of their contribution, not only through stimulating specific questions, but in general through their challenge to present ideas clearly and concisely. Faculty colleagues at both institutions have similarly greatly stimulated my thinking—particularly Gerald Pomper and Gordon Schochet of Rutgers University, Joseph Haberer now of Purdue University, and Dick W. Simpson, George D. Beam, Doris A. Graber, and Kaye Miller of the University of Illinois at Chicago Circle. Professor Neal Riemer of the University of Wisconsin–Milwaukee initially suggested the preparation of this anthology and critically commented on an early version. Manfred Halpern made extremely helpful and insightful comments. Last, but hardly least, my family may be surprised to learn how much their stoic sufferance of the erratic schedule dictated by such a venture is appreciated.

FRANK TACHAU

Contents

INTRODUCTION

HISTORIANS a century or two from now may well characterize our time as the age of emergent world civilization. For one of the distinguishing features of this age has been the breakdown of barriers of physical isolation which insulated the great societies of the past from one another. A profound result of this breakdown has been the rising demand of ordinary people everywhere for a say in the decisions which affect their individual lives. In the process, time-honored traditions have been undermined. The search for new institutions and values has been marked by grave social and political instability. The effects have been especially dramatic and revolutionary among the peoples of Asia, Africa, and Latin America. They are undergoing what Robert L. Heilbroner calls the "Great Ascent." In his words, it is "a process through which the social, political, and economic institutions of the future are being shaped for the great majority of mankind. On the outcome of this enormous act will depend the character of the civilization of the world for many generations to come, not only in the poor and struggling nations, but in the rich and privileged ones as well. Whatever the outcome of the Cold War—indeed, whatever the outcome of a Hot War—more and more will civilization, or what is left of it, reflect the emergent societies of the newly incorporated parts of the world." [1]

If Heilbroner is correct, then close study of the basic forces at work in these "newly incorporated parts of the world" becomes vitally necessary. This study may be approached in two ways. On the one hand, understanding may be sought through analysis of basic social, economic, and political processes and their interaction in the developing nations. A second approach focuses on the impact of these processes on the world community.

In this collection of readings, we attempt to combine these two approaches, which are interrelated. The instability and crisis that has

[1] Robert L. Heilbroner, *The Great Ascent: The Struggle for Economic Development in Our Time* (New York: Harper and Row, 1963), p. 10.

1

characterized the developing nations has already threatened on occasion to engulf the world, as illustrated by the Indochina conflict and the Arab-Israeli dispute. It is policy-makers who are chiefly responsible for managing such crises. Unless they have a clear understanding, however, of the fundamental social and political factors underlying the upheavals with which they must deal, their task will be a hopeless one—like King Canute commanding the sea to retreat.

A basic theme of this reader is that such understanding is to be found in the concept of *modernization*. Modernization refers to the series of economic, social, and political changes which began in Europe toward the end of the Middle Ages, and which have continued with accelerating speed until our own day. Not only has the speed of change accelerated, but the arena within which the changes have occurred has expanded to a global stage. There is no continent, and hardly any sizable community of men anywhere that has not been affected in some way by the winds of change.

What is modernization? We may define this concept by positing two abstract models, one of traditional society, the other of modern society. Modernization is the process of change—transition—from one model to the other. Neither of the models is an accurate image of the real world; they are abstractions drawn from elements of reality in order to enhance understanding.

The model of traditional society is one in which the economy is generally based on production for subsistence and exchange by barter. The dominant world view emphasizes man's subjection to supernatural forces beyond his control, and these are often thought to include the political authorities which govern the society. The social structure is "marked by inequalities based on kinship ties, hereditary privileges and established (frequently monarchical) authority." [2] The focus of identification for the bulk of the population is at the level of the local community, whether it be rural village, town, or city. Except for religious ritual and belief, contact with broader political and cultural institutions tends to be peripheral and spasmodic. As indicated, religion and politics overlap, with the authorities viewed as distant, exalted, and beyond the control of the individual.

Modern society, by contrast, is a mass society. Cash, commercial credit, advanced technology, and specialized production underlie an extensive market economy based on mass production and consumption. Mass media of communication and universal public education help to instill a common set of values, a common ideology, and common aspirations among all groups in the society. Mass transportation enables individuals to become

---

[2] Reinhard Bendix, "Tradition and Modernity Reconsidered," *Comparative Studies in Society and History*, IX, No. 3 (April 1967), 293.

mobile in the physical as well as the psychic sense, and thus to associate with members of social groups who might be culturally alien and physically far removed. Election of government officials means mass participation in the political system, whether there are actually meaningful choices among alternate sets of leaders or merely plebiscites which legitimize the rule of those already in power. In sum, modern society is geographically extensive—often of continental proportions—possessed of a large and diverse population, but highly integrated in terms of values and communications. The bulk of the population identifies closely with the symbols of political authority. Governments impinge visibly on the lives of the members of the society; governments demand and usually receive overt signs of active support and allegiance from the bulk of the population. Finally, the predominant world view is secular and rationalist; natural and social forces are typically viewed as subject to purposeful human control.

As we have indicated, modernization refers to the transition of societies from the traditional to the modern model. It is a transition which is profound and extensive; no aspect of the life of individuals or the society is unaffected. In the words of a prominent sociologist, this transition amounts to a "transformation . . . [which] is comparable in magnitude only to the transformation of nomadic peoples into settled agriculturalists some 10,000 years earlier." [3]

It is relatively easy to say what modernization is, but it is not so easy to explain why it has followed a certain course in the past, nor what course it is likely to take in the future. This point becomes painfully evident when we turn from the modernization of Europe to modernization in other parts of the world. Modernization in Europe occurred earliest and has continued for over five hundred years, with perhaps the most dramatic developments occurring in the late eighteenth and nineteenth centuries. Modernization in other parts of the world, however, began only in the twentieth century. In retrospect, modernization in Europe proceeded relatively slowly and smoothly, while modernization elsewhere has developed rapidly and unevenly, resulting in severe social and cultural dislocation as well as violence. Modernization in Europe, because it occurred there first, took place without the benefits or disadvantages of an alien model to emulate or to compete against. Above all, European modernization produced the greatest concentration of economic and political power in history. Through colonial expansion, this power eventually penetrated the farthest reaches of the earth. In fact, the encroachment of European power triggered the process of modernization in most non-European countries, with many leaders of these countries seeking to adopt modernization as a means of fending off European power. In

[3] *Ibid.*, p. 292.

short, while the essence of the process of modernization may be the same everywhere, the precise course which it runs in any given culture, or the precise effects it has on any given society are bound to be quite different. Modernization has developed furthest in Europe and North America and has resulted in the most complex, powerful, and prosperous societies in history. As a result, many writers have been misled into universalizing the specific European experiences. This has been particularly true of some American observers. They have tended to see the ideal model of modern social and political systems in terms of the pluralistic society; the two-party or multiparty competitive political system; government of separated functions, if not powers; and an economic system that is relatively decentralized and relatively competitive.[4] This tendency is based on a static and undifferentiated conception of traditional society on the one hand, and the assumption of a wide gap—amounting to a dichotomy—between tradition on the one hand and modernity on the other, a tendency enhanced by the abstract models described above. The two are assumed to be mirror images of one another. Thus, while traditional society is permeated by sacral values, modern society is secular. Traditional society is dominated by primary associations and groups, modern society by secondary associations. Traditional society embodies an economy based on barter and subsistence; modern society employs cash, commercial credit, and specialized and surplus production. Traditional society is hierarchical, elitist, authoritarian, and parochial; modern society is equalitarian, democratic, and national.

Reinhard Bendix has suggested that this tendency to portray tradition and modernity as opposite numbers is due to the sudden and dramatic impact of the Industrial Revolution and the French Revolution. The result is that most nineteenth-century writers ". . . exhibit the same burning sense of society's sudden, convulsive turn from a path it had followed for millennia. All manifest the same profound intuition of the disappearance of historic values—and, with them, age-old securities, as well as age-old tyrannies and inequalities and the coming of new powers, new insecurities, and new tyrannies. . . ."[5]

And, we might add, if the transition from tradition to modernity seemed sudden and convulsive in the European context, how much more

---

[4] Even Gabriel Almond, one of the leading theorists in this general area, inadvertently revealed his ethnocentrism in one of his early statements on the general nature of political systems. His listing of the functions of political systems amounted to a generalized model of the American system. See his introduction to *The Politics of the Developing Areas* (Princeton, N.J.: Princeton University Press, 1960). S. M. Lipset also tends to portray developed political and social systems in terms of the American model.

[5] Carlo M. Cipolla, *The Economic History of World Population* (Baltimore: Penguin Books, 1964), pp. 24–28; quoted by Bendix, *op. cit.* (above, n. 2), p. 293.

disruptive of the values, securities, and institutions of ancient Asian and African cultures did the impact of modernization on those societies seem. The dichotomous conception outlined here is not necessarily wrong or inaccurate. Its use of a static and undifferentiated model of tradition, and a uniform model of modernity, is, however, misleading. The crucial point is that we must extrapolate from the process of social change that which is universal as opposed to that which is the particular product of a specific historical tradition and social system. We cannot expect the societies of Asia, Africa, and Latin America to emerge from the process of modernization as undistinguished models of the contemporary societies of the United States or Western Europe—or for that matter of the Soviet Union. Indeed, insofar as modernization involves the institutionalization of continuing rapid social change, the contemporary societies of the developed nations may themselves undergo radical alterations in the immediate future.

In short, the process of modernization is exceedingly complex. The selections included in this reader have been chosen with a view not only to underline this complexity, but also to suggest the uncertainties inherent in attempts to generalize from the evidence at hand. It is hoped that a reading of this volume will dispel some of the many misconceptions that prevail. In particular, the following may be mentioned:

1. *Traditional societies are rigidly static, steeped in ignorance, and bound to disappear.* By comparison with modern societies, traditional societies change slowly, leading to the misconception that they do not change at all. Because men tend to prefer the familiar to the unknown, they clothe traditional institutions and values in garments of authority and moral sanction. Moreover, as L. I. and S. H. Rudolph point out in the selection reprinted below, change itself is often either deliberately or unconsciously made to appear as part of an unchanging tradition, in order to render it more easily acceptable.

Seen from the perspective of modern science and secular rationalism, the prevalence of devout belief in traditional societies—often mixed with superstition—and the relatively limited scope or minimal character of literary tradition, often creates the impression of benighted illiteracy and ignorance. This impression overlooks the importance of functional intelligence. Innumerable anecdotes illustrate the case of the foreign-aid adviser in an underdeveloped rural village who ridicules some superstition of the local villagers which is hostile to a particular scientific innovation which he seeks to introduce. These anecdotes invariably conclude with the discomfiture of the foreign adviser upon discovering that the hoary superstition of the villagers does, in fact, have a solid empirical base which renders his rational innovation useless or at best ineffective.

Similarly, there is a tendency to predict the displacement of traditional elites by new groups performing modern functions and espousing modern ideas. This misconception overlooks the adaptability of individuals and groups. The selection by Wolfram Eberhard illustrates how traditional tribal leaders may actually solidify their elite status by means of manipulating modern institutions and laws to their benefit. This case could be multiplied with other examples from elsewhere in the Middle East, as well as parts of Africa. Such evidence suggests that the process of modernization is not necessarily either inevitable or unilinear, and that traditional groups, institutions, and values cannot be written off as merely the dead hand of the past.

2. *Modernity is an improvement over tradition and therefore much to be preferred.* Improvement in the material standard of living is perhaps the most visible aspect of modernity. But modernization does not guarantee happiness. Indeed, the impersonality and anonymity of much of modern life may even produce unhappiness. It is thus an error to assume that the potential which modernity offers mankind will necessarily be fulfilled.

The opposite notion—that traditional values and institutions embody the wisdom of the ages and are thus preferable to their modern counterparts—is also mistaken. The typical member of a traditional society may indeed be happier and better adjusted than the average citizen of a modernized country. But this is not necessarily the case. Where it is not, an additional problem will be encountered: the avenues for physical and social mobility which in a modern society provide opportunities to escape burdensome or unfavorable conditions are generally lacking in traditional environments. The case of a young Iranian village girl comes to mind. In keeping with tradition, this young girl moved into the household of her bridegroom's family—a household dominated by an exceedingly authoritarian mother-in-law. The strains of this relationship produced a severe case of ulcers in the girl, and even the availability of modern medical facilities failed to alleviate her condition permanently. In a modern social setting, the solution would have been simple: the girl could have offered her husband the choice of establishing a separate household of their own, or divorce. But for a person steeped in the traditions of a society based on kinship ties and respect for elders, neither of these possibilities offered anything but dishonor and disgrace.

Every society combines some elements of its unique tradition with elements of modernity. It is possible to describe and analyze the particular combination that is manifested in any given society. It is, however, exceptionally difficult if not impossible to say authoritatively which combination is best.

3. *Tensions and conflict, particularly on the international scene, are primarily the result either of interference from an external and alien*

power, or the spillover effects of modernization within national societies. This misconception most often takes the form of linkage between the so-called population explosion and international crisis. No doubt the continued pressure of population on resources in the lesser developed countries produces tensions which may be reflected in the international arena. Were this the main source of international tensions, the solution would be simple to conceive, though possibly difficult to implement.

In fact, however, the international conflicts and crises which have occurred in Asia and Africa since the end of World War II have a far more immediate and evident cause: the erosion or disappearance of the political power primarily of European nations. Typically, these conflicts have revolved around questions of what groups or countries are to inherit the power most recently exercised by Europeans, and in what fashion that power is henceforth to be exercised. Population pressure is indeed a deep-seated problem, but it has been at best peripheral to the conflicts involving Korea, Indochina, the Sino-Indian border, the Sino-Soviet border, Israel, Cyprus, the Congo, or Nigeria.

This is not to say that these conflicts have nothing to do with modernization. They are very much a product of that process. What is involved here is the regulation of relations between nations which have already undergone a good deal of modernization and those which are still in the relatively early stages of the process. This brings us back to a point raised earlier in this discussion. We have noted that Europe was the first part of the world to modernize. Now we must add the further contention that "late" modernizers are deeply affected not only by the prior experience of "early" modernizers, but also by continuing relations with them. Some writers refer to this point by use of the term "defensive modernization." We mean by this the attempt to deliberately introduce and control the process of modernization as a means of equalizing a power relationship between two or more societies. Indeed, the introduction of modern, especially military, techniques and institutions during the nineteenth century in such countries as Japan, China, and Turkey was regarded by those countries as necessary in order to resist further encroachment of European armies and navies on territorial integrity and political independence. Defensiveness of this type remains uppermost in the minds of leaders of the developing nations today, as some of the selections that follow illustrate.

Similarly, the relations among the more modern states will also affect the process of modernization in the so-called developing nations. Thus, the course of modernization in the latter cannot be divorced from the cold war and other relationships prevailing among the great powers. On occasion, modernizing nations may benefit from competition among more powerful and wealthy states, as in Afghanistan, where the United

States built a large multipurpose dam while the Russians paved the streets of Kabul. On other occasions, great power rivalry may lead to frustration for the developing nations, as was the case in 1956, when U.S. Secretary of State John Foster Dulles abruptly canceled an offer of American aid for the Aswan Dam project. These power relations are part of the environment within which all nations, modern and developing, must strive for survival.

Thus, we have returned to the starting point of our discussion. The survival of the nation-states of the world is specifically the problem of policy-makers. Insofar as this survival depends on the management and control of the process of modernization, we need to apply an understanding of the vagaries of that process to the solution of specific policy problems.

The selections were chosen with two basic criteria in mind: to illustrate the two approaches to the study of forces at work in the developing nations, and to emphasize the controversial nature of the problems at issue by presenting differing and contrasting points of view. The selections in Part One are intended to give a basic description of the process of modernization, both as a problem of conceptualization and as a policy problem in its contemporary international setting. Part Two presents a series of analyses of the operation of various factors in the process of modernization. Part Three raises questions of the future course of modernization in Asia, Africa, and Latin America as seen from the perspective of the more developed nations of Europe, North America, and the Soviet Union. Part Four includes several examples of the perspectives of the developing nations themselves. Finally, in Part Five, we present two articles which again illustrate the interweaving of basic theory and practical policy-making. Robert L. Heilbroner examines the question of appropriate American policy towards modernizing nations, while Manfred Halpern returns to the basic question of the nature of modernization itself, particularly in view of continuing change in developed nations.

The reader may find some of the arguments presented in this book more convincing or congenial than others. There is much conventional— and some unconventional—wisdom in these arguments. Perhaps the most important lesson to be gleaned from the confusion of conflicting opinions is that there is no single path to modernization. Rather there are many alternate routes, some more hazardous than others.

Part One

TRADITION AND MODERNITY: DICHOTOMY OR DIALECTIC?

W E begin our examination with a discussion of the material basis of the process of modernization—specifically, the conditions of economic growth.

Without technological development and economic growth modernization is inconceivable. A mass society cannot come into being unless the means for mass participation—mass communications, mass transportation, mass production—exist. The creation of these facilities presupposes the availability of economic resources such as capital, natural resources, and technical skills. This is undoubtedly why economists were the first to turn their attention to problems of development and modernization.

Economic analysis is attractive because it deals in quantitative terms, which have the appearance of precision. It is necessary to keep in mind, however, that economic development is integrally related to social and cultural factors. Capital formation or savings, for example, are intimately affected by cultural attitudes toward material goods and commercial activities. In some cultures, such as Islam, business and commerce are held in low esteem. The same was true at one time in parts of Europe. Thus, the question of what is the single most important causal factor in economic development has not been finally answered. Secondly, it is necessary to remember that the use of quantitative expression is no guarantee of precision. For one thing, the collection of statistics, particularly in underdeveloped nations, is not always a reliable function. Many official statistics are nothing more than educated guesses. Furthermore, statistical quantities often express averages or general tendencies, and thus do not give a full picture of the real world from which they are derived. Kuwait and the United States, for example, have per capita production figures that are very similar (see Table 1), but it would be a gross error to assume that the average Kuwaiti is as well off as the average American.

The first selection by Richard T. Gill presents the basic facts of material

9

poverty and economic stagnation as viewed from the perspective of the economist. Gill also discusses the distinctions between the poor of our day and those of the past, the obstacles that hinder the drive for economic development, and the amount of development that the poor countries may realistically anticipate.

In the second selection, Cyril E. Black explores the meaning of the process of modernization with all its ramifications. His discussion focuses on five aspects: intellectual, political, economic, social, and psychological. Black adopts the perspective of comparative history, which makes it possible to focus on the similarities and differences between the experiences of Europe and North America on the one hand, and the rest of the world on the other.

L. I. and S. H. Rudolph, in the third selection, argue that the concepts of tradition and modernity are abstractions only. They point out how these abstractions have misled some observers, and remind us that in the real world every society combines some elements of modernity with elements of tradition. The significant question in each case is how these elements are brought together and assimilated. The Rudolphs prefer to emphasize the continuity of cultural change rather than the disruptiveness of rapid modernization.

Irving L. Horowitz, in a provocative study of the "three worlds of development," descriptively analyzes three patterns of modernization that are historically observable. The "first world" pattern has been distinguished by the activities of a moneyed middle class, backed by the legal authority and political power of the sovereign state. The state in turn has demanded and won the loyalty of all its citizens. The product of this combination of economic and political forces has been a pluralistic political and social system that is highly integrated. The best examples are the countries of Western Europe and North America.

The "second world" pattern of modernization is typified by the model of the Soviet Union, where political development preceded economic development. The consolidation of the sovereign state came first, with the state again demanding and receiving the loyalty and commitment of the mass of citizens. The political power of the state was then used for the purpose of bringing about economic development. The result was the growth of a highly integrated political and social system under much more centralized control than was the case in the Western world. The second world pattern, therefore, is not one of either social or political pluralism; moreover, it has been sanctioned by the militant ideology of Marxist communism, which seeks to justify the system by proving its historical inevitability.

Unlike the first and second worlds, the "third world"—including most of the lands of Asia, Africa, and Latin America—is still in the early stages of the process of change.[1] The circumstances that prevail in the third world are substantially different from those of the first and second worlds, and the shape of the final product is by no means clear. With the waning of the tide of European colonial empire and the achievement of political independence, almost all of these countries have established the form of the sovereign state. They have not yet succeeded in filling this form with modernized social and political processes, however. In particular, the masses do not yet identify culturally or politically with the formal institution of the state. In the economic sector, there is no sizable middle class, such as there was in the West, capable of accumulating the necessary capital for purposes of large-scale productive investment. Because extreme poverty is the rule, even governments which are committed to policies of economic development are unable to marshal the necessary resources without massive aid from abroad. As a result, the third world is characterized by a nonintegrated or malintegrated political and social system, with a relatively high degree of pluralism and low level of political power and economic resources.

1. THE ECONOMIC PROBLEMS OF THE UNDERDEVELOPED COUNTRIES

Richard T. Gill

RICHARD T. GILL took his A.B., *summa cum laude* in economics, at Harvard College and, following study at Oxford University as a Henry Fellow, returned to Harvard for his Ph.D. He has served in a number of administrative capacities at Harvard, including Assistant Dean of Harvard College, and is now Master of Leverett House and Lecturer on Economics. His books include *Economic Development: Past and Present* (1967), *Evolution of Modern Economics* (1967), *Economics and the Public Interest,* and *Economics and the Private Interest* (1970).

In the age of jet aircraft, the time distance which separates the United States from one of the underdeveloped countries of Asia, Africa, or Latin America is only a matter of hours. Measured in economic distance, the gap is more like that between the present and the Dark Ages. Over the

---

[1] It should be noted that not all third world countries are necessarily "new nations." Politically, some of them are over one hundred and fifty years old, as in most of Latin America. Others embody a culture with an unbroken history stretching thousands of years into the past, as in the case of India and China. Some, such as Thailand, can lay claim to both cultural and political continuity with the ancient past.

past century the time distance has been constantly narrowing; during the same period the economic distance has become immeasurably wider. The United States and the other economically advanced countries of the world have been growing steadily richer at rates never before dreamed of. The poor countries of the world, with a few exceptions, have remained poor; in many cases, conditions have notably deteriorated. It is all told in the Bible:

For unto every one that hath shall be given, and he shall have abundance; but from him that hath not shall be taken away even that which he hath. (St. Matthew, xxv, 29)

The story of the "hath nots" is the story of the modern underdeveloped countries.

MEANING OF ECONOMIC UNDERDEVELOPMENT

One cannot, of course, divide the world quite so neatly into economically advanced countries, on one hand, and underdeveloped countries, on the other. We have a whole spectrum of degrees of development depending on when a country embarked on the path of modern growth and on the progress it has achieved. From the point of view of the United States, the Soviet Union is still, in most respects, an underdeveloped nation. Much the same can be said of Europe in general. For that matter, if we are thinking of growth *potentialities,* the United States with its continuing favorable prospects is itself an "underdeveloped" country.

Even when we limit our attention to the definitely poorer countries of the world, moreover, we still find a great variety of conditions. Some are much poorer than others. Some are growing; some are not. In a country like India there is a civilization which is, in many respects, older than that of the West. By contrast, in certain regions of Africa and Oceania we find a tribal organization of the most primitive kind. In some countries, such as Ceylon, Colombia, Peru, and Indonesia, there is a relatively rich endowment of natural resources; in others, such as Jordan and Yemen, the poverty of resources may be a major deterrent to development. There are, moreover, very significant differences in the densities of population as between these various countries. Brazil, for example, has roughly 30 times as much land per capita as does Taiwan. Broadly speaking, Africa and Latin America tend to be relatively underpopulated while Asia is heavily overpopulated, but even here there are important exceptions to the rule.

In short, the problem is not one of a single situation but of a whole complex of different situations in which the obstacles to progress are likely to be extremely varied. What unites this group and makes the notion of "underdeveloped countries" a meaningful one, however, is that all these countries have just begun to experience, or have yet to experience, the phenomenon of rapid economic growth which has become so characteristic in the economically advanced nations. In one way or another, they are all still wrapped up in what we have called the problem of "getting started." While the nations of Europe, North America, and Australasia were one by one entering the development race, these countries remained at the post. The result has been persistent, grinding poverty in a world where affluence was, at last, becoming conceivable.

HOW POOR IS POOR?

Poverty means one thing to an American wage-earner; it means quite a different thing to the beggar in the streets of Calcutta. How can we measure in quantitative terms the degree of poverty existing in the underdeveloped countries of the modern world?

The problems we encounter here are very similar to those . . . in connection with the measurement of long-term economic growth. Accurate statistics are seldom available; many of the relevant items are all but impossible to include; the differences in the kinds and relative quantities of goods produced in a poor country as opposed to a more advanced country make international comparisons extremely difficult; and so on. Despite these problems, however, various attempts have been made to estimate the levels of output per capita in the underdeveloped countries of the world as compared with their more favorably situated neighbors. The truth is that the differences are *so* enormous that even the most defective measuring sticks could not fail to detect them.

In Table 1 some estimates of output per capita in the various countries of the world . . . are presented. These particular estimates have been converted to United States dollars. . . .

. . . [W]hen all is said and done, the striking thing which emerges from Table 1 is *how very low* the level of output per capita in most of the world's countries is. According to these estimates, roughly . . . [one quarter of] the world's population produces less than $100 of output per person per year. . . . Another . . . [third] of the world's population has an annual output per capita of between $100 and $300. Together, these two groups of countries present us with a clear problem of economic underdevelopment. In terms of population, they comprise [almost] two-thirds of the world. In terms of geography, they include . . . [much] of Latin America, and virtually all of Asia and Africa. . . . Even if the estimates of output per capita in these regions were low by two, three or even four times, the central conclusion would remain—two-thirds of the world is extremely poor and a sizable fraction is living in circumstances which can only be called desperate.

Table 1. Per-Capita Gross National Product *
(converted to U.S. Dollars)

Group A: Annual Per-Capita Gross National Product of $0–100 (Includes approximately 26% of the World's Population)

Latin America	Asia and Middle East	Africa
Haiti	Pakistan	Nigeria
	Vietnam Republic	Somaliland
Asia and Middle East	(North)	Tanzania
Afghanistan	Yemen	Togo
Bhutan		Uganda
Burma	Africa	
India	Angola	Oceania
Indonesia	Ethiopia	Western Samoa (N.Z.)
Muscat and Oman	Gambia	
Nepal	Mozambique	

Group B: Annual Per-Capita Gross National Product of $101–300 (Includes approximately 36% of the World's Population)

Latin America	Africa	Asia and Middle East
Bolivia	Congo	China (Taiwan)
Brazil	Ghana	China (Mainland)
Dominican Republic	Kenya	Iran
Ecuador	Liberia	Iraq
El Salvador	Madagascar	Jordan
Guatemala	Morocco	Korea (South)
Honduras	Rhodesia	Philippines
Paraguay	Sudan	Saudi Arabia
Peru	Tunisia	South Viet Nam
		Thailand
Africa	Asia and Middle East	Turkey
Algeria	Cambodia	United Arab Republic
Cameroons	Ceylon	

Group C: Annual Per-Capita Gross National Product of $301–600 (Includes approximately 8% of the World's Population)

Latin America	Africa	Asia and Middle East
Argentina	Mauritius	Hong Kong
British Honduras	Union of South Africa	Lebanon
Chile		Libya
Colombia	Europe	Malaya
Costa Rica	Bulgaria	North Korea
Cuba	Czechoslovakia	Singapore
Mexico	Greece	Ryukyu Islands
Nicaragua	Malta	
Panama	Portugal	
Surinam	Spain	
Uruguay	Yugoslavia	

Group D: Annual Per-Capita Gross National Product $601–1,600 (Includes approximately 8% of the World's Population)

Latin America	*Asia and Middle East*	*Europe*
Netherland Antilles	Israel	Hungary
Puerto Rico	Japan	Ireland
Venezuela		Italy
	Europe	Netherlands
Asia and Middle East	Albania	Norway
Brunei	Belgium	Poland
Cyprus	Finland	Rumania

Group E: Annual Per-Capita Gross National Product $1,600 and above (Includes approximately 20% of the World's Population)

America	*Oceania*	*Europe*
United States	Australia	Luxembourg
Canada	New Zealand	Sweden
		Switzerland
Asia and Middle East	*Europe*	United Kingdom
Kuwait	Denmark	West Germany
	East Germany	U.S.S.R.
	France	

NOT LISTED: Approximately 2% of World Population

SOURCES: *United Nations Statistical Yearbook,* 1968.
The New York Times Encyclopedic Almanac 1970 (New York: The New York Times, Book and Educational Division, 1969).
* Table 1 has been updated by substituting new data, with the permission of Professor Gill. (Editor)

THE DEMAND FOR DEVELOPMENT

Poverty, even desperate poverty, is not a new phenomenon in many of these countries. It may be true, as some economists have argued, that the industrial development of the economically advanced countries has sometimes had adverse effects on the standards of living of the poorer countries; but, whether true or not, this is not the essential explanation of why these countries are poor. The fact is that they were poor at the time of the English Industrial Revolution; in most cases, they have been poor since the dawn of history. Poverty is an ancient, not a modern, condition.

What is new in the modern underdeveloped countries, then, is not the fact that they are poor but the fact that they have become *aware* of being poor and have grown increasingly determined to *do something* about it. This awareness and determination, in turn, are largely a product of the exposure of these countries to the economic achievements of the industrialized world. There has been what economists sometimes call an international "demonstration effect."[1] Because of the colonial interpenetration of the East by the West during the nineteenth century, and because of the dramatic improvements in the means of communications in the twentieth, the poor countries have had a constant "demonstration" of the economic superiority of Western ways. The sharp contrast in standards of living between the economically advanced peoples and their own has not escaped them. On the contrary, it has led to constantly growing demands for rapid development at no matter what the cost.

This insistence on quick progress has given rise to many problems. Politically, it has often been associated with a violent rejection of the ways of the former colonial powers and a susceptibility to slogans and ideologies which find scapegoats in the past and give easy promises for the future. Moreover, it sometimes poses obstacles to the achievement of the very economic development which is desired. In some underdeveloped countries, the emulation of Western achievements has led governments to adopt many of the social-security and other "welfare" measures which, in the case of the economically advanced nations, came only at a very late stage of their forward progress. A poor country, in trying to do more than it can afford, can easily sap the strength of the forces which might make for permanent economic development.

In the final analysis, however, it should be said that this awakened desire for improvement is the main driving force capable of dislodging the modern underdeveloped country from its rut of ancient poverty. Without such an awakening, the tense problems of economic development might disappear. But it would not be poverty that had disappeared—only the will to overcome it.

THE OBSTACLES TO DEVELOPMENT

If the demand for economic development in the modern underdeveloped countries is great, so also are the obstacles to its achievement. In fact, most economists believe that the problems of "getting started" in these countries may be much more difficult than those which faced the developing nations of the nineteenth century.

[1] The term "demonstration effect" was originally developed by Harvard University's James S. Duesenberry (*Income, Saving and the Theory of Consumer Behavior* [Cambridge: Harvard University Press, 1949]), to explain how consumers might be affected by the living standards of other consumers within the domestic economy. This general notion was applied to the international sphere by the late Ragnar Nurkse in his important book, *Problems of Capital Formation in Underdeveloped Areas* (New York: Oxford University Press, 1953). The idea is that awareness of higher living standards elsewhere may bring pressure for an increase in one's own living standards. Of course, a simple desire for better living does not necessarily *bring* better living. Indeed, Nurkse feared that poor countries in trying to raise their immediate consumption levels might actually impede the process of long-run capital formation, and therefore, long-run growth.

In a way this is a rather surprising conclusion because the modern underdeveloped country does have at its disposal a most potent instrument of growth—namely, the whole apparatus of modern technology which has been developed in the industrial countries. The potentialities for "borrowing" techniques are now enormous. It is typical—and a little paradoxical—that a country like India, with an output per capita of less than $100 a year, already has her own Atomic Energy Commission. With a similar level of income, China already has the atomic bomb.

However, . . . there are often difficulties as well as advantages in following after. And, in the case of the modern underdeveloped countries, these difficulties, plus a variety of special circumstances, have created what often seem to be virtually insurmountable obstacles to progress. Here are a few of the problems which may make the process of "getting started" more difficult for these countries than it was for their predecessors:

1. *The difficulty of adapting Western technology.* Advanced Western technology, on which most hopes for progress are pinned, is by no means ideally suited to the conditions of the typical underdeveloped country. By and large, this technology has evolved along lines appropriate to the conditions of the countries which created it, meaning that it uses (relatively) little labor and a great deal of capital, and depends in its operations on the existence of a reservoir of skilled labor and technically trained personnel. Such a technology is quite inappropriate to most underdeveloped countries where: (a) labor is abundant or super-abundant; (b) capital is extremely scarce; and (c) there is often an acute shortage of skilled labor and management. Ideally, the underdeveloped countries would employ a technology which is neither the Western technology of a century ago (which is defective) nor the most modern Western technology (which is adapted to a different kind of economic context), but a *third* technology which consists of an adaptation of modern methods to the special conditions of the underdeveloped world. Despite some efforts in this direction, however, this third technology does not really exist. Lacking it, the modern underdeveloped country typically tries to import the "latest" Western methods, with the consequence that it faces acute shortages in certain areas (capital and trained personnel) while it has idle surpluses in others (large numbers of unemployed, unskilled workers).

2. *Lack of preparation for an industrial revolution.* In the nineteenth century, industrial revolutions were launched primarily in Europe or in countries linked with Europe where the social and economic groundwork was reasonably well-laid. In the typical modern underdeveloped country, an attempt is being made to accomplish simultaneously both the industrial revolution and the preparations *for* such a revolution. The difficulties

here are sometimes extreme, particularly in the political sphere. Consider, for example, the political unrest and frequent changes of government in the Congo since independence. Even the economically hopeful country of Nigeria has recently been subjected to considerable interregional strains. In Southeast Asia, Indonesia has . . . experienced a major political upheaval and bloodbath. In many underdeveloped countries a complete social and political revolution is required while the industrial revolution is getting underway. In general, the lack of prior preparation means that these countries are economically poorer than their nineteenth-century predecessors; it means that their agricultural and commercial sectors have not developed to the point where they can easily sustain rapid industrial progress; it means, above all, that there has been little or no time for their institutions and value systems to adapt themselves to modern economic change. A sharp desire for material betterment, a willingness to work hard and in a regular, punctual manner, an awareness of the future benefits of present sacrifices—these attitudes may be the prerequisites of economic growth; yet they may be largely absent in many underdeveloped countries.

3. *Population problems.* Most modern underdeveloped countries face population problems of a different and much more serious sort than did the nations of the West a century ago. Partly this is a matter of the rate of increase of population; partly it is a matter of population density in relation to land and other resources.

As we know, the modern underdeveloped countries have undergone a "public health revolution" which has made possible a fall in the death-rate and consequently rapid population growth even in the absence of substantial economic development. In India and China—comprising over a third of the world's population—population is now increasing at 2 per cent or over per year. In Latin America the rate of increase is between 2½ per cent and 3 per cent. These are very rapid rates of increase and they pose serious difficulties for poor countries in which the rate of capital formation tends to be low. The danger is that such capital as is accumulated may simply go into spreading a larger quantity of tools over a larger number of people without actually raising per-capita productivity. This problem is likely to continue, moreover, because death-rates in these countries are still high relative to the economically advanced countries and therefore may continue to fall in the future.

Furthermore, the increase in population is all the *more* serious in those countries where population is already dense in relation to land and other resources. Generally speaking, this is the situation in Asia, where the great majority of the poverty-stricken of the world are located. In many of these Asiatic countries, population is already pressing against the available cultivable land in a thoroughly "classical" manner. In some extreme cases, such as Java, there are well over 1,000 persons per square mile. Under such circumstances, population growth is not a stimulant to development, as it was in the United States, but a depressant. Because of the lack of industrial capital, the growing labor force cannot find jobs in the city and therefore adds itself to the already congested rural areas. Rapid population growth in such "labor surplus" economies may mean that despite the attempts to increase industrial employment, the absorption rate is insufficient, and that open and disguised unemployment increase as a percentage of the labor force—the reverse of successful development.

4. *The international context.* Finally, many economists would add that the modern underdeveloped countries face a rather different and generally less favorable international environment than did the developing countries of the nineteenth century. Often this problem is put in terms of the degree to which private investors in the economically advanced countries are willing to provide sources of capital to their poorer neighbors. In the nineteenth century, British foreign investment flowed freely and massively to the then developing areas of the world. By contrast, in the twentieth century, the flow of private capital from rich to poor countries has been a mere trickle in relation to their needs. In the case of the United States, much of our private foreign investment goes to economically advanced countries (e.g., Canada and Western Europe), and a large fraction of the rest is devoted to extractive products, like oil, where the impact on the over-all development of the poor country may be relatively limited.

In general, and in part due to the attitudes of the underdeveloped countries themselves, the current climate for private foreign investment is a rather unfavorable one. With former colonial abuses in mind and with a strong upsurge of nationalistic feeling, many of these countries have effectively restricted both the kinds and the terms of investment open to foreign investors. Even where restrictions do not exist, the danger of nationalization and expropriation is always present. Under such circumstances, American investors will often prefer to employ their capital in more familiar and secure surroundings, particularly when—as, for example, in the case of the Common Market countries—economic progress is continually creating new and favorable opportunities.

To a degree, of course, this deficiency is made up for by the increase in intergovernmental aid—loans and grants from the United States and other countries and international agencies—which has taken place during the past 15 years. Because of the comparative lack of private investment, however, the gap to be filled by these aid programs is a very substantial one.

These, then, are some of the special problems which a modern underdeveloped country faces in its attempts to achieve rapid growth. The advantage of having a ready-made foreign technology is considerably qualified by the fact that that technology makes severe demands on its scarce supplies of capital and skilled labor and management. It faces the herculean task of transplanting an industrial revolution into a social and economic context which has not naturally been prepared for it. It suffers from acute population problems. And its hopes for foreign assistance have come to rest more and more on the largess of friendly governments and international organizations.

This list, of course, does not include anything like all the obstacles to development which these countries face. It merely suggests some of the ways in which the problem of "getting started"—difficult enough at best —may be even *more* difficult for the modern underdeveloped countries than it was for those who accomplished the breakthrough in the nineteenth century. We can now understand why many economists feel that the "vicious circles of poverty" may be particularly "vicious" in these countries and why the initial push may have to be an especially big one.

THE SCALE OF POSSIBLE DEVELOPMENT

The combination of an intense demand for rapid growth and the existence of severe obstacles to growth is the source of profound social and political tensions in many modern underdeveloped countries. For the student of economic development, it raises a number of interesting and difficult problems. Can these demands for growth actually be met? Have these countries any reasonable hope of closing or at least narrowing the gap between themselves and the economically advanced countries? What, realistically, is the scale of possible future development that may be achieved in the underdeveloped areas?

Such questions have no definite answers, but they do raise certain points which it is well to keep in mind. In the first place, it should be said that experience, both past and present, suggests that modern economic growth can be launched in a wide variety of apparently unlikely contexts. The achievement of Japan during the past 75 years is an historical case in point. In recent years we have the fact that many of the underdeveloped countries have, indeed, shown an acceleration in their rates of progress. See Table 2 for a few examples from the past 15 years. These rates, after all, compare quite favorably with that of the United States (a little over 3½ per cent) during most of its historic development. Some countries are doing better than others and, of course, the per-capita rate of advance is lessened by dint of the great population upsurge. Nevertheless, in the underdeveloped world as a whole, the past 15 years have seen definite forward strides as compared to times past.

Having said this, however, we should counter with a second point which is this: Any hope that these countries might have of closing or even seriously narrowing the economic gap which separates them from

Table 2. Rates of Growth of Modern Underdeveloped Countries

Nation	*Average Annual Rate of Growth of GNP*	
	1950–1960	*1960–1964*
Ceylon	6.1 [a]	2.2
Chile	3.6	3.5
Colombia	4.6	4.4 [b]
Ecuador	4.9	4.0
Guatemala	3.8	6.1
Honduras	3.5	4.0 [b]
Jamaica	7.7 [c]	4.0
Korea, Rep. of	4.8 [c]	6.2
Malawi	4.0 [d]	1.0 [b]
Paraguay	2.7	3.5
Peru	4.9	6.4
Philippines	4.5 [e]	4.1
Sudan	5.0 [e]	6.9 [f]
Taiwan	7.9 [g]	7.1 [b]
Uruguay	0.0 [c]	−0.1 [b]
Zambia	8.2 [e]	3.4

[a] 1958–1960 [e] 1955–1960
[b] 1960–1963 [f] 1960–1962
[c] 1953–1960 [g] 1951–1960
[d] 1954–1960

SOURCE: United Nations, Department of Economic and Social Affairs, *Statistical Yearbook, 1965,* pp. 562–564.

a country like the United States is—at least for the foreseeable future—an unrealistic one. This point is brought home very forcibly by some arithmetic calculations which were made a few years ago by the Economic Commission for Latin America.[2] These calculations, it should be remembered, pertain to Latin America where the average level of per-capita output is already considerably higher than that of Africa or Asia.

The Commission asked, in effect, how long it would take, under various assumptions, for output per capita in Latin America as a whole to reach a level equal to *one-third* of the United States level. Assuming that output per capita in Latin America were to rise by a healthy 2.4 per cent per year, they found that it would take 42 years for it to equal one-third of the present U.S. output per capita. But that, of course, is the *present* level of U.S. output per capita. If one is thinking in terms of narrowing the gap, one would have to take into account the fact that the level of U.S. output per capita would *also* be continuing to rise during this period. On

[2] UN Department of Economic and Social Affairs, *Analyses and Projections of Economic Development: A Study Prepared by the Economic Commission for Latin America: I.* "An Introduction to the Technique of Programming" (New York: UN, 1955). Cf. discussion in Benjamin Higgins, *Economic Development* (New York: Norton, 1959), pp. 432–440.

the assumption that U.S. output per capita were to rise at the rate of 2 per cent per year, the Commission found that it would take 252 *years* for the level of output per capita in Latin America to reach one-third of the then current U.S. output per capita!

Needless to say, these assumed rates of increase for both the United States and Latin America are arbitrary, and the conclusions therefore are necessarily arbitrary too. Nevertheless, the calculations do bring out clearly the scope of the problem facing the modern underdeveloped countries. For all practical purposes, and barring completely unforeseen circumstances, there is no reason to expect that the gap between the highly advanced and economically underdeveloped countries will be closed or even appreciably narrowed over the course of the next century or more. In the year 2060 there will still be rich nations and poor. Or, if there are not, it will most likely be because of political and military circumstances, not the economic.

All of which suggests that the goals of most underdeveloped countries must be on a considerably more modest scale. This is not a counsel of despair, however. For certainly *the* most important goal of any poor country must be the removal of the extremes of poverty which shorten, cripple, and undermine the value of human life. The goal of "catching up" with the West may be morally defensible, but it is not crucial. What *is* crucial is that children should not die of malnutrition and exposure and that adults should enjoy life with that minimum of health, comfort, and leisure necessary to physical and mental peace. And this goal, given modern technology, should lie within the realm of the possible. Its achievement, moreover, is to the interest of every nation, rich or poor. For, as the former Ambassador to India, John Kenneth Galbraith, has remarked, this is "without question . . . the most important and humane task on which men are now engaged." [3]

2. THE DYNAMICS OF MODERNIZATION

Cyril E. Black

CYRIL E. BLACK has been a member of the History faculty at Princeton University since 1939. He is also Director of the University's Center of International Studies. He has served in the U.S. State Department, and as a faculty

[3] John Kenneth Galbraith, *Economic Development in Perspective* (Cambridge: Harvard University Press, 1962), p. vi.

member of the National War College. In addition to *The Dynamics of Modernization* (1966), from which excerpts are presented here, he has written, co-authored, and edited a number of books, including *The Establishment of Constitutional Government in Bulgaria* (1943), *The Transformation of Russian Society* (1960), *Rewriting Russian History* (revised edition, 1962), *Communism and Revolution* (1966), *Neutralization and World Politics* (1968) and (with Richard A. Falk) *The Future of the International Legal Order* (1969–), of which the first two of five volumes have been published. He is also an editor of the journal *World Politics*.

"Modernization" as it is used here refers to the dynamic form that the age-old process of innovation has assumed as a result of the explosive proliferation of knowledge in recent centuries. It owes its special significance both to its dynamic character and to the universality of its impact on human affairs. It stems initially from an attitude, a belief that society can and should be transformed, that change is desirable. If a definition is necessary, "modernization" may be defined as the process by which historically evolved institutions are adapted to the rapidly changing functions that reflect the unprecedented increase in man's knowledge, permitting control over his environment, that accompanied the scientific revolution. This process of adaptation had its origins and initial influence in the societies of Western Europe, but in the nineteenth and twentieth centuries these changes have been extended to all other societies and have resulted in a worldwide transformation affecting all human relationships. Political scientists frequently limit the term "modernization" to the political and social changes accompanying industrialization, but a holistic definition is better suited to the complexity and interrelatedness of all aspects of the process.

The culture-bound or deterministic character of most of the widely accepted explanations has obstructed efforts to understand this process. It seems clear that the liberal view of "progress" was a projection for the whole world of a conception of change that was believed, erroneously, to be true of the societies of Western Europe and of the English-speaking world. Other widely held views have more often than not been characterized by a narrow-minded determinism that has sought to explain all change in terms of some simple original cause or motivating factor. A characteristic reflection of a lack of appreciation on the part of these theories of the ultimate complexity and unpredictability of the social process is the assurance they offer that a resolution of fundamental problems lies just ahead, perhaps even within one's own lifetime, if only the program implied by the theory is generally accepted. The advantage of a term such as "modernization" is not only that it has a broader scope than

"Westernization," "Europeanization," "industrialization," or even "progress," but also that it is less encumbered with accretions of meaning.

What would an educated man from fifteenth-century England find familiar and what would he find strange in contemporary Britain? The written language he might be able to understand in some measure, some aspects of religious services might be familiar, a few of the great architectural monuments of his day would still be standing, and in the countryside there might be features of rural life that at least at first glance would not appear to have changed a great deal. Yet how much more striking has been the transformation, and how completely new and incomprehensible would be most of what he saw and read.

The process by which this transformation has taken place may be discussed in terms of the adaptation of a given set of institutions to changing functions. In historical perspective, the institutions undergoing this process may be defined as the traditional institutions of the societies of the world. "Traditional" and "modern" are, then, relative terms, but they are used here in a specific sense. For the societies of Western Europe, the traditional institutions are those of the Middle Ages, and the challenge of modernity to the traditional system occurred between the twelfth and eighteenth centuries. Comparable traditional periods before the challenge of modernity may be discerned in all other societies. In the least developed societies, the traditional period has lasted until well into the twentieth century. Since the challenge of modernity in the societies that modernized earliest was primarily internal, the process of transformation took place gradually over several centuries. In the later-modernizing societies this challenge has been increasingly external, hence more rapid and even abrupt. These traditional eras were, of course, diverse, highly sophisticated in some cases and no more than tribal in others, but the common factor is that in each case they formed the setting for the particular pattern of historically evolved institutions that is adapted to the functions of modernity and that gives each modernized society its distinctive character.

The modern does not share the diversity of the traditional, insofar as the particular functions characteristic of modernity tend to be common to all mankind, but the identification of these common characteristics is fraught with problems. The principal of these is that most societies, embracing the great majority of human beings, have not advanced to the point where these characteristics can be fully discerned. Even the most advanced countries are still modernizing, and it is only by an effort of the imagination that one can conjecture which of their features are likely to be characteristic of all modern societies and which are simply culture-oriented idiosyncrasies of individual societies.

TRADITION AND MODERNITY

All aspects of human activity have been undergoing transformation at the same time, and the process of modernization is too complex to be reduced to simple terms without the danger of grave distortion. Assume for the purposes of this study, however, that all of human activity can be discussed in terms of five aspects: intellectual, political, economic, social, and psychological. It is clear that these are essentially arbitrary categories adopted for the sake of convenience, familiar terms that it would probably be a mistake to try to define too closely. It should also be apparent that the various aspects of human activity, however categorized and defined, are continually interacting and can be discussed in discrete compartments only by a deliberate act of gross oversimplification.

Intellectual. It is appropriate to start with the intellectual realm, since the growth of man's understanding and control over his environment in all of its complexity plays such a vital role in the process of change in modern times. Indeed, it is clear that in a sense little has changed except man's knowledge, for the diversity of the physical environment was present before man began to understand its potentialities, and evolutionary changes in man and his environment have not been significant in historical times. Historians trace the immediate origins of modern knowledge in Western Europe to the renaissance of the twelfth century, when the writings of Greek and Arabic scholars became available and creative work of a lasting order was initiated in many fields. The basis of this renaissance was the recognition that it was possible to seek a rational explanation of physical and social phenomena. In the natural sciences, which have stamped such a forceful impression on the modern era, the level of achievement of the Greeks and Arabs was reached in Western Europe in the thirteenth and fourteenth centuries. By the sixteenth century the revolutionary growth in the understanding of nature, which has placed in man's hands instruments of great power and peril, was under way.

The revolution in science has no doubt fostered the most dramatic change in man's understanding of his environment, but it was in fact only one part of a much more comprehensive re-evaluation of accepted ways of doing things. Indeed, all of man's conceptions were subjected to scrutiny, and all fields of intellectual activity underwent a rapid transformation. Each generation toppled the idols of the last, in one respect or another, and the view came to be generally accepted that change was the normal state of all knowledge. . . .

Historians of Europe have found it convenient to describe the evolution of man's understanding in terms of a Renaissance, a Reformation and Counter Reformation, an Age of Enlightenment, and perhaps an Age of

Materialism, and a traditional periodization such as this remains a useful frame of reference. What is particularly significant is that from the twelfth to the nineteenth century this intellectual revolution was almost exclusively the product of Europe. The earlier debt to the Greeks, the Arabs, and the Hindu mathematicians and astronomers is well known, and there were significant parallel and contributing developments in China and Southeast Asia. The great modern effort to understand the world of men and matter was nevertheless essentially a European achievement until the nineteenth century, when other societies attained the sophistication necessary to participate in this great adventure. Even today, when universities and research institutes encircle the globe, the original intellectual centers of Europe still possess the greatest accumulation of talent in many fields of endeavor, and are rivaled in some fields and surpassed in others chiefly by the English-speaking countries overseas and by the peoples of Russia who have been their pupils. It is in this sense that many think of modernization as being "Europeanization" or "Westernization." The accumulation of knowledge, and the methods of rational explanation by which it was achieved, is no doubt the most generally recognized aspect of modernization, and as an attitude of mind it lies at the center of this process.

An important feature of the intellectual revolution was the application of science to the practical affairs of man in the form of technology. One of the most consistent themes of the modern era has been the opportunity offered by the new knowledge for the betterment of man's material life, and this is a sphere where great achievements have been registered. Whether in manufacturing, transportation, communications, agriculture, or medicine, the new technology has revolutionized the ways in which man conducts his affairs. For the first time in the history of mankind it is possible to anticipate that adequate food, shelter, education, and medical care can eventually be made available to everyone and that want can be abolished forever. Not only do goods and services multiply in ever-increasing quantities, but the amount of energy available per capita is continually growing. The further reduction through automation of the need for human exertion is advancing rapidly, and the possibility of significant man-made modifications in the climate can now be envisaged.

The scientific attitude has also influenced the values by which men live. Theological systems and religious beliefs based on earlier conceptions of the nature of the world have been confronted with the need for a reassessment of the distinction between those aspects of a faith that represent eternal verities and those that reflect the outlook of particular periods and cultures. Beliefs and values are always subject to change, but the modern age is one in which particular emphasis has been placed on a critical approach. In this reassessment of values it is natural that the welfare of man should have become a matter of primary concern. The potentialities of the modern age for the material betterment of the conditions of human existence are so great that this concern has taken precedence over others. History has become increasingly preoccupied with economic and social matters. In literature the novel has become a favorite form of expression, perhaps because it is particularly suited to the exploration of the infinitely complex problems characteristic of the modern age. The great works of modern literature have been deeply concerned with social change, the conflicts between traditional and modern values, and the fate of man in an era peculiarly lacking in stable norms of behavior. In all these respects, man—his nature, well-being, and prospects—has become the central concern of modern thought. . . .

Political. The political implications of modernization are most strikingly apparent in the consolidation of policy-making that has occurred in both the public and the private domains. This consolidation has doubtless been the result in part of technical developments in communications and transportation that permit the administration of increasingly larger enterprises and areas from a single base. It is due more, however, to the desire on the part of modernizing leaders in both government and private enterprise to mobilize and rationalize the resources of society with a view to achieving greater control, efficiency, and production.

In the public domain this has taken the form of the increasing centralization of the administrative organs of the state. Although traditional political forms have varied greatly around the world, the authority of the state has in the past not normally reached down to every citizen. It has tended to be limited to defense against foreign attacks, the preservation of law and order at home, the maintenance of essential public works, and the collection of sufficient taxes to perform these functions. Even in the case of such exceptionally authoritarian and centralized traditional states as China and Russia, the authority of the central government reached down to the individual peasant only indirectly and through a variety of intermediaries. Before modern times, political power was in most instances shared by numerous authorities, and only after a long struggle did kings and emperors succeed in subduing the various bodies that exercised power at the local level and in consolidating their power on a nationwide basis. Some of the most dramatic pages in the history of political modernization have been concerned with the civil wars in which the struggle between centralizing, regional, and local authorities was waged.

The modern state arose from this consolidation of local authorities and then proceeded to extend its power on a functional basis to many activities that had hitherto been in the private or local domain. Functions that the family, the village, the landlord, the church, and a variety of other agencies had originally performed all tended to be gathered into the hands of the state. In some societies practically all education, communications, transportation, and social security, as well as much manufacturing, are functions of the state, and most other activities come under state regulation in one form or another. Even in societies with a strong tradition of local rights, such as Switzerland and the United States, the trend over the years has been for the central authorities to increase their power at the expense of the local. Private enterprise in those societies where it is firmly rooted is not incompatible with a strong central government, and is generally the most efficient method of production. Where the state has traditionally played a large role, or where war and other catastrophes have undermined private enterprise, modernization is often accompanied by one form or another of statism. In either case, the state tends to absorb functions that other agencies are not able to perform effectively, and the relationship between public and private enterprise varies with the traditionally evolved capabilities of the particular society. Modern states today collect revenues in an amount equivalent to between one-quarter and one-half of the gross national product to reimburse the costs of general administration, public enterprises, and social security, whereas in traditional societies such revenues may be as low as 5 percent or less of the wealth produced.

The relatively centralized and rationalized functions of a modern state would not be possible without the rule of law maintained by a highly organized bureaucracy, and a close rapport between the state and every member of society. Indeed, the replacement of the arbitrary administration of individuals by a legal system is the hallmark of modernization in the political realm, for modern administration with its vast undertakings would not be able to operate effectively on any other basis. Arbitrary decisions are still necessary at a high level of policy, and even at lower levels a legal system does not rule out a wide variety of choices, but unless the range of choices is restricted by generally accepted norms, a modern state will not function well. Large bureaucracies are called for, manned by persons who devote their lives to civil service. Principles of organization suitable for a wide variety of organizations have been evolved, and modern methods of administration and techniques of management permit the effective implementation of complex policies.

A closer rapport between the modern state and its citizens is necessitated by the fact that for the first time, the state has direct relations with every member of society. The state cannot fulfill its functions in regard to taxation, foreign policy, education, social security, and a myriad of other matters unless the citizenry understands and in considerable measure accepts its role. Public participation in politics may nevertheless take many forms. In societies with a deeply rooted tradition of individual rights, modern government has typically been democratic in the sense that all citizens participate to some degree in the choice of political leaders and policies, and that the right of individual choice is guaranteed by effective civil liberties. In other societies this rapport is maintained by various forms of popular enlightenment and propaganda, and the consensus is enforced by police methods when it cannot be won by other means. Even in the most tightly controlled police states, however, great reliance is placed on propaganda and economic incentives to gain the necessary degree of acceptance and participation on the part of the public. It is not possible to run a modern political system by sheer terror, and modern dictators depend on their ability to win public support through thought control, plebiscites, and nominally representative bodies.

Modern societies rely to such a degree on the acceptance and participation in one form or another of its inhabitants that the structure of the state has been determined to a large extent by its ability to gain such acceptance. Geography, economic viability, or security might dictate very different political units from those that have emerged. Indeed, some would argue that continentwide or worldwide political systems are the only ones that make sense today. In fact, however, a state can be no larger than the basis of its support, voluntary or enforced, and this basis has generally been the result of a variety of factors among which common historical experience is no doubt the most significant. In most cases a common language has been the principal feature of this experience, and nationalism has been a characteristic rallying point for modern states. It has proved to be the most effective means of consolidating loyalties that would otherwise be divided by attachments to many other associations. Yet linguistic nationalism is by no means the only, or even a necessary, prerequisite of nationhood; and there are numerous instances of states that are multinational or that are held together by religious or other beliefs. Indeed, state boundaries have rarely coincided precisely with those of linguistic or other forms of nationality, and efforts to bring the two into close rapport have led to endless strife. The location of groups of peoples with common linguistic traditions is often such as to make discrete political entities out of the question, and a variety of provisions for federalism and minorities rights have been evolved in an effort to bridge this gap. . . .

Economic. Economic development may be discussed in terms of the two essential and interrelated functions of saving and investment. Traditional economies tend to consume virtually all that is produced, leaving little for investment and growth. Even modest savings may be of no avail in an undeveloped economy if the population grows more rapidly than production. The saving of resources for investment presupposes a net surplus per capita, and it is the availability of this surplus that makes development possible. When rapid economic development was getting under way two or three centuries ago in the countries that are now advanced, it had the benefit of rather high levels of income and of agricultural land per capita. This was certainly one of the reasons that the countries of Western Europe got a head start. These levels were on the whole several times higher than those of undeveloped countries today, and the application of the new technology to this relatively prosperous economy resulted in very rapid growth. Accompanying this growth was a degree of specialization that permitted the production of a much greater surplus than before, hence greater savings.

Specialization was accompanied in turn by an expansion of domestic and foreign trade that made it possible to integrate a wide range of resources and peoples into a relatively well-knit economic system. A traditional rural community may be virtually self-sufficient, producing most of its food, clothing, and implements from resources available locally and only occasionally purchasing goods from itinerant merchants, whereas a modern community may devote all of its efforts to a few products and purchase the greater part of its needed supplies from outside. Savings may take the form of private profits or of public taxes, and in either case many problems of policy are raised concerning the means by which savings should be achieved.

Investment is the complementary function of allocating resources, and saving and investment are generally performed by the same institutions: governments, banks, business enterprises, and individuals. The policy of investment depends on the capabilities of an economy and on the purposes and sophistication of the investor. Generally speaking, a large investment in producer goods—transportation, the production of raw materials, factories, and heavy machinery—will result in more rapid economic development but will impose a heavier burden on the population. A large investment in consumer goods, on the other hand, will benefit the population but will reduce the productive capacity of the economy. Societies, moreover, do not always have a free choice in this matter, for emphasis on consumer goods is not possible until a society is relatively well developed. Yet at every stage there exists a choice between patterns of investment, and this choice is essentially a political one. Some political leaders are prepared to demand maximum sacrifices of the people in the interest of the rapid development of producer goods, whereas others will prefer to provide for annual increments in the standard of living even in the earlier stages of development.

The economic aspect of modernization has been so dramatic that many have regarded it as the central and determining force in this process. In fact, however, economic development depends to a great extent on the intellectual and political aspects of the process, the growth in knowledge and the ability of political leaders to mobilize resources. Yet economic growth has no doubt been compelling in its effect on individuals. It seems likely that in the more advanced societies real income per person may have increased ten to twenty times or more in the past two or three centuries. At the heart of this growth has been the scientific and technological revolution, which has made possible a phenomenal increase in production through the mechanization of labor. Here, as in other fields, innovation in its modern form can be traced back to the Middle Ages, but it was the rapid industrialization of the nineteenth and twentieth centuries that brought this process to its most dynamic phase.

As a result of increased specialization the area in which goods and services are exchanged has been expanded, and barriers to travel and trade within and between states have gradually been broken down. This has permitted the creation of mass markets, supplied by mass production, with a corresponding reduction of costs per unit and increase in real income per hour of work. This expansion has affected agriculture no less than industry and trade, and the machine has come to the aid of man in every sphere of his activity.

The difference between tradition and modernity in the economic sphere can be graphically illustrated by a variety of quantitative measures. In gross national product per capita, a widely employed indicator despite many shortcomings, the dozen or more most advanced societies range from $800 to $2,500, whereas the twenty-five least developed countries with about one-half of the world's population have a gross national product per capita of less than $100. In modern societies one-sixth to one-quarter of the gross national product may be reinvested each year, stimulating a continuing rapid growth over a period of many decades. In traditional societies, by contrast, only one-twentieth or less of the gross national product may be so invested, and in some cases the rate of economic growth is slower than the growth of population, so that the inhabitants become gradually poorer over the decades. This profound difference in economic levels and patterns of growth between the societies that make effective use of technology and those that do not may be seen in the contrast both between advanced and undeveloped societies of today and between these advanced societies and the same societies several centuries ago. Differences between societies as to resources and skills are such that one cannot assume that all societies are capable of the same rates and levels of development as those that are now the most advanced, and indeed it appears that during the first half of the twentieth century the gap between the advanced and the undeveloped has grown. In seeking an explanation for this diversity of growth trends one must look beyond economics to the political, social, and psychological factors.

Social. Profound social changes have accompanied and complemented the intellectual, political, and economic aspects of modernization. In the course of this process societies that for many generations were composed predominantly of peasants, with perhaps no more than 10 percent of the population engaged in administration, manufacturing, and trade, may within a few generations change to the extent that a relatively small minority remains rural. A phenomenal migration to the cities accompanies this change in occupations, and within a few generations three-quarters or more of the population may live in urban areas. This urbanization generally involves a significant transformation of the family from the larger kinship units normally associated with agrarian life to the much smaller nuclear family consisting only of parents and younger children. In advanced societies there is also much more geographical mobility, and as much as one-fifth of the population may move each year from one locality to another in response to occupational demands.

These trends have been associated with a considerable leveling in terms of income, education, and opportunities. This is not matched by a similar leveling of social or political roles, however, and one may in fact question whether such distinctions will ever disappear. Not only do the natural endowments of individuals vary considerably but also the functional requirements of a society call for a wide variety of roles, ranging from imaginative leadership at the highest level to the equally necessary but less dramatic tasks of tending cattle and cleaning streets. What is called for by the rationalizing tendencies of modernization is less a leveling than an equalization of opportunity, so that the members of a society will find the roles best suited to their abilities and predispositions. In any society the composition and training of the leaders—or the "elite," as it is sometimes called—is a matter of the highest importance.

Modernization is also accompanied by the extension of literacy from a small proportion of the population in traditional societies to a practically universal ability to read and write. The associated expansion of education, to the point where in some societies virtually the entire population completes secondary education and as much as one-third of the relevant age group receives formal education at a higher level, has resulted in a revolution in the acquisition and dissemination of information.

Relations between men and women also undergo a marked change, for until the modern era the status of women was based on the circumstance that the livelihood of most people depended on heavy physical labor, which men are best able to perform. The gradual replacement of physical with mechanized labor and with clerical and intellectual work, greatly reducing this age-old functional inequality, has challenged the pattern of relations that had been accepted for many centuries. This change in the relationship of men and women is fraught with problems, and appropriate institutional forms to meet them are only now being elaborated in the more advanced societies. Education has been the principal vehicle for the emancipation of women, making professional, managerial, and clerical occupations available to them. At the same time, the legal and social status of women has undergone a transformation designed to give them opportunities and responsibilities equal to those of men.

Through a wide variety of media, interested persons can keep in touch with developments in many fields. This growth of the communications network contributes greatly to the integration of society and permits the maintenance of a close rapport among its many divergent elements. Modern societies have annual newspaper circulations of 250 to 500 per 1,000 population, exchange each year 100 to 350 items of domestic mail per capita, own 250 to 950 radios and 50 to 300 television sets per 1,000 population, and have an annual cinema attendance of 10 to 25 per capita. Traditional societies had none of these means of communication a century or more ago, and even today possess them in a limited degree.

With the aid of mechanization, only a small proportion of the population is needed to raise food, whereas in earlier times agriculture occupied the bulk of the population. In advanced societies the differences in income and conditions of labor between the various occupations are greatly reduced. Indeed, the role of labor itself assumes much smaller proportions as machines increasingly take over work formerly done by muscles. In such societies more than one-half of the population is engaged in the professions, services, and clerical work, and the role of manual labor is correspondingly reduced.

Equally striking has been the improvement of health as a result of modern medicine. In traditional societies the rates of both birth and death are normally between 3 percent and 4 percent, and have tended to remain relatively stable over long periods of time. With the advent of modern medicine and sanitation the death rate has been rapidly reduced, but the birth rate has remained high for much longer. In the advanced countries, as a result both of external pressures and of changes in family practices, the birth rate has been significantly reduced and the rate of population growth has become more gradual. Earlier, however, the population of Europe had grown from 188 million in 1800 to 462 million by 1914. In the countries that developed later, the impact of modern medicine has been much more strongly felt, but the birth rate has continued to follow traditional patterns, so that their populations have grown at an unprecedented rate. Infant mortality is as low as 16 to 30 per 1,000 live births and life expectancy as high as 70 to 75 years in modern societies. In traditional societies the corresponding levels may be as high as 100 to 225 for infant mortality and as low as 25 to 50 for life expectancy.

In modern societies there is a trained physician for every 500 to 1,000 inhabitants, in traditional societies one for every 10,000 to 100,000.

At the same time, modernization fosters a more equal distribution of income. This is the case not only because graduated income taxes and provisions for social security tend to reduce differences of income in the more advanced societies but also because mass production is inexorably dependent on mass consumption. As societies industrialize, all of their members tend in the long run to become better off, and those with modest incomes benefit relatively more than those with large ones. Indeed, a mass-production economy would collapse if it did not have a mass of consumers capable of absorbing its products. In some traditional societies the upper 5 percent of the population may have fifteen to twenty times as much income as the lower 50 percent. In highly industrialized societies this ratio is closer to four or five to one. Distribution of income is not tied solely to the level of development, but this is the most important single factor. Distribution of income in a "capitalist" United States is similar, then, to that of "socialist" societies in Western Europe, whereas in a "socialist" Soviet Union distribution of income is relatively more unequal and resembles that in other societies at its level of development.

This complex of changes constitutes a process sometimes referred to as social mobilization—the transfer of the main focus of commitment for most individuals from community to society and from the local to the national sphere. Social mobilization follows from the physical migration of the bulk of the population in a modern society from its traditional rural habitat. It also follows from the people's heightened awareness, through vastly expanded means of communication, of a national sphere of interest and of a much larger world beyond. In modernizing countries the flow of domestic mail relative to foreign mail tends to increase significantly; similarly, domestic commerce plays an increasingly more important role than international commerce in national income. Such trends, although they are by no means uniform for all countries, appear to reflect the increasing mobilization of resources and skills at the national level in terms of culture, political loyalties, economic interest, and social dependence, as well as a corresponding weakening of ties to both the local and the international spheres. The political significance of social mobilization is that it promotes the formation of a consensus at the national level by encouraging nationalism and economic and social integration, strengthening, in the process, the hold of the national community over all of its citizens.

Psychological. The psychological aspect of modernization is of fundamental importance, for in the last analysis it is on the perceptions of individual human beings that everything depends. The manner in which an individual adapts to his environment is a result of the conditioning received in the early years of life in the home setting and also of influences in later life that may be sufficiently powerful to affect the firmly set pattern established in childhood. In a typically stable traditional society a child is able to model itself after adults whose behavior follows reasonably predictable patterns. Within the local community children learn the range of problems they will face in later life and the accepted manner of handling them. When they reach adulthood, most individuals cope with life's problems in accordance with the age-old customs of the locality, and under these circumstances the range of initiative and original behavior is narrowly restricted.

The rather rigid social structure of traditional societies also tends to inhibit individualism. Most peasants never expect to change their occupation, and the relatively small numbers of large landowners, warriors, merchants, priests, and rulers, constituting narrow strata within the society, also tend to remain within the confines of their inherited status. The sense of achievement inspired by a desire to get ahead or to gain new privileges is consequently limited. The relatively static life of most members of a traditional society likewise protects them from the need to adapt themselves to peoples and situations not encountered in childhood, and few have any conception of the larger world beyond the mountains or even across the river. One should not, of course, exaggerate the static quality of traditional life. As each person went through the life cycle the pattern of his relations with others constantly changed. In all ages each individual lived in a state of balanced tensions, both between his conscious and unconscious strivings and between himself and others. Yet in a relative sense the traditional world was socially stable, with patterns of behavior tending to remain constant from generation to generation, even during periods of war and migration.

The fundamental problems of human nature and relations do not alter as societies modernize, but they are dealt with in a different environment. The essential difference is that the relative stability of traditional society is lacking under modern conditions. The norms by which parents live may be out of date by the time children grow up, and behavior patterns are constantly changing as a result of altered social conditions and the influence of foreign ways of life. The social fluidity underlying these changes also affects the relationships of individuals in adulthood. In circumstances under which peasants move in masses to the cities, artisans become managers, and privileged elites must compete with the formerly underprivileged for a multitude of new jobs, the qualities that make for success are adaptability, initiative, and empathy. Young people tend to imitate their peers rather than their parents, and individualism has a higher value than conformity. Opportunities for upward mobility are available to a large proportion of the population that in a traditional society would never have thought of changing occupation or residence, and man is emancipated from the vast accretion of customs and beliefs that in traditional societies tend to smother individuality. Possibly at some future time a new plateau in the growth of knowledge may permit a new stability, but that time is not in sight. Indeed, the advanced societies are today undergoing more profound and rapid changes than ever before.

In traditional societies individuals are normally involved in relations principally with the family, the local community, and the functional group to which they belong. They tend to look upon others in terms of the narrow viewpoint, bred by the restricted range of acquaintances, in which their personal security is invested. Having little ability to see other points of view or appreciate different ways of doing things, they regard all alien persons and customs as hostile. Moreover, individuals in traditional societies have little expectation of change in their status and believe that the age-old social order is divinely ordained and unchangeable. Clearly in all ages there have been widely traveled and sophisticated individuals, as well as a measure of innovation and social change; and revolts and migrations of various types have testified to the presence of unrest. From a relative point of view, however, traditional societies are static, closed, and quiescent.

THE AGONY OF MODERNIZATION

This rapid and rather impressionistic review of the main differences between tradition and modernity has purposely stressed the elements of expansion and amelioration, and may have conveyed the idea that mankind has benefited greatly from this process. This is certainly the case up to a point; indeed, it has often been asserted that an era of "progress" has arrived in which the benefits of man's new knowledge can be made available to all. A variety of utopias have been conceived of, in which it is anticipated that all manner of human ills will be overcome; even serious students of society with less utopian goals discuss the possibility of a world rid of war and poverty within a foreseeable future. Yet it is well known that modernization has been accompanied by the greatest calamities that mankind has known. Now that man has perfected weapons capable of destroying all human life, it is unavoidably clear that the problems modernity poses are as great as the opportunities it offers.

Of these problems, one of the most fundamental has been that the construction of a new way of life inevitably involves the destruction of the old. If one thinks of modernization as the integration or the reintegration of societies on the basis of new principles, one must also think of it as involving the disintegration of traditional societies. In a reasonably well-integrated society institutions work effectively, people are in general agreement as to ends and means, and violence and disorder are kept at a low level. When significant and rapid changes are introduced, however, no two elements of a society adapt themselves at the same rate, and the disorder may become so complete that widespread violence breaks out, large numbers of people emigrate, and normal government becomes impossible—all of which has happened frequently in modern times.

Modernization must be thought of, then, as a process that is simultaneously creative and destructive, providing new opportunities and prospects at a high price in human dislocation and suffering. The modern age, more than any other, has been an age of assassinations, of civil, religious, and international wars, of mass slaughter in many forms, and of concentration camps. Never before has human life been disposed of so lightly as the price for immediate goals. Nationalism, a modernizing force in societies struggling for unity and independence, easily becomes a force for conservatism and oppression once nationhood is achieved. Few political leaders have had the vision to place the human needs of their peoples above national aims. Too often the means for achieving modernization have become ends in themselves, and are fought for with a fanaticism and ruthlessness that risk the sacrifice of these ends. . . .

An inherent contradiction in the process of modernization is the tendency toward the concentration of authority at the level of politically organized societies and at the same time toward the integration of most aspects of human activity within a much larger framework, in some cases embracing all of mankind. When for the first time systems of knowledge of universal validity have been developed; when societies are increasingly dependent for their security on factors that extend far beyond their boundaries; when systems of production require raw materials, markets, and skills that no one society can provide; when social relationships and cultural institutions overlap national confines; and when the orientation of the individual is developing toward acquiring values that know no national frontiers—at this very time the effect of organizational controls within which all aspects of human activity must operate is being concentrated increasingly at the level of national states, of politically organized societies. This growing contradiction between independence and interdependence at the present stage of modernization lies at the heart of the contemporary international crisis.

One sometimes thinks of the modern age as being especially conducive to internationalism, but this has not thus far been the case. In traditional societies diverse peoples often have shared common religions, enjoyed fluid political allegiances and economic ties within large and loosely knit empires, and in a few cases employed languages recognized to some extent as universal. Today the inexorable requirements of modernization have been concentrated to such an extent at the national level that international organizations vital for national security can be formed only on the condition that they be forbidden to intervene in matters that are essentially within the domestic jurisdiction of member states. Intervention is permitted only if there is a threat to peace so grave that the great powers are willing to compromise their differences and take appropriate measures to prevent a major war.

Another source of unrest characteristic of the modern age has been the threat that the developing modern integrated society has posed to traditions and values evolved at a time when these were nurtured by a relatively small group of privileged leaders. The problem has led serious students to question whether education of a high quality can survive if everyone must be educated, whether ideas and standards will not erode if they must be presented in a form in which everyone can understand them—indeed, whether democracy is workable if everyone can make his influence felt. To some extent such fears no doubt are present among the former privileged leadership groups, which resent the necessity of sharing their privileges. Yet the problems of maintaining quality in an integrated or mass society cannot be said to have been solved. When a national budget must be approved by persons representing innumerable discordant interests, and when literature and art must be adapted to a mass audience at the risk of losing financial support—to cite only two examples—the problem is real.

Other social concomitants of modernization are equally grave. In many undeveloped countries, where the birth rate has remained high long after the death rate has declined, the growth in population may outstrip by a considerable margin any possible expansion in the output of food and manufactured goods. In these cases, even though agriculture and industry are stimulated by local efforts and foreign aid, production per capita may decline. The reluctance of the peoples of these countries to adopt methods of birth control is due to traditional values and behavior patterns that in their rate of change lag far behind medical care. In India, which has a serious population problem, not only are birth-control methods not employed but the many millions of Hindus refuse to eat the cattle that wander uncontrolled and often damage crops, or to kill the monkeys that devour enormous quantities of fruit and nuts. In such a case traditional scruples take precedence over human needs, and millions suffer.

The population problem is further compounded by the fact that in the early stages of economic growth, consumption on the part of the bulk of the population must be kept stable in order to provide the necessary investments. But how can this be done when the population is already growing faster than the production? In the more acute cases the answer has not yet been found. In the relatively developed countries, such as Britain in the mid-nineteenth century and Russia in the twentieth, the real income of wage earners appears to have declined absolutely for a generation or more before the benefits of the new industrial production became widely available. These countries started their growth at a much higher level than that of the newer states, however, and enjoyed more favorable conditions of development.

The effects of modernization on the stability and identity of personality have also been serious. The relatively stable personality characteristic of traditional societies is formed by an environment in which the elders are the unquestioned trustees of a cultural heritage that has changed only slowly through the centuries. Children are brought up within the immediate family in an atmosphere of emotional security, and enjoy face-to-face relations with the members of their community in relative isolation from peoples of a different heritage. This environment and set of relations make for a strong sense of identity and self-assurance, which for the overwhelming majority of members of traditional societies is never strained by confrontations with conflicting norms and values.

Although the fundamental psychological problems of individual adjustment may not change through the ages, and the incidence of aggressive and passive personalities and of neurotic and psychotic individuals may vary little, the environment in which these adjustments are made is greatly altered in the course of modernization. The traditional cultural heritage, rapidly undermined, gives way to a fundamental uncertainty as to norms and values. The environment in which children are raised and the norms that govern their upbringing are directly affected by a number of trends. Urbanization alters the family structure, and the local community dissolves as rural inhabitants desert the villages for cities and not infrequently for foreign countries. Changes in the relations between men and women attendant upon the mechanization of labor profoundly affect the centuries-old patterns of identity that have distinguished masculine and feminine roles.

The individual is less under the domination of his environment in modern than in traditional societies, and to this extent he is freer, but at the same time he is less certain of his purpose and in times of great unrest is prepared to surrender his freedom in the interest of purposeful leadership. This is what is meant by the loss of identity characteristic of individuals in societies undergoing rapid social change. The modern environment tends to atomize society, depriving its members of the sense of community and belonging without which individual fulfillment cannot be satisfactorily achieved. Many regard personal insecurity and anxiety as the hallmarks of the modern age, which can be traced directly to the profound social disintegration that has accompanied modernization.

This disintegration of traditional norms and values is apparent in the many forms of pathology that characterize modern societies. It is generally believed, although it is difficult to prove, that all categories of social disorganization—crime, delinquency, divorce, suicide, mental illness

—have seen an increase in frequency as societies have become more modern. Underlying this trend is the circumstance that the close ties of individuals to others in the immediate environment are loosened as individuals by the millions migrate from rural to urban areas and the conformity to norms and effectiveness of sanctions characteristic of traditional societies are weakened. In a general sense this isolation of the individual is referred to as alienation.

At the heart of alienation is the impersonality of the societies in which the entire life of an individual—work, home, nourishment, health, communication, recreation—is managed by a variety of bureaucratic organizations that tend to treat individuals as numbers, bodies, or abstract entities. People may live in apartment houses where they do not know their neighbors, work in offices or factories where their colleagues change every few months, prepare food purchased from or delivered by unknown persons, eat among strangers in restaurants, enjoy entertainment either transmitted by electronic devices or seen in theaters or stadiums filled with persons one has never seen before, worship in churches where ceremony, clergymen, and congregation are unfamiliar, and grow up as children without close relations with parents and in environments where danger lurks in the street, and trees and animals are rarely seen. Indeed, individual social and spiritual needs receive more attention in modern armies than they do in the ever-growing metropolises in advanced societies. In terms of the relations of individuals to their environment this impersonal way of life in a modern metropolis—perhaps somewhat overdrawn for emphasis, but not untypical of the way many millions live— lies at the opposite extreme from life in the closely knit communities of traditional rural societies. No large numbers of individuals have been able thus far to adjust satisfactorily to the modern environment, and forms of social organization conducive to healthy personal adjustments have yet to be developed.

Related to these changes, in ways that are not entirely clear, is the increase in violence that has accompanied modernization. Painstaking but inevitably inconclusive worldwide estimates for the period 1820– 1949 indicate that large wars have become more frequent and have taken a toll of 46.8 million lives. By comparison, 2.9 million lives have been lost in the same period from minor forms of group violence, and 9.7 million lives have been lost in murders involving one to three persons. One may gain some comfort from the fact that the increase in loss of life through violence has not exceeded the growth in world population. It nevertheless seems clear, although comparable statistics are not available for earlier periods of history, that the loss of life due to violence is significantly greater in proportion to population in modern than in traditional societies. Some of this violence may be attributed no doubt to the willful malevolence of political leaders, but most of it can be explained by the radical character of the changes inherent in modernization. Involving the totality of human behavior patterns, these changes are correspondingly unsettling in terms of the identity and security of individuals and institutions. Traditional functions and institutions must be changed, but they do not surrender without a struggle. At the domestic level violence has taken the form of efforts to consolidate national authority, to suppress revolts, and to overthrow governments. The transition from traditional to modernizing political leaders has invariably involved violence and not infrequently civil wars of considerable intensity and duration. At the international level the dissolution of multinational empires, the liberation of subject peoples, the unification of territories to form new states, and the preservation of the national security of states both new and old have likewise been fraught with violence. Much of this violence has centered in the European and English-speaking societies that were the first to modernize, and it is possible that the inventiveness and vigor that enabled these peoples to develop modern knowledge and apply it to human affairs may be accompanied by an unusual bellicosity. It remains for the societies of Latin America, Asia, and Africa to demonstrate that they can achieve a comparable level of modernity with less violence.

The more modern societies are not freer than traditional societies from the problems inherent in personal and social relations; nor are they more civilized in any general or absolute sense. Modern societies, with a greater understanding of their physical and human environment, have a greater capacity for assuring the material welfare of mankind; yet at the same time, they face more complex personal and social problems and possess a greater capacity for violence and destruction. It is the task of the modern societies to make the best of their opportunities and to safeguard themselves as best they can against the destructive capabilities of their power.

3. THE MODERNITY OF TRADITION

L. I. and S. H. Rudolph

LLOYD I. RUDOLPH is Associate Professor of Political Science at the University of Chicago. He has done research in India on four occasions over the past fourteen years. In addition to *The Modernity of Tradition*, the introductory chapter of which is presented below, he has co-edited and contributed to *Education and Politics in India* (1971) and has written many articles on various aspects of Indian politics.

SUZANNE HOEBER RUDOLPH is Associate Professor of Political Science, and a member of the Social Science Faculty in the College of the University of Chicago. In addition to *The Modernity of Tradition*, she has co-edited *Education and Politics in India* and has written numerous articles on Indian politics, particularly on Gandhi's asceticism. In 1970–71, she held Guggenheim and Fulbright-Hays grants for a fourth year of research in India.

Modernity has generally been opposed to tradition in contemporary analyses of social and political change. . . . The roots of the opposition of modernity and tradition go back at least as far as the Enlightenment. Condorcet's unilinear vision of progress found nothing of value in the past and saw the hope of mankind in the future. His perspective is still to be found in the assumptions of those concerned to understand the course of modernization in new nations. So, too, is Marx's variant of the Enlightenment attitude. The idea of dialectical conflict denigrates the past in its assumption that "theses" will be consumed in the fires of revolutionary change. Building on such assumptions, theorists of social change in new nations have found a dichotomy between tradition and modernity. Useless and valueless, tradition has been relegated to a historical trash heap. Modernity will be realized when tradition has been destroyed and superseded.

The assumption that modernity and tradition are radically contradictory rests on a misdiagnosis of tradition as it is found in traditional societies, a misunderstanding of modernity as it is found in modern societies, and a misapprehension of the relationship between them.[1] There is a striking contrast between the image of modern society developed by scholars whose purview is Europe and America and the image drawn by those whose aim is to compare such modern Western societies with traditional non-Western ones.

Scholars who confine their attention to their own or other modern

[1] Despite our reservations concerning models of tradition and modernity, we find certain contrasts heuristically useful: "modernity" assumes that local ties and parochial perspectives give way to universal commitments and cosmopolitan attitudes; that the truths of utility, calculation, and science take precedence over those of the emotions, the sacred, and the non-rational; that the individual rather than the group be the primary unit of society and politics; that the associations in which men live and work be based on choice not birth; that mastery rather than fatalism orient their attitude toward the material and human environment; that identity be chosen and achieved, not ascribed and affirmed; that work be separated from family, residence, and community in bureaucratic organizations; that manhood be delayed while youth prepares for its tasks and responsibilities; that age, even when it is prolonged, surrender much of its authority to youth and men some of theirs to women; that mankind cease to live as races apart by recognizing in society and politics its common humanity; that government cease to be a manifestation of powers beyond man and out of the reach of ordinary men by basing itself on participation, consent, and public accountability.

societies have in our generation increasingly stressed traditional survivals. Studies of American political behavior suggest the persistence of such traditional forces as local history, ethnicity, race, and religious community. American sociologists studying the fate of the melting pot emphasize the importance of ethnic and religious solidarities and structures. The literature on organization reveals that the modern corporation attempts with considerable success to create diffuse affective bonds among not only its employees but also their wives, families, and neighbors. Corporate concerns and private interest become inextricably entangled. Economic relations among and between employers and employees take on affective dimensions and assume aspects of traditional patron-client relationships. The new urban sociology tells us that the metropolis produces collectivities of urban villagers. In sum, the literature focusing exclusively on so modern a society as America tends to contradict the notion that tradition and modernity are dichotomous. It suggests instead that there may be certain persistent requirements of the human condition that tradition, as it is expressed in the past of particular nations, can and does satisfy.

When we turn, on the other hand, to the image of modern society that emerges from much of the literature comparing it to traditional society, we find that its traditional features have either disappeared from view or are pictured as residual categories that have failed to yield, because of some inefficiency in the historical process, to the imperatives of modernization. In this literature, tradition lives on today only in new nations that stand at or near the beginning of a historical process that modern Western nations have already traversed.

The misunderstanding of modern society that excludes its traditional features is paralleled by a misdiagnosis of traditional society that underestimates its modern potentialities. Those who study new nations comparatively often find only manifest and dominant values, configurations, and structures that fit a model of tradition and miss latent, deviant, or minority ones that may fit a model of modernity. All civilizations and complex cultures, predominantly traditional or modern, encompass a range of sentiments, psychological predispositions, norms, and structures that "belong" with an ideal type other than their own. Analyses that aim to validate heuristic theories may obscure or ignore these deviations, but theories concerned to encompass social change do so at their peril.

Comparative stratification studies, for example, have tended to use a reified conception of the Indian caste system as an approximation of the ideal type of traditional stratification: a system in which rigidly ascribed and closed status groups whose superordinate and subordinate relationships are legitimized by a comprehensive sacred ideology block social mobility and change. Much of that image has always been correct. But we are now beginning to recognize that earlier interpretations based on sacred texts took too literally their descriptions of social organization and assumed too readily the social validity of their legitimizing values. These texts' Brahmanic ideology in fact masked considerable mobility and social change. Conquest and novel economic opportunities often enabled alien or subordinate peoples or castes to establish themselves within the traditional system. These groups were provided with names, symbols, genealogies, and ritual rank appropriate to their newly won power and status. By the time British ethnographers got to work, these events and processes had disappeared from view; castes who might have established themselves in the fifteenth or seventeenth century were presented in terms of Vedic social structure, with the clear implication that they had been in place since time immemorial. Subsequent interpretations of the caste system based on sacred texts and deductions from an ideal-typical model of a traditional stratification system led to systematic inattention to the evidence of mobility and social change.

Psychological theories of entrepreneurship provide another example of how potentially modern features of traditional Indian society have been hidden from view. Entrepreneurship in the modern West has often been linked to a character structure associated with Protestantism or early liberalism, both conspicuous in India by their absence. Yet new historical and anthropological research suggests that the ethic and character of traditional merchant castes could be channelled into behavior appropriate to capitalist entrepreneurship within the framework of continuing familial and community obligations. Even more recently, new studies have revealed how Brahmans, socialized as a literary and priestly class but blocked by contemporary events from occupying such roles or their modern equivalents, have harbored recessive capacities for economic enterprise. And Gandhi's this-worldly ascetism translated a variant of traditional merchant entrepreneurship into political terms.

The cumulative effect of the misdiagnosis of traditional societies and the misunderstanding of modern societies has been to produce an analytic gap between tradition and modernity. We find the literature speaking of an abyss between them; stressing incompatibilities between their norms, structures, and personalities; and describing the hollowness of men and institutions in midpassage. Because they are seen as mutually exclusive, to depart from one is disorienting and traumatic, to enter the other alienating and superficial. Nor does the notion of transitional society escape the preoccupation with the dichotomy between tradition and modernity, for it assumes rather than challenges it. If the two systems are taken to be fundamentally different and incompatible, then social engineers working with new blueprints and new materials are required. Change takes on a systemic rather than adaptive character.

The opposition of modernity and tradition is also a natural consequence of the comparative method of analysis. Students of American society who examined it in isolation tended to stress the importance of class differences and conflict, whereas those who did so comparatively tended to stress class homogeneity and the absence of ideological conflict. To some extent, the one-sided view of traditional and modern societies that emerges from the comparative view of new and old nations arises out of similar differences of assumptions and perspectives. We recognize how modern we are by examining how traditional they are. One of the great attractions of comparative analysis has been to correct excessively narrow perspectives and the parochial judgments they produce by placing any particular instance in the context of plausible alternatives. But comparative analysis can also mislead if the questions that are built into the terms of comparison are a product of unproved assumptions.

Interest in comparison has not always been combined with knowledge of and sensibility toward particular non-Western nations. The strongest impulse for comparative work has come from those familiar with Western comparative politics and political sociology. They have, characteristically and understandably, been influenced by categories of analysis and historical possibilities fashioned in their own familiar context. It is in this sense that the comparative approach has found it hard to avoid an imperialism of categories and historical possibilities. Comparison becomes a way of measuring, and the standards of measure have a way of carrying normative implications. Has a particular new nation approximated the standards of the context out of which the comparison and the comparativist arose? One result has been comparative inquiry aimed at discovering whether the non-West has or can have such characterological, structural, or philosophic features as an achievement ethic, modern bureaucracy, individualism, or an attitude of mastery toward the physical and human environment. Because Western nations have realized certain objective conditions such as industrialization, urbanization, and literacy before political democracy, they are often assumed to be requisites of it. Such assumptions and inquiries have the effect of limiting the models of modernity and the processes and sequences of modernization to the experience of Western nations. The myths and realities of Western experience set limits to the social scientific imagination, and modernity becomes what we imagine ourselves to be.

The difficulties that can arise from the use of ideal-typical concepts in empirical investigation have often been recited. They can screen out perceptions of the particular and the exceptional that contradict dominant trends and motifs. Such theoretical screening is especially inimical to the analysis of social change because it eliminates from consideration latent, deviant, and minority alternatives. With some alteration in historical circumstances, such alternatives may become the source of new or transformed identities, structures, and norms. Social change and the new realities it creates arise not only from the impact of objective, exogenous, or revolutionary forces on established systems but also from alternative potentialities within such systems. Marxist theory brilliantly stresses this insight when it emphasizes the creative possibilities of historical contradictions. Ideal-typical or heuristic analyses of modernity and tradition in particular historical and national settings are likely to miss these creative possibilities in so far as they assume that the characterological, structural, and ideological components of each are absent in the other and thereby place modernity and tradition in a dichotomous rather than a dialectical relationship. Such a divorce of modernity and tradition can be and sometimes is compounded by deducing a model of tradition from a model of modernity and proceeding, in the study of modernization in particular traditional societies, on the assumption that the deduced model provides the point of departure for change.

Probably there was no better way to begin the comparative enterprise than with the ideal-typical categories suggested by Western experience. But if we are right in believing that tradition and modernity are internally varied, then research and findings that proceed on the assumption of a dichotomous relationship between internally relatively consistent models are serious obstacles to understanding social change and modernization. Systematic social science schemes fed by non-contextual behavioral data selected with a view to filling in the outlines of ideal types may ignore, obscure, or falsify more than they reveal.

The separation of tradition and modernity has not been alleviated by those on speaking terms with the particulars of traditional societies. Area scholars have rarely exhibited strong predilections for comparative theory. Their strength has lain in a concern for the integrity, the autonomous meaning, and the inner logic of their subjects, civilizations, institutions, religions, philosophies, and individuals. They have appreciated the way chronology, by excluding some possibilities and including others, shapes consciousness and the subsequent course of historical events. The strength of historical particularism lies in aesthetic and philosophic empathy, in the sensitivity for process in time and context, and in the discipline, not of a discipline, but of the experience of mastering and understanding a subject from within as well as from without.

An exclusive preoccupation with historical particularism is, of course, inimical to the growth and refinement of theory, particularly theory arising from comparative studies and knowledge. On the other hand, it possesses the resources for exposing and correcting the biases and limitations of theory whose origin lies in other historical contexts. By insisting on the independent significance of alien particulars, making clear that they are not always or merely the source of instances and illustrations, the small Arabic numerals to be ordered (or excluded) beneath the Roman in an imported conceptual scheme, historical particularism can suggest the inappropriateness of dichotomies and ideal types derived from Western historical experience and normative concerns. Properly attended to, they can, of course, provide insights and instances for new and more valid general theory.

The separation of tradition and modernity may arise from still another source, from the distortions that influence the view held by historically ascendant classes, races, or nations of those that are or were subject to them. Dominant classes, races, and nations attribute causal potency to those attributes associated with their subjection of others. The mirror image of others as the opposite of oneself becomes an element in civilizational, national, and personal esteem. Africans, including American Negroes, long appeared to Americans as black, lazy, cannibalistic, chaotically sexual, childish and incapable of social organization and government. We liked them that way because it strengthened the mirror image we had of ourselves as white, industrious, self-controlled, organized, orderly, and mature. India seen as a mirror image of the West appears otherworldly, fatalistic, unegalitarian, and corporate. It is as though we would be less ourselves, less this-worldly, masterful, egalitarian, and individualistic if they were less what they are. Occasionally one comes away from a colleague's work with the impression that he is reassuring himself and his readers of the uniqueness of the Western achievement, a uniqueness that would be endangered by recognition of the cultural, functional, and structural analogues to be found in non-Western, traditional societies.

If there have been false starts and enthusiasms in the exploration of tradition and modernity and their relation, there have also been promising beginnings. Greater familiarity and appreciation of non-Western traditional societies have already acted as correctives in lay as well as scholarly circles. So, too, has the changing power relationship between old and new states. Non-Western scholars who command the attention and respect of their Western colleagues have helped disabuse them of an overly simple and Occident-centered view of the relation between tradition and modernity. The too easy equation of Western and modern has become increasingly apparent in the face of studies that focus on the varieties of modernity, including the Japanese and Russian cases, and the ways in which the traditions of particular modern nations, Western and non-Western alike, have made them as unlike as like each other. Renewed attention to economic, political, and social modernization in Western nations has led to a more differentiated view of the conditions and processes involved and has drawn attention to the parallels and analogues between the past circumstances of modern nations and those of contemporary traditional societies.

Our concern . . . is to accord tradition a higher priority in the study of modernization than has often been the case in previous analyses of it. By placing Indian manifestations of tradition in the foreground of observation, we are better able to explore its internal variations and potentialities for change. The examination of internal variations within traditional and modern societies draws attention to those features of each that are present in the other. If tradition and modernity are seen as continuous rather than separated by an abyss, if they are dialectically rather than dichotomously related, and if internal variations are attended to and taken seriously, then those sectors of traditional society that contain or express potentialities for change from dominant norms and structures become critical for understanding the nature and processes of modernization. Classes and castes, religions and sects, statuses and roles that represent deviations from dominant motifs; stresses within dominant ideologies; and recessive themes in cultural patterns and psychological makeup that can be mobilized by somewhat changed historical circumstances become grist for the mill of social change. The components of "new" men may exist among the "old"; it is not always necessary for new men to be the progenitors or creators of a modern economy or polity. Cultural patterning is rarely homogeneous nor does it always command total compliance among social groups and individuals. Those qualities of groups or individuals or structures that produce incongruence and strain in relation to a society's dominant motifs, or those points at which socialization creates friction or conflict rather than integration and control, can become at critical historical moments the sources of incremental or fundamental social change.

Gandhi's leadership . . . illustrates some of these observations. It would be difficult to place him with either the new or old society, although his symbolism was traditional. His ideology and tactics stressed non-violence, asceticism, compromise, and consensualism, themes that are as susceptible to a fatalistic and otherworldly interpretation as to an activist and this-worldly one. Whether one or another of these interpretations is valid depends upon the meaning with which they are infused and the purposes to which they are put. In fact, Gandhi harnessed them to the requirements and purposes of a modern mass movement whose goals were national independence, coherence, and self-esteem. The potential for activism and mastery of the environment had always been there; changed historical circumstances provided an opportunity for its expression.

The introduction of new ideas and objective forces that followed British conquest and rule mobilized latent, deviant, or minority qualities within traditional Indian society that were like or compatible with them. For example, . . . horizontal solidarities and interests latent in the caste system have been used in its structural, functional, and cultural transformation. In its transformed state, caste has helped India's peasant society make a success of representative democracy and fostered the growth of equality by making Indians less separate and more alike. Traditional law . . . was characterized by simultaneous conflict and integration of parochial customary law and an overarching pattern of sacred law that was cultivated and interpreted by Brahmans. The need for more uniform law that followed the introduction of the British raj strengthened the second at the expense of the first. For some time in a variety of ways, indigenous high-culture law aided in establishing a national legal framework.

Increased attentiveness to the variations and potentialities of traditional society not only yields insights into the connections between it and "modernity" but also, when combined with attentiveness to "traditional" aspects of modern societies, raises questions about the meaning of modernity. The modernization of traditional new nations has begun to suggest that established notions of modernity may have to be amended and revised. Our study of Indian law suggests how and why Indians, still closer to the consensual and face-to-face procedures of traditional law, might choose, even as modern Western law of late has, to incorporate such "traditional" aspects into their legal system. The persistence of caste communities in contemporary Indian politics and ethnic and religious ones in modern American politics . . . suggests that political modernity, contrary to broadly shared assumptions, may involve ascriptive and corporate features. Paracommunities, associations combining traditional and modern features, are not merely transitional phenomena but a persistent feature of modernity.

Our argument concerning the modernity of tradition and its correlate, that modernity incorporates traditional aspects, is based on a rather different view of historical processes, sequences, and end products than many comparative analyses of modernization in new nations. The latter are often expressed in terms of requisites or conditions, certain levels of industrialization, urbanization, literacy, mass communications, and so on, which must be realized before modern behavior and structures in the economic, social, and political realms can be independently and effectively established. By relating such factors, through multivariate analysis, to aggregate characteristics of systems, these theories attempt to establish when and under what conditions such aspects of modernity as political democracy or social mobilization are possible and viable. Although there is no mention of necessity or inevitability in such theories, they do tend to assume that some processes and sequences are related in predictable ways to certain historical end products, including political democracy. But must we assume, as such theories tend to, that because in modern Western nations particular conditions preceded the emergence of modern societies and democratic politics they will or must be replicated in our own era to produce the same results? Will the muse of history, having prescribed a particular historical sequence for the Atlantic nations, suffer a failure of imagination and repeat herself endlessly into future historical time?

Although certain historical reiterations and coincidences are surely to be expected, there are compelling reasons to believe that different processes, sequences, and relationships are probable. Knowledge of what has happened in history, of what is available from the political, economic, and administrative experience of "modern" nations, and of what is transferable from the accomplishments of science and technology creates new historical possibilities. Scenarios of modernization have been repeated often enough for their significance and lessons to become part of elite world consciousness. The muse may be susceptible to feedback. To be sure, nations and their leaders do not always learn, nor are they always receptive to such knowledge. But certain possibilities, certain alternatives that were not available to seventeenth and eighteenth century Europeans and Americans, are today not only available but taken for granted in many new nations.

Western observers often view the aspirations and ambitions of new nations in the spirit of the father who finds his son taking for granted the birthright that he has labored long and arduously to produce. He mistrusts the son's assumption that he can take as a starting point what his father has made available without experiencing in considerable measure similar trials and tribulations. There is, however, another side to such historical moments. The techniques and methods, the values and structures, the character and behavior for satisfying the aspirations of new generations and new nations, are known and available. They can be used or abused. New nations do not find themselves in the situation that Europeans did two hundred years ago. The world knows how to build a steel mill, both in the narrow technical sense and, to some extent, in the wider social sense. It knows the capacities of scientific agriculture even though poor and ignorant Indians, like poor and ignorant Tennesseeans, may take some time to use them effectively. Experience with cultural and technical innovation has made it abundantly clear that we cannot expect lessons that history has to teach to be easily or happily learned. At the same time, there is no doubt that the environment of change and innovation in the mid-twentieth century is radically different from that of the eighteenth: many historical processes and sequences have been telescoped or eliminated.

Some have also been reversed. What was in one context a culmination may in another be a cause. Because modernity has been realized in history, it is possible to imagine, anticipate, and produce reversals in the order of its achievement as well as modifications in its form and meaning. The initial act of creation may require different social and psychological qualities than adaptability to its fruits. The presence of models, the fact that a certain kind of history has already been experienced and that this experience is susceptible of vicarious meaning for others, means that the history of modernization will not be the same for all nations and for all time.

There is of course nothing natural or inevitable about modernization that connects congenial elements of the old society to the needs of the new. Nothing may happen; tradition and modernity may not connect. There must be apparent incentives on the side of adaptation, innovation, and change before some kind of dialogue between the new and the old arises. Such situations have not been established in all new nations. . . .

4. THREE WORLDS OF DEVELOPMENT

Irving Louis Horowitz

IRVING LOUIS HOROWITZ is Professor of Sociology at Rutgers University, and Chairman of the Department of Sociology at Livingston College of Rutgers University. Before coming to Rutgers, he taught at Washington University, the universities of Buenos Aires, California, Wisconsin, the State University of New York at Buffalo, and the London School of Economics. He is Director of *Studies in Comparative International Development* and Editor-in-chief of *Trans-Action* Magazine. Among his major publications in the area of development are *The Three Worlds of Development* (1966), *Revolution in Brazil: Politics and Society in a Developing Nation* (1964), *Masses in Latin America* (1970), and *Latin American Radicalism* (1969), of which he is co-editor. He has also written *The Rise and Fall of Project Camelot* (1967).

[T]he phrase "The Third World" is generally attributed to the Algerian writer, Frantz Fanon. His book on Algeria is probably the first to use it as a colloquial expression for the newly emergent nations. While the French phrase *le Tiers Monde* is quite well known at this point, the English language equivalent is only now entering the vernacular. . . .

At the outset we must undertake to sketch the features of the First and Second Worlds so that differentiation from the Third World is substantially free of clichés or stagnant notions. The "three worlds" are contrasts in social structural evolution, contrasts too in their appearance in historical time.

What is meant by the First World is basically that cluster of nations which were "naturally" transformed from feudalism into some form where private ownership of the instruments and means of production predominated. If these nations did not evolve out of feudalism, they at least grew out of the soil of Western Europe and started as capitalist states. Certain properties of this First World are clear: historically they had their initial take-off in the banking houses of sixteenth-century Italy, in the middle-sized industry of seventeenth-century France, and in the industrial mechanization of eighteenth-century England and nineteenth-century United States and Germany. Economically, they share an emphasis on industrialization and technology used for private enrichment and public welfare in uneven dosages.

The First World nations have in common an internal generative power. Changes which took place in Western European nations and the United States have usually come about as a result not of invasion or of foreign conquest, but through the internal breakdown of the older landed classes, a general disintegration of agricultural societies, or through the initiative and creation of new life styles. The basic characteristic of the First World is that economic development was a consequence of the internal machinery of each nation and not the result of international planned agreement. As a matter of fact, there was not even agreement between the nations on a nation-state system until very late in the development of capitalism—the late nineteenth century.

The First World has two geographical parts: Europe and North America. The break with traditionalism in the United States occurs differently as compared with Western Europe. For it gained its national independence only through a struggle with England; and only then could it adopt a central parliamentary system. But it is important to note that in both sectors of the First World the formation of the parliamentary state system followed the bourgeois dominance over the forms of economic production. While they were often supportive of each other, political styles and structures in the First World emerged from the class conflicts of an economic system based on laissez-faire.

The rise of industrial capital was preceded by a profound expansion in commercial capital. In this, the United States only repeated the "phasing in" process of capitalism previously undergone in Europe. The factory unit became the keystone of the industrial system and its by-products:

hardened national boundaries, protectionist tariff arrangements, heavy migration from countryside to city. And when trade relations became socially expensive, technology stepped in to prevent the premature disintegration of private capital investment. Invention promised savings on labor costs and raw materials, to the point that the factory itself, rather than any individual labor units, became the principal investment unit. It will be seen that this economic interpretation, however suited it may be for the study of classical capitalism, can hardly be applied to the Third World—since the relationship of politics to economics is reversed.

The system of competitive capitalism which developed in Western Europe was forced to go beyond its own domestic markets. The First World became colonialist as well as capitalist. It established overseas bases from which to draw raw materials or develop potential markets for the purchase of finished products; in so doing it created out of its own dilemmas the master dilemma of colonialism.

Even the most rabid believer in European preeminence would be hard put to deny that the United States of America is the best example extant of the First World—of the highly mobile, commodity oriented, and ideologically egalitarian social system. It witnessed the development of capitalism not only unfettered by feudal structures, but assisted by political legislation. There occurred a crystallization of the state and the economy at roughly the same time and by roughly the same socio-economic groups; asynchronous and unstable elements were held in check during its development. And whatever interpretation of the origins of the United States is preferred, economist or revisionist, one ineluctable fact emerges —the United States is the most perfect representative of parliamentary democracy and capitalist economics. . . .

The United States should not be dismissed as a model of development for the Third World. The fact that the United States has performed a colonial role is a poor and inadequate explanation of why it does not serve as the perfect model. There are, after all, many cases of the oppressed adopting the methods and philosophies of their exploiters. What is more, the imperialism of the United States was until recently ambivalent and half-hearted. Economically self-sustaining and unlike nineteenth-century England, it was totally independent of imperial holdings. It is only very recently that efforts of the United States to shape the world in its image have given impetus to its imperial thrust in international politics. Still, its anti-colonial sentiments, if not always behavior, set definite limits to its pursuit of influence.

Then why has the United States, despite its enormous power and prestige, failed to capture the imagination of the Third World bloc? It is a failure not of propagandistic devices, but rather of structural inefficiencies. One could say, the failure of success.

First: The United States remains the classic case of national development without a national plan. This is an historical possibility denied to those nations now emerging as economic entities. Indeed, the United States itself, through its various agencies, simply refuses to entertain requests or demands for loans or financial support without some blueprint or plan for over-all growth. Thus, what the United States expects from other nations was not a condition of its own growth. In this, the classic explanation of the mystic hand of the free and mysterious market looms as an apologia for capitalism, while powerful nations like the United States reject the possibility that other nations are entitled to the same sort of laissez-faire apologetics.

Second: Despite the enormous amount of earned income in the United States, distribution of this income continues to be very uneven. Distribution of wealth, in the form of monies and bonds, has remained virtually the same since 1929. The distribution of wages and salaries in the United States also indicates the gap between classes—with the lowest income fifth receiving only 2.5 per cent of the national wage and salary income, while the highest fifth receives an extraordinary 47.0 per cent. Thus, the United States has not solved its class problem, despite the existence of an incredibly high standard of living—the style of life has grown evenly, but economic social division has remained disparate. In the Third World nations, it is precisely the problem of income, wage, and salary equity which looms large, if social development is to be achieved with relative harmony, that is, with a relative absence of class warfare.

Third: Monopolistic and oligopolistic situations obtain in nearly every sector of the American society. This means that competition between private sectors and public sectors continues in the United States with an unabated fury. This can be seen with especial clarity in the "space-race" —where a multiplication of agencies and organizations have arisen, often in competition, for control of everything from property rights on the Moon to domination of the earth satellites. But whatever the net benefits or deficits of this for the United States, it is clear that such competition is precisely what prevents planning for the whole society and inhibits a full drive toward economic equity. The First World has become such an incredible plethora of money and material wealth, that the Third World can no more meet the requirements of this system than it could the traditional, rigorous nineteenth-century capitalist model.

Finally, certain structural weaknesses in the Third World also serve to reduce the role of the United States as a model. The Third World presents a picture of multiplying nations and contrasting politics. Uncritical emulation of the United States social system would mean reversing the current vast trend toward national separatism. Both the United States and the Soviet Union have adopted a cultural pluralism which enables them to absorb rather than crush separatist claims without lessening the quality or the extent of development. The situation in the Third World remains such that ecumenicism of such a variety remains a dream for some, a nightmare for others—but a reality for none.

The Second World is historically the Russian orbit, the Soviet Union and its bloc. The center of the Second World presents an ambiguous situation, for the old Russian world was colonized by Poles, Germans, and other Europeans, including the Swedes. Yet Russia also remained a colonial power. While Russian feudalism was accommodating capitalism, the emergence of revolutionary forces in the late nineteenth century inhibited this accommodation. Thus, instead of a movement from feudalism to capitalism, there took place a radical shift from feudalism to socialism. The period of capitalist survival in Russia was extremely short-lived; no more than 25 years. Thus, one can speak neither of the failure nor success, obsolescence nor abortiveness, of capitalism in Russia.

The politics of old Russia was fatally centralized in official functions, residing in the divine royal person of the Czar. Economic and political initiative lay in his hands. For this reason "modernizing" Czars like Catherine or Peter the Great, no less than "backward" Czars, left Russia a legacy of a stagnant agriculture on one hand and an advanced industrial complex on the other. Commercial middle-class elements were considered traitors to Russia's aspirations because of their contacts with foreigners. These business transactions were in turn perceived as direct challenges to royal supremacy; they were thus despised by the traditional and nascent classes alike.

No social class could really carry forward industrialization without the aid of the throne. While Peter the Great's Westernization policy fostered both industrialization and centralization of political authority, it remained for the Bolsheviks to renovate the social structure so as to make possible the completion of industrialization. This combination of an autocratic-Byzantine heritage, and a modern industrialized self-conception arising from a revolutionary movement dedicated to removing this past, makes the Soviet Union a world apart.

In its pre-revolutionary, semi-backward condition Russia resembles the Third World. In its post-revolutionary industrialized status, it resembles the First World. While this descriptive picture helps to explain the Soviet reality, the fact that the Soviet society is also an ideological society further complicates matters. Marxism-Leninism, the ideological context within which all Soviet self-reflection takes place, makes the U.S.S.R. a unique entity, differentiated from China, since the latter's entry in the modern world has compelled numerous doctrinal accommodations. By its past the Soviet Union is an Eastern culture forcibly Westernized under the impact of European powers. Its revolutionary withdrawal from the capitalist sphere of influence gave it a new pride, and also a new destiny—that of being the first socialist state in the world. That it *was* in fact first, further enhances its uniqueness. The advantage of being first separates the Soviet Union from the Third World; while at the same time, being first makes it a model for the Third World. The Soviet Union, unlike Czarist Russia, is no longer a prostrate nation rent by foreign intervention and, even worse, by foreign debts. In its socialist orientation the Soviet Union stands as a model; but in its Russian traditions it stands apart. . . .

Why has the Soviet Union, despite the enormous impetus it has given to developmental theory and ideology, actually had a relatively slender role in directly affecting the institutions of the Third World? It will be noted that there seems to be a reversal—Third World nations seem to reproduce Soviet ideology (although this is in need of great qualification), while at the same time seeking to reproduce American technology. The first and most obvious reason is that American technical achievement is far greater than Soviet technical achievement. The emergence of socialism in one country, in Russia, has bred a rigid giganticism. Customarily, size is mistaken for efficiency, design has been isolated from function. Hence, in the Soviet developmental process, functions may be modern, but form remains baroque. Soviet satellite nations of a more independent persuasion have had to repudiate this strain between social function and cultural norm. And such imbalance stands as a warning to Third World nations.

The Soviets also resolved ethical and political decisions by administrative fiat and bureaucratic enlargement. It is this very institutionalization of a command society that the Third World is subjecting to skeptical scrutiny. Such problems as the dysfunctionality of large-scale organization units, techniques of increasing productivity (which are at the same time not disguised techniques of exploitation), and political tests of bureaucratic enterprise have not been seriously faced by the Soviets, precisely because of their rigid commitment to an ideology. But all of these are now under consideration in subtle ways within the Soviet Union, and even in bolder ways in the Third World nations. The classical nineteenth-century dialogue between capitalism and socialism has yielded to searches for options to both. Economic and political experimentation is nearly as intense within the classic capitalist and socialist blocs as in the Third World itself.

Many of the obstacles which prevent the United States from serving as an effective "model of models" also serve to obstruct, *mutatis mutandis*, the growth of Russia as the model of models. Furthermore, the Soviet Union faces two additional handicaps in its struggle for universal recognition: its own ideological commitments to national self-determination . . . and the hostility of the United States, a nation superior in power to itself and one quite ready to support any nationalist movements which adopt an anti-Communist posture. . . .

Finally, the phrase "Third World" itself indicates that a narrow choice between inherited industrial forms is no longer possible. The "natural dyad" which Soviet ideologists have long labored under has in fact been changed into a "natural triad." The Third World is a Third Force and a Third Position, irrespective of the canons of Marxism-Leninism which say that such a situation is impossible, except as a temporary aberration.

Russian development may be considered a pivot between the First and Third Worlds of development. Russia is both European and Asian. It has looked to the West for its political ideology and turned to the East for its political domain. Russia is both liberator and exploiter, a nation which makes revolution in the name of all humanity, and yet imposes the strictest class and party dictatorship on a nation. Russia is both technologically advanced and artistically backward; jet design aircraft must compete with decadent Edwardian interior decorations. Russia is both a land of advanced workers and of backward peasantry. It represents an imperfect fusion of urban sophistication and industrial secularization. The Soviets substitute giganticism for miniaturization (refined perfecting), size for quality. Such a society cannot provide a "model of models" when it is still in the process of finding its own self-image and its own clear-cut directions. . . .

We might say that the Third World is characterized by the following set of conditions: First, it tends to be independent of both power centers, the United States-NATO complex and the Soviet Warsaw-Pact group. Second, the bulk of the Third World was in a colonial condition until World War Two. Third, it draws its technology from the First World while drawing its ideology from the Second World. Thus, the Third World is non-American, ex-colonial, and thoroughly dedicated to becoming industrialized.

The Third World is a self-defined and self-conscious association of nation-states. Definitions of the Third World position have been made at the Bandung Conference of Colored Peoples in 1955; the Belgrade conference of Non-Aligned Powers in 1961; the Congress of African States in Addis Ababa in 1963; and the Second Conference of Non-Aligned Nations held in 1964 at Cairo. The leading nations involved in formulating the politics and ideologies of the Third World at this point are India, Ceylon, United Arab Republic, Yugoslavia, Indonesia, and Ghana. This informal web of association extends to every continent, with a nucleus of membership in Africa, Asia, and Latin America. Marginal membership must be accorded such nations as Canada (a new arrival on the scene of Third World politics), China (which prefers to consider itself "aligned" but "independent"), and Algeria (which although only recently independent is already a powerful voice in the formulation of policies for the Third World). . . . At one level, the designation Third World is a strategy for economic development rather than a type of economic or social structure. The "mix" in the Third World is ostensibly between *degrees of* (rather than *choices between*) capitalism and socialism at the economic level, and libertarianism and totalitarianism politically. It is not a new synthesis of political economy. One of the typical self-delusions of Third World nations is that they perceive themselves as developing new economic forms, when as a matter of fact this has not been the case thus far. There is little evidence that there will be any real new economic alternatives to either capitalist or socialist development in the immediate future. In the political sphere, however, the Third World seems to have added a new style if not a new structure.

The Third World is a mixture of different adaptations of capitalism and socialism but not an option to either of them at the economic level. The Third World is transitional. It is in a state of movement from traditional to modern society. It is the forms of transition which therefore have to concern us.

The fact that the First and Second Worlds are always in competition within a relative balance of power makes possible the exercise of Third World strategies in determining the role of foreign capital and aid, and not being determined by such capital. To be a member of the Third World, in short, is not to make a choice in favor of one political bloc or another. As a matter of fact, it is to be very conscious and deliberate about not making this decision for the present. . . .

Part Two

FACTORS OF MODERNIZATION

M OST of the countries of the third world are determined to bring
about the process of social and economic transformation quickly.
The issue before them is what means and instrumentalities are best suited
for this purpose. In one sense they have already made a choice: one of
their chief instruments will be the machinery of the sovereign state. In
order for this machinery to function effectively, however, the state as a
political institution will have to be brought into a rational working relationship with the social and cultural community which it encompasses.
The selection by Myron Weiner addresses itself to this problem. Weiner
suggests that integration is the key to the problem, and spells out five
aspects or senses in which third world countries will have to achieve
integration if their political institutions are to become viable tools for
purposes of modernization. The achievement of integration, then, is the
primary political task confronting these countries.

Weiner's discussion of political integration touches on the relationship
between the state and the social and cultural community. A critical factor
which determines this relationship is nationalism. For just as the state
defines the legal and political boundaries of the political community, so
nationalism defines its psychological boundaries. In other words, nationalism defines the ideal community with which the members of the group
are expected to identify. If this ideal community roughly corresponds
to the body of citizens encompassed by the state, then state and nation
will mutually reinforce one another. Nationalism then provides moral and
emotional sanction for the authority of the state, while the legal and political institutions of the latter provide concrete expression for the idealized
concept of the national community. If, however, the psychological
boundaries of the nation do not correspond to the political boundaries of
the state, severe political instability will probably develop.

The complete congruence of nation and state has historically been a
rare occurrence. In almost all cases, the consolidation of the state has

either left some elements of the national community outside the bounds, or has included more than one national community within its bounds. In the former cases, irredentism has often developed and become a source of international tensions. In the latter cases, separatism and ultimately civil wars have ensued.

Nationalism thus plays a crucial role in the formation of the state. To understand the precise relationship of nationalism to the process of modernization, however, we must note one additional feature. As an ideology of group cohesiveness, nationalism is exceptionally well suited to bridge the gap between traditional institutions which have been undermined and modern institutions still in the process of formation. This is particularly true of the concept of the tribe as the focus of group cohesion. Based on kinship ties, tribalism has been one of the chief foci of group identity throughout history. By adopting the terms and emotions of tribal solidarity, nationalism has in many cases been the means by which group loyalty was transferred from the relatively restricted scope of kinship to the more extensive base of the modern state. Nowhere was the potency of this process better illustrated than in the streets of the major cities of Turkey during a tense confrontation between students and Army troops in 1960. The students effectively nullified the government's authority and control of the troops by simply asking: "Can a brother strike a brother?" Rupert Emerson's book *From Empire to Nation* explores these aspects of nationalism with particular reference to the emergence of independent states in Asia, Africa, and Latin America. The excerpts presented here also touch on significant similarities and differences between nationalism in Europe, and in Asia and Africa.

Communication is basic to the formation of community. It is no accident that language has played a prominent role in nationalism. For without a vehicle for communication—language—how are the members of the nation to become conscious of their common identity? Thus, language has either been a major catalyst in the formation of national entities, or has subsequently become a prime concern of nationalist leaders. But there is more to the function of communication than language, and there is more to the sense of community than national identity. The two selections from the coauthored volume on *Communications and Political Development* by Lucian W. Pye and Daniel Lerner elaborate the characteristics and role of the communications process in traditional, modern, and transitional social environments. As is pointed out in those selections, communications may either enhance or impede modernization.

Lerner in particular emphasizes the contrast between the oral system of communications, which predominates in traditional societies, and the mass media, which are characteristic of modern societies. One of the fundamental skills required to function in an environment dominated by the mass media is literacy. So basic is this skill that at one time one could deduce the relative achievement of modernization of a society by noting the proportion of its adult population that was literate. Most governments of modernizing countries have proclaimed the establishment of a system of universal public education as one of their chief goals.

A universal system of public education produces social and cultural effects that extend well beyond the essentially mechanical skills of reading and writing. For example, public schools may foster a strong sense of national identity among young citizens, as indeed they have done throughout the first and second worlds of development. The selection by James S. Coleman examines the relation between education and political modernization and integration. Coleman points out, however, that education may also become dysfunctional in a modernizing society; that is, it may hamper political and social integration rather than enhance it.

Traditional or pre-modern societies are typically elitist in character. What is more, there are few links that bridge the gap between the elites and the masses. In the changing environment that prevails throughout the third world, this gap is reinforced by the fact that the dominant elites are in many cases committed to modern values and modern institutions, while the masses remain largely steeped in traditionalism. Yet, as Myron Weiner points out, one of the major aspects of the process of integration is the closing of this gap between elites and masses. The selection by Harry J. Benda explores the nature of elites (particularly the intelligentsia and the military) and the problems which confront them in their efforts to provide leadership for their societies.

One of the supposed benefits of European colonial rule in the third world has been the establishment of modern instruments of government, particularly the civil service or bureaucracy. The training of large numbers of native citizens in the skills necessary to the operation of the machinery of government is generally cited to explain the relatively smooth transition from colonial dependency to independence, on the part of former British colonies throughout the world. Obviously, without a minimum standard of governmental services, no political community can long survive. Maintenance of law and order and security of person and property are basic. Provision of minimal communications and transportation facilities as well as the normal public utilities is essential. Reasonable efficiency in the collection of taxes and disbursement of public funds is also necessary. Without maintaining at least minimal standards in these areas, no government can expect to survive for long in a modern political and social environment.

Fred W. Riggs suggests, however, that if government services are too far advanced, the society may not be able to support them, and serious social and political imbalance may result. He argues that a well-developed bureaucracy may actually impede the process of development or modernization in a highly traditional society, for it may monopolize the political arena and prevent the emergence of independent centers of power. Such a bureaucratic machine may thus accentuate existing cultural and social gaps and fail to bring about the kind of integration which is necessary.

Among the political forces operative in modern times, the political party is perhaps unique. It appears to be ideally suited to bridge the elite–mass gap, to provide a communications link between the top and the bottom of the political pyramid. It serves both to inform the political leadership of the demands and sentiments of the public, and to mobilize public support for governmental programs. These functions are performed equally well in a competitive political system, where there is open debate and a measure of choice for the citizen among competing parties, and in authoritarian systems, where only one party legally exists and there is no freedom of choice. The selection by Manfred Halpern examines some of the more specific ways in which political parties affect the process of modernization. Although Halpern's analysis deals primarily with the Middle East, it is generally valid for the other countries of the world.

The final selection in Part Two consists of an account by Wolfram Eberhard of the adjustment of a traditional tribal elite to the changing political and social environment of a modernizing society. The locale described here is in southern Turkey, but as Professor Eberhard notes, it illustrates a number of factors common to modernizing societies elsewhere. The conclusion we may draw from this account is that traditional elites need not be destroyed by modernization; they may instead manipulate the situation in such a way as to gain control of new institutions which are in the process of formation, and thus entrench themselves more firmly in positions of dominance.

5. POLITICAL INTEGRATION AND POLITICAL DEVELOPMENT

Myron Weiner

MYRON WEINER is Professor of Political Science and senior staff member of the Center for International Studies at Massachusetts Institute of Technology. He has been a consultant to the U.S. State Department and the Calcutta Metropolitan Planning Organization, and a member of the Committee on Comparative Politics of the Social Science Research Council, the board of directors of the Association of Asian Studies, and the editorial board of the *American Political Science Review*. He has written or edited the following books, among others: *Political Change in South Asia* (1963), *Modernization: The Dynamics of Growth* (1966), *Political Parties and Political Development* (1966), and *Party Building in a New Nation: The Indian National Congress* (1967).

It is often said of the developing nations that they are "unintegrated" and that their central problem, often more pressing than that of economic development, is the achievement of "integration." . . .

The term "integration" . . . covers a vast range of human relationships and attitudes—the integration of diverse and discrete cultural loyalties and the development of a sense of nationality; the integration of political units into a common territorial framework with a government which can exercise authority; the integration of the rulers and the ruled; the integration of the citizen into a common political process; and, finally, the integration of individuals into organizations for purposive activities. As diverse as these definitions are, they are united by a common thread. These are all attempts to define what it is *which holds a society and a political system together*. Scholars of the developing areas have groped for some such notions of integration, for they recognize that in one or more of these senses the political systems they are studying do not appear to hold together *at a level commensurate with what their political leadership needs to carry out their goals*. . . .

FORMS AND STRATEGIES

Transitional or developing political systems are generally less integrated than either traditional or modern systems. This is because these systems cannot readily perform the functions which the national leadership—or in some instances, the populace too—expects them to perform. In other words, as the functions of a system expand—or the political leadership aspires to expand the functions of the system—a new level of integration is required. When we speak of political development, therefore, we are concerned first with the expanding functions of the political system, secondly with the new level of integration thereby required to carry out these functions, and, finally, with the capacity of the political system to cope with these new problems of integration. It is necessary, therefore, that we now take a more concrete look at the kinds of expanding functions which occur in the course of political development, the specific integrative problems which these pose, and the public policy choices available to governmental elites for coping with each of these integrative problems.

National integration. It is useful to ask why it is that new nations with pluralistic social orders require more national integration than did the colonial regimes which preceded them. The obvious answer is that colonial governments were not concerned with national loyalties but with creating classes who would be loyal to them as a colonial power. Colonial governments, therefore, paid little or no attention to the teaching of a "national" language or culture, but stressed instead the teaching of the colonial language and culture. We are all familiar with the fact that educated Vietnamese, Indonesians, Nigerians, Indians, and Algerians were educated in French, English, and Dutch rather than in their own languages and traditions. Although the colonialist viewed the development of national loyalties as a threat to his political authority, the new leadership views it as essential to its own maintenance. Moreover, since the colonial rulers permitted only limited participation, the parochial sentiments of local people rarely entered into the making of any significant decisions of essential interest to policy makers. Once the new nations permit a greater measure of public participation, then the integration requirements of the system are higher. Moreover, the new elite in the new nations have higher standards of national integration than those of their former colonial rulers and this, too, creates new integration problems.

So long, for example, as export-import duties were imposed by a colonial ruler whose primary concern was with the impact of commercial policies upon their trade and commerce, then no questions of national integration were involved. Once these areas of policy are in the hands of a national regime, then issues immediately arise as to which sections of the country—and therefore which communities—are to be affected adversely or in a beneficial fashion by trade policies. Once educational policy is determined by national rather than colonial needs, the issues of language policy, location of educational facilities, the levels of educational investment, and the question of who bears the costs of education all affect the relations of culturally discrete groups. Finally, once the state takes on new investment responsibilities—whether for roads and post offices or for steel mills and power dams—questions of equity are posed by the regions, tribes, and linguistic groups which make up plural societies. Even if the assent of constituent groups is not necessary for the making of such decisions—that is, if an authoritarian framework is maintained—at least acquiescence is called for.

How nations have handled the problems of national integration is a matter of historical record. Clifford Geertz [1] has pointed out that public policy in the first instance is affected by patterns of social organization in plural societies. These patterns include (1) countries in which a single

---

[1] See Clifford Geertz, "The Integrative Revolution: Primordial Sentiments and Civil Politics in the New States," *Old Societies and New Nations*, ed., Clifford Geertz (New York: Free Press of Glencoe, 1963).

group is dominant in numbers and authority and there are one or more minority groups; (2) countries in which a single group is dominant in authority but not numbers; (3) countries in which no single group by itself commands a majority nor is a single group politically dominant; and (4) countries of any combination in which one or more minorities cut across international boundaries. Examples of the first group are prewar Poland (68 per cent Polish), contemporary Ceylon (70 per cent Sinhalese), and Indonesia (53 per cent Javanese). The dominant minority case is best exemplified by South Africa (21 per cent "white"). The best examples of complete pluralism with no majorities are India, Nigeria, and Malaya and, in Europe, Yugoslavia and Czechoslovakia. And finally, among the minorities which cross international boundaries, the most troublesome politically have been the Kurds, the Macedonians, the Basques, the Armenians, and the Pathans. In contemporary Africa, there are dozens of tribes which are cut by international boundaries, and in Southeast Asia there are substantial Chinese and Indian minorities.

In general there are two public policy strategies for the achievement of national integration: (1) the elimination of the distinctive cultural traits of minority communities into some kind of "national" culture, usually that of the dominant cultural group—a policy generally referred to as assimilationist: "Americanization," "Burmanization," "detribalization"; (2) the establishment of national loyalties without eliminating subordinate cultures—the policy of "unity in diversity," politically characterized by "ethnic arithmetic." In practice, of course, political systems rarely follow either policy in an unqualified manner but pursue policies on a spectrum somewhere in between, often simultaneously pursuing elements from both strategies.

The history of ethnic minorities in national states is full of tragedy. If today the future of the Watusi in East Africa, the Hindus in East Pakistan, the Turks in Cyprus and the Greeks in Turkey, and Indians in Burma and Ceylon is uncertain, let us recall the fate of minorities in the heterogeneous areas of East Europe. Poland in 1921 had minorities totalling 32 per cent of the population. Since then 2.5 million Polish Jews have been killed or left the country and over 9 million Germans have been repatriated. Border shifts and population exchanges have also removed Ruthenian, white Russian, and Lithuanian minorities, so that today only 2 per cent of the population of Poland belongs to ethnic minorities. Similarly, the Turkish minority in Bulgaria was considerably reduced at the end of the Second World War when 250,000 Turks were forced to emigrate to Turkey in 1950, and three million Germans and 200,000 Hungarians have been repatriated from Czechoslovakia since the war. Killings, the transfers of populations, and territorial changes have made most Eastern European countries more homogeneous today than they were at the beginning of the Second World War. Yugoslavia and Czechoslovakia are the only remaining East European countries which lack a single numerically dominant ethnic group.[2]

It is sad to recount an unpleasant historical fact—that few countries have successfully separated political loyalties from cultural loyalties. The dominant social groups have looked with suspicion upon the loyalty of those who are culturally different—generally, though not always (but here, too, we have self-fulfilling prophecies at work) with good reason. Where killings, population transfers or territorial changes have not occurred, the typical pattern has been to absorb the ethnic minority into the dominant culture or to create a new amalgam culture. Where cultural and racial differences continue in Europe or the United States, they are generally accompanied by political tensions. No wonder that so many leaders of the new nations look upon assimilation and homogenization as desirable and that strong political movements press for population transfers in Cyprus, India, and Pakistan, and are likely to grow in importance in sub-Sahara Africa. It remains to be seen whether the ideal of unity and diversity, that is, *political* unity and *cultural* diversity, can be the foundation for modern states. Perhaps the most promising prospects are those in which no single ethnic group dominates—Nigeria, India, and Malaysia. The factors at work in prewar Eastern Europe seem tragically in the process of being duplicated in many of the developing nations: the drive by minorities for ethnic determination, the unsuccessful effort by newly established states to establish their own economic and political viability, the inability of states to establish integration without obliterating cultures —and often peoples—through assimilation, population transfers or genocide, and, finally, the efforts of larger more powerful states to establish control or absorb unintegrated, fragile political systems.

Territorial integration. The associations of states with fixed territories is a relatively modern phenomenon. The fluctuating "boundaries" of historic empires, and the fuzziness at the peripheries where kinship ties and tributary arrangements marked the end of a state are no longer acceptable arrangements in a world where sovereignty is characterized by an exclusive control over territory. In time the control over territory may be accompanied by a feeling of common nationality—our "national integration," but there must first of all be territorial integration. For most new states—and historic ones as well—the establishment of a territory precedes the establishment of subjective loyalties. A Congo nation cannot be achieved, obviously, without there being a Congo state, and the first order of business in the Congo has been the establishment by the central government of its authority over constituent territorial units. Some scholars

[2] These figures are taken from Lewis M. Alexander, *World Political Patterns* (Chicago: Rand McNally), pp. 277–325.

have distinguished between the state and the nation, the former referring to the existence of central authority with the capacity to control a given territory and the latter to the extent of subjective loyalty on the part of the population within that terriory to the state. There are, of course, instances where the "nation" in this sense precedes the "state"—as in the case of Israel and, according to some, Pakistan—but more typically the "state" precedes the "nation." "Nation-building," to use the increasingly popular phrase, thus presumes the prior existence of a state in control of a specified—and, in most instances, internationally recognized—territory. Territorial integration is thus related to the problem of *state-building* as distinct from *nation-building.*

Colonial rulers did not always establish central authority over the entire territory under their *de jure* control. The filling of the gap between *de jure* and *de facto* control has, in most instances, been left to the new regimes which took power after independence. Thus, the areas under *indirect* control by colonial authorities have been placed under the *direct* control of the new governments—in India, Pakistan, Malaya and in many areas of Africa. This process has been accomplished with relatively little bloodshed and international disturbance—although the dispute over Kashmir is an important exception—largely because the colonial regimes denied these quasi-independent pockets of authority the right to create their own armies.

The more serious problem of territorial integration has been the efforts of the new regimes to take control over border areas which were, in effect, unadministered by the colonial governments. Since both sides of a boundary were often governed by the same colonial power—as in French West Africa—or by a weak independent power—as in the Indian-Tibetan and Indian-Chinese borders—the colonial government often made no effort to establish *de facto* authority. Moreover, some of these areas are often occupied by recalcitrant tribes who forcefully resisted efforts toward their incorporation in a larger nation-state.

Some of the new governments have wisely not sought to demonstrate that they can exercise control over all subordinate authorities—wisely, because their capacity to do so is often exceedingly limited. But no modern government can tolerate for long a situation in which its laws are not obeyed in portions of its territory. As the new regimes begin to expand their functions, their need to exercise control grows. As an internal market is established, there is a need for a uniform legal code enforceable in courts of law; as state expenditures grow, no area can be exempt from the tax collectors; with the growth in transportation and communication there is a need for postal officers and personnel for the regulation in the public interest of communication and transport facilities. Finally, there is pride, for no government claiming international recognition will willingly

admit that it cannot exercise authority in areas under its recognized jurisdiction, for to do so is to invite the strong to penetrate into the territory
of the weak.

Value integration. The integration of values—whatever else it encompasses—at a minimum means that there are acceptable procedures for the
resolution of conflict. All societies—including traditional societies—have
conflicts, and all societies have procedures for their resolution. But as
societies begin to modernize, conflicts multiply rapidly, and the procedures for the settlement of conflict are not always satisfactory. There
are societies where the right of traditional authority to resolve conflict
remained intact during the early phases of modernization—Japan comes
readily to mind—and were thereby able to avoid large-scale violence. But
these are the exceptions. Why does the system require a new level of
value integration?

First of all, the scale and volume of conflict increases in societies experiencing modernization. The status of social groups is frequently
changed, even reversed, as education opens new occupational opportunities, as the suffrage increases the political importance of numbers, and
as industrial expansion provides new opportunities for employment and
wealth. A caste or tribe, once low in status and wealth, may now rise or
at least see the opportunity for mobility. And social groups once high in
power, status, and wealth may now feel threatened. Traditional rivalries
are aggravated, and new conflicts are created as social relationships
change.

The modernization process also creates new occupational roles and
these new roles often conflict with the old. The new local government
officer may be opposed by the tribal and caste leader. The textile manu-
facturer may be opposed by producers of hand-loomed cloth. The doctor
may be opposed by a traditional healer. To these, one could add an enormous list of conflicts associated with modernization: the conflicts between
management and labor characteristic of the early stages of industrial
development, the hostility of landlords to government land-reform legislation, the hostility of regions, tribes, and religious groups with one another
as they find it necessary to compete—often for the first time—in a common
political system where public policies have important consequences for
their social and economic positions. Finally, we should note the importance of ideological conflicts so often found in developing societies as
individuals try to find an intellectually and emotionally satisfying framework for re-creating order out of a world of change and conflict.

There are two modal strategies for integrating values in a developing
society. One stresses the importance of consensus and is concerned with
maximizing uniformity. This view of consensus, in its extreme, emphasizes
as a goal the avoidance of both conflict and competition through either

coercion or exhortation. A second view of the way integrative values may be maximized emphasizes the interplay of individual and group interests. Public policy is thus not the consequence of a "right" policy upon which all agree, but the best policy possible in a situation in which there are differences of interests and sentiments.

Since most developing societies lack integrative values, political leaders in new nations are often self-conscious of their strategies. In practice, of course, neither of these two strategies is pursued in a "pure" fashion, for a leadership which believes in consensus without conflict may be willing to permit the interplay of some competitive interests while, on the other hand, regimes committed to open competition often set limits as to which viewpoints can be publicly expressed.

Though movements often develop aimed at the elimination of conflict— Communists, for example, see class harmony as the culmination of a period of struggle—such movements in practice simply add another element of conflict. The problem has been one of finding acceptable procedures and institutions for the management of conflict. It is striking to note the growth of dispute-settling institutions in modern societies. When these bodies are successful, it is often possible to prevent conflicts from entering a country's political life. Here we have in mind the social work agencies, churches and other religious bodies, lawyers and the courts, labor-management conciliation bodies and employee councils, and interracial and interreligious bodies. The psychiatrist, the lawyer, the social worker, and the labor mediator all perform integrating roles in the modern society. In the absence of these or equivalent roles and institutions in rapidly changing societies in which conflict is growing, it is no wonder that conflicts move quickly from the factory, the university, and the village into political life.

A modern political system has no single mechanism, no single procedure, no single institution for the resolution of conflict; indeed, it is precisely the multiplicity of individuals, institutions, and procedures for dispute settlement that characterizes the modern political system—both democratic and totalitarian. In contrast, developing societies with an increasing range of internal conflict, typically lack such individuals, institutions, and procedures. It is as if mankind's capacity to generate conflict is greater than his capacity to find methods for resolving conflict; the lag is clearly greatest in societies in which fundamental economic and social relationships are rapidly changing.

Elite-mass integration. The mere existence of differences in goals and values between the governing elite and the governed mass hardly constitutes disintegration so long as those who are governed accept the right of the governors to govern. British political culture stresses the obligations of citizens toward their government; the American political culture stresses the importance of political participation. In both, a high degree of elite-mass integration exists. At the other extreme are societies faced with the problem of internal war, and in between are many countries whose governments are so cut off from the masses whom they govern that they can neither mobilize the masses nor be influenced by them. The integration of elite and mass, between governors and the governed, occurs not when differences among the two disappear, but when a pattern of authority and consent is established. In no society is consent so great that authority can be dispensed with, and in no society is government so powerful and so internally cohesive that it can survive for long only through the exercise of cohesive authority. We need to stress here that both totalitarian and democratic regimes are capable of establishing elite-mass integration and that the establishment of a new pattern of relations between government and populace is particularly important during the early phase of development when political participation on a large scale is beginning to take place.

It is commonplace to speak of the "gap" between governors and the governed in the new nations, implying that some fundamental cultural and attitudinal gaps exist between the "elite" and the "mass," the former being secular-minded, English- or French-speaking, and Western-educated, if not Western-oriented, while the latter remain oriented toward traditional values, are fundamentally religious, and are vernacular-speaking. In more concrete political terms, the government may be concerned with increasing savings and investment and, in general, the postponement of immediate economic gratification in order to maximize long-range growth, while the public may be more concerned with immediate gains in income and, more fundamentally, equitable distribution or social justice irrespective of its developmental consequences. Often the governmental elite itself may be split with one section concerned with satisfying public demands in order to win popular support while the other is more concerned with maximizing growth rates, eliminating parochial sentiments, establishing a secular society, or achieving international recognition. The elite-mass gap also implies that communications are inadequate, that is, that the elite is oriented toward persuading the mass to change their orientation, but the feedback of political demands is not heard or, if heard, not responded to.

Perhaps too much is made of the attitudinal "gap" between governors and governed; what is more important perhaps is the attitude of government toward its citizens. Nationalist leaders out of power are typically populist. They generally identify with the mass and see in the "simple peasant" and the "working class" qualities which will make a good society possible. But once the nationalist leadership takes power and satisfies its desire for social status it tends to view the mass as an impediment to its goals of establishing a "modern," "unified," and "powerful" state. From being the champion of the masses the elite often becomes their detractor.

In all political systems, those of developing as well as developed societies, there are differences in outlook between those who govern and those who are governed. In a developed system, however, those who govern are accessible to influence by those who are governed—even in a totalitarian system—and those who are governed are readily available for mobilization by the government. In modern societies governments are so engaged in effecting the economy, social welfare, and defense that there must be a closer interaction between government and the governed. Governments must mobilize individuals to save, invest, pay taxes, serve in the army, obey laws. Modern governments must also know what the public will tolerate and must be able to anticipate, before policies are pursued, what the public reaction to a given policy might be. Moreover, the modern government is increasingly armed with sophisticated tools of economic analysis and public opinion surveys to increase its capacity to predict both the economic and political consequences of its actions. In contrast, the elites of new nations are constantly talking to the masses; it is not that they do not hear the masses, but what they hear is often so inappropriate to what they wish to do. To ban opposition parties, muzzle the press, and restrict freedom of speech and assembly does indeed close two-way channels of communication, but often this is precisely what is intended.

But whatever their fear of the masses, governmental elites in new nations cannot do without them. While the elite may be unsympathetic to mass efforts to exercise influence, the elite does want to mobilize the masses for its goals. In some developing societies an organizational revolution is already under way as men join together for increasingly complex tasks to create political parties, newspapers, corporations, trade unions, and caste and tribal associations. Governmental elites are confronted with a choice during the early stages of this development. Should they seek to make these new organizations instruments of the authoritative structures or should these organizations be permitted to become autonomous bodies, either politically neutral or concerned with influencing government? When the state is strong and the organizational structures of society weak —a condition often found in the early phases of postcolonial societies with a strong bureaucratic legacy—then government leadership clearly has such an option. It is at this point that the classic issue of the relationship of liberty and authority arises, and the elite may choose to move in one direction rather than the other.

The choices made are often shaped by dramatic domestic or international crises of the moment. But they are also affected by the society's tradition of elite-mass relations. The traditional aloofness, for example, of the mandarin bureaucracy toward the Vietnamese populace and the traditional disdain of the Buddhist and Catholic Vietnamese toward the *montegnards* or "pagan" hill peoples have probably been more important factors affecting elite-mass relations in contemporary Vietnam than any strategic or ideological considerations on the part of the Vietnamese government. Similarly, the behavior of many African leaders can often be understood better by exploring the customary patterns of authority in traditional tribal society than by reference to any compulsions inherent in the development process.

In the analysis of elite-masses relations much attention is rightly given to the development of "infra-structures"—that is, political parties, newspapers, universities, and the like—which can provide a two-way communication channel between government and populace.[3] Much attention is also given to the development of a "middle strata" of individuals who can serve as links—newspapermen, lobbyists, party bosses, and precinct workers. While in the long run these developments are of great importance, in the short run so much depends upon the attitude of the governmental elites, whether the elites fundamentally feel—and behave—as if they were alienated from and even antagonistic to the masses as they are, or whether the elites perceive the values of the masses as essentially being congruent to their own aims.

Integrative behavior. The readiness of individuals to work together in an organized fashion for common purposes and to behave in a fashion conducive to the achievement of these common purposes is an essential behavioral pattern of complex modern societies. Modern societies have all encountered organizational revolutions—in some respects as essential and as revolutionary as the technological revolution which has made the modern world. To send a missile into outer space, to produce millions of automobiles a year, to conduct research and development, to manage complex mass media all require new organizational skills. During the last few decades we have begun to understand the nature of managerial skills and the complexity of organizations—how they carry out their many purposes, how they adapt themselves to a changing environment, and how they change that environment. We know less about why some societies are more successful than others in creating men and women capable of establishing, maintaining, and adapting complex organizations for the achievement of common purposes.

The consequences of an organizational lag as an impediment to development are, however, quite apparent. The inability of many political leaders to maintain internal party and government unity in many new nations has resulted in the collapse of parliamentary government and the establishment of military dictatorships. The much vaunted organizational

---

[3] For a discussion of the role of infra-structures in political development, see Edward Shils, *Political Development in the New States* (The Hague: Mouton, 1962).

skill of the military has also often failed in many new nations. In Ceylon a planned military coup collapsed when several of the conspirators spoke of their plans so openly that even a disorganized civilian government had time to take action, and in many Latin-American countries, and now in Vietnam, the military has proven to be as incapable of maintaining cohesive authority as their civilian predecessors.

The capacity—or lack of capacity—to organize with one's fellow men may be a general quality of societies. A society with a high organizational capacity appears to be organizationally competent at creating industrial organizations, bureaucracies, political parties, universities, and the like. Germany, Japan, the United States, the Soviet Union, Great Britain come quickly to mind. In contrast, one is struck by a generalized incompetence in many new nations where organizational breakdowns seem to be greater bottlenecks to economic growth than breakdowns in machinery. In some new countries technological innovations—such as industrial plants, railways, telegraph and postal systems—have expanded more rapidly than the human capacities to make the technologies work, with the result that mail is lost, the transport system does not function with any regularity, industrial managers cannot implement their decisions, and government administrative regulations impede rather than facilitate the management of public sector plants. Though some scholars have argued that the skill to create complex institutions will accompany or follow technological innovation, there is good reason to think that organizational skills are a prerequisite for much political and economic development. In fact, the pattern of interpersonal relations appears to be more conducive to organization-building in some traditional societies than in others. Just as the presence of entrepreneurial talents in the traditional society is a key element in whether or not economic growth occurs, so may the presence of organizational talents be an important element in whether there emerges a leadership with the capacity to run a political party, an interest association, or a government.

Surprisingly little is known about the conditions for the development of effectual political organizations. If the modernization process does produce political organizations, why is it that in some societies these organizations are effectual and in others they are not? By effectual, we mean the capacity of an organization to establish sufficient internal cohesion and external support to play some significant role in the decision-making or decision-implementing process. The multiplication of ineffectual political organizations tends to result either in a highly fragmented unintegrated political process in which government is unable to make or implement public policy, or in a political system in which the authoritative structures make all decisions completely independently of the political process outside of government. In the latter case we may have a dual political process, one inside of government which is meaningful and one outside of government which, in policy terms, is meaningless.

Some scholars have suggested that political organization is a consequence of increased occupational differentiation which in turn results from economic growth and technological change—an assumption, incidentally, of much foreign economic assistance. The difficulty with viewing political change as a consequence of social changes which in turn are the consequence of economic development is that, however logical this sequence may appear to be, in the history of change no such sequence can be uniformly found. Indeed, political organization often precedes large-scale economic change and may be an important factor in whether or not there is large-scale economic change.

In recent years greater attention has been given to the psychocultural components of political organization. Attention is given to the existence of trust and distrust and the capacity of individuals to relate personal ambition with some notion of the public good and of moral behavior. For explanations, psychologists focus on the process of primary socialization.

While psychologists focus on the working of the mind, sociologists and social anthropologists have been concerned with the working of society, and focus on the rules that effect the relationship among men—why they are kept and why they are broken. Sociologists have given attention to the complex of rules that organize social relationships, the patterns of superordination and subordination as among and between groups and individuals, how these change, and what effects they have on political and social relationships. While psychologists give attention to the primary process of socialization, sociologists and social anthropologists are concerned with the way in which the individual, during his entire life, comes to learn the rules and, under certain circumstances, to break them. It is from these two complementary views of man that we may expect the more systematic study of politically integrative and disintegrative behavior.

CONCLUSION

We have tried to suggest in this essay that there are many different kinds of integration problems faced by developing nations, for there are innumerable ways in which societies and political systems can fall apart. A high rate of social and economic change creates new demands and new tasks for government which are often malintegrative. The desire of the governing elite or the governed masses, for whatever reasons, to increase the functions of government are often causes of integration problems. Since modern states as well as modernizing states are often taking on new functions, it would be quite inappropriate to view integration as some terminal state. Moreover, the problems of integration in the developing areas are particularly acute because so many fundamentally new tasks or major enlargements of old tasks are now being taken on. Once the state actively becomes concerned with the mobilization and allocation of resources, new patterns of integration between elite and mass are called for. Once the state takes on the responsibilities of public education and invokes sentiments of "national" solidarity, then the integration of social groups to one another becomes an issue. And once men endeavor to create corporations, newspapers, political parties, and professional associations because they perceive their individual interests served by common actions, a new set of values is called for which provides for the integration of new structures into the political process. The challenges of integration thus arise out of the new tasks which men create for themselves.

6. NATIONALISM

Rupert Emerson

RUPERT EMERSON is Professor of Government, Emeritus, at Harvard University. He has also taught at the University of California at Los Angeles and Berkeley, and at Yale University. He has held a number of government positions, including the directorship of the Division of Territories of the U.S. Department of the Interior. He has published *Malaysia. A Study in Direct and Indirect Rule* (1937 and 1964), *Representative Government in Southeast Asia* (1955), and *Africa and United States Policy* (1967).

The nation is today the largest community which, when the chips are down, effectively commands men's loyalty, overriding the claims both of the lesser communities within it and those which cut across it or potentially enfold it within a still greater society, reaching ultimately to mankind as a whole. In this sense the nation can be called a "terminal community" with the implication that it is for present purposes the effective end of the road for man as a social animal, the end point of working solidarity between men. "In our world, it is still as citizen of a national state that one is oppressed or liberated; willy nilly, one lives the destiny of one's nation." Within it there is the assumption of peaceful settlement of disagreement, based on the supreme value of national unity, whereas in conflict between it and other communities there is an assumption of the possibility of violence.

Since the state is in modern times the most significant form of organization of men and embodies the greatest concentration of power, it is inevitable that there should have been, and should still be, a great and revolutionary struggle to secure a coincidence between state and nation. The nation seeks to take over the state as the political instrument through which it can protect and assert itself. Less than a century ago Lord Acton could lay down the dictum that "A state may in course of time produce a nationality; but that a nationality should constitute a state is contrary to the nature of modern civilization"; but the nation has in fact become the body which legitimizes the state. As in earlier times the state achieved legitimacy through, say, its monarch or its religion, it is now legitimate if it is the embodiment and expression of a nation. Where the state is based on any principle other than the national one, as is by definition the case in any imperial system, its foundations are immediately suspect in a nationalist age. Once the people of such a state have come to a consciousness of national identity, the presumption is that the state will shortly be swept away, to be replaced by another cleaving as closely as possible to the national foundations. Where the peoples of several nations are seriously intermingled, as they are at so many points on the face of the globe, discord and trouble are the almost inevitable result. . . .

The nation is not only a community of brethren imbued with a sense of common destiny. It is also a community which, in contrast to others such as family, caste, or religious body, is characteristically associated with a particular territory to which it lays claim as the traditional national homeland. The emotional and intellectual tie in the minds of men is buttressed by a location in space which anchors the nation with permanence on the face of the earth. When the nation achieves its full self-realization in the form of a sovereign state this double base of spirit and soil emerges in a perplexing and often dangerous contradiction which lies embedded at the heart of the national concept.

In accord with the fundamentals of the political structure of the modern world the state asserts jurisdiction over all persons within its borders, but the nation on which it is based and from which it derives its legitimacy is likely neither to be wholly confined within the state frontiers nor to have its state domain all to itself, unencumbered by other peoples. The national principle and the state principle, despite the close ties which have grown up between them in modern times, are far from being identical and not infrequently come into dramatic conflict with each other. The existence in almost all corners of the earth of explosive minority issues and in others of troublesome irredenta is the political expression of this disparity. . . .

Many doctrinal disputes divide those who have attempted to explore the nature of the nation and its making, but there is a wide measure of agreement that nations differ so greatly from each other in their make-up and historical antecedents that no single set of factors can serve as more than a useful check list. Of the many and complex forces which have entered into the shaping of the nations one which may be singled out as having distinctive importance is the role of the state. Stretching the matter to its furthest limits Rudolf Rocker went so far as to say, in terms similar to those of Lord Acton: "The nation is not the cause, but the result, of the State. It is the State which creates the nation, not the nation the State." For the sake of achieving a single and coherent theory it might be very nice if this were true, but the historical evidence indicates clearly that it cannot be sustained in any such across-the-board fashion. Another more acceptable version of the same proposition is that of Ortega y Gasset who suggested in relation to Europe that "every linguistic unity which embraces a territory of any extent is almost sure to be a precipitate of some previous political unification. The State has always been the great dragoman."

Over and over again, if the inquiry is pressed back in time, it will be found that there was a state structure, or at least a political system approximating a state, which coincided to a striking degree with the modern nation in terms of territory and people. The nation is in a very large number of instances a deposit which has been left behind by the state—although this evades the query as to whether the state itself was perhaps the product of prior ethnic unity. Where the state has survived for many generations reasonably intact within an approximation of the same frontiers, as is the case with France, England (though here Great Britain becomes more problematical), Ireland, Spain, Portugal, Egypt, China, Japan, and certain others, the argument is so obvious as to need no elaboration. In such cases the territory claimed as the national homeland is substantially identical with that enclosed within the boundaries of the state. Poland, Hungary, Bohemia, and Bulgaria may serve as good examples of states which vanished from the historical scene for longer or shorter periods of time but left behind them firmly established national precipitates.

These and similar examples indicate a coincidence which is too striking to be ignored, but, as with so many other aspects of the analysis of nationalism, a certain amount of legerdemain is necessary. While it is possible and plausible to single out those periods in history during which, say, the Hungarian and the Bohemian people were given a national mold by a state which had, prospectively, a "national" base, these peoples were at other considerable periods of their history incorporated in quite differently oriented state structures. For one phase of it, if Poland be taken as an example, a glance at an historical atlas establishes that the Polish state extended to vastly different expanses of territory in the course of its long existence. Coming at the problem from another angle, the peoples of eastern and central Europe and the Balkans have over the centuries lived their lives in a number of different state and imperial systems. An arbitrary trimming of the facts to fit the theory inevitably attaches to any effort to single out some one era of their political experience as the determinative one while others are ignored or minimized. Yet the fact remains that in many instances communal identity appears related to an identifiable prior state structure. . . .

Nowhere is the significance of the state in its capacity as nation-maker more inescapably evident than in the colonial sphere. In some instances, such as those of the Burmese and the Vietnamese, the peoples who have recently claimed nationhood had achieved a vigorous earlier communal identity, despite the annoying presence of minorities. In other instances, such as those of the Philippines and Indonesia, the lines drawn on the map by the imperial power were the determining element in establishing the boundaries within which peoples have developed national awareness. The common government was a major instrument in pressing diversity into a common mold.

The way in which the existence of a single political authority works to knit together the people over whom it rules is easy enough to lay out in general terms, including the special consequences which flow from alien rule of the colonial variety. Subjection to a common government immediately operates to impose some elements of a common destiny on the people embraced within the political boundaries and to mark off the territory from neighboring countries, facilitating personal intercourse within and erecting barriers to easy intercourse with peoples outside. The growth of a single network of communications is encouraged. The public educational system is based upon a common body of ideas, principles, and materials. In all probability a single common language of administration is utilized at least by the central government, and that language is likely to become the language of education at one or another level. For the country as a whole a common body of law and a common administrative system reflect something of a single political philosophy, although the effective impact of unity of law and administration may dwindle off to a vanishing point under indirect rule. The consolidation of a political system is an almost indispensable pre-condition for the building of an integrated economy. More broadly, if less tangibly, the government reflects a common cultural pattern brought to bear on all the people within its domain.

Of the limits within which these forces of consolidation are effectively operative two are perhaps particularly worth taking into account, especially within a colonial context. One concerns the nature, strength, and stage of development of the peoples concerned, and the other the type of policies adopted by the colonial power.

On the first score, it is evident that the human material involved sharply limits the effect of the forces set in motion by the achievement of political unification. Integration is far more likely to occur where peoples have an original similarity than where they are divided by large-scale disparities in such basic elements as race, culture, religion, and language. Thus the closely related indigenous communities of the Indonesian archipelago lent themselves to an approximation of a general national pattern when they were brought under a single roof by Dutch rule, while the Chinese in Indonesia presented almost insuperable barriers to any comparable assimilation. To cite again the familiar cases of Malaya and Palestine, one may doubt that any government, whatever its policies, would have been able to bring about a national consolidation of the Malays, Chinese, and Indians in the one case and the Arabs and Jews in the other. In such instances the bonds of prior communal attachment were too deeply rooted and the differences between the peoples too profound to allow the state to play its role as the great dragoman. Similarly in Africa, through the superimposition of a colonial government, a group of African tribes may achieve a sense of national identity into which Europeans and Indians living under the same government are highly unlikely to be drawn.

In addition to mere difference, both qualitative and quantitative distinctions enter in. The presumption in favor of integration becomes greater if the people to be integrated accept the culture of those to whom they might be assimilated as being at a higher level than their own, and the presumption declines to the extent that they look down upon the other as inferior. The working of the American melting pot was eased by the frequent readiness of the immigrant to accept assimilation to "Americanism" as desirable. The European in Africa, on the other hand, or the Chinese in Malaya looked down upon the people to whose country he had come and regarded acceptance of their culture as a descent in the scales. Where one side has a great overbalance in numbers, as in the different African multi-racial societies, the vast majority cannot be expected to make a speedy or complete transition even to a culture accepted as higher. The more highly developed peoples are likely to have passed through the formative stage in their evolution and to be no longer readily susceptible to remolding. In particular, Islam appears to set a stamp upon peoples which is immensely resistant.

As for the bearing of colonial policy, in the past it could be taken for granted that there would be a lack of zeal on the part of the imperial power to achieve the national welding together of peoples over whom it ruled. What emerged in the way of national unity was an accidental by-product rather than an intended result. Even in the present changed imperial climate, where nation-building has found some acceptance as a proper colonial goal, colonial administrators cannot take on the tasks which only a national government can assume. The persons who head the administration and determine its policies are by definition alien; their values and outlooks are foreign to the peoples ruled; and the potentially national symbols and traditions cannot be drawn upon effectively. Where a national government encourages the development of a rounded national economy, colonial governments have typically developed colonial economies—the *pacte coloniale* of the French—directed toward the export of raw materials and foodstuffs in exchange for the manufactures of the mother country. Lines of transport and communication, which in other circumstances aim at knitting the country together, tend to flow from inside the dependency outward to serve the purposes of the alien government, investors, and traders. In one unique fashion, however, the colonial government serves the national cause: in the hostility to itself which it generates it pulls together the heterogeneous segments of the people under its sway.

Any colonial system which builds on ethnic diversity as one of its fundamental elements is sure to impede the processes of national integration. Whatever the virtues of indirect rule, one of its effects is undisputably to hold peoples apart rather than to bring them together. While direct rule will not necessarily produce a merger of disparate ethnic groups, the acceptance as the base of the colonial structure of traditional societies, each equipped with its own body of law and custom and its own native authorities, is to emphasize diversity rather than to encourage homogeneity. In West Africa the French policy of direct rule appears to have subordinated tribal differences to a greater extent than the indirect rule which has until recently dominated British practice. The difficulties which the British have encountered in promoting the development of Uganda as a unitary state derive in considerable part from their earlier acceptance of Buganda and other African polities as the building blocks with which they worked. There is no occasion to accept as valid across the board the customary contention of the nationalist that indirect rule, whether in its Lugardian African form or in such devices as the princely states of India, reflects the evil intent of the imperialist to divide and rule, but the nationalist has good reason to view such practices with dismay.

The same kind of results flow from other systems which take as their starting point the racial or other diversity of the peoples concerned. At the extreme, the South African doctrine of *apartheid* explicitly rejects any conception of building a single national community out of the peoples to whom the state's authority extends. At a lesser level obstacles to nation building are intruded wherever communalism comes to official recognition, as in the systems of election and representation in India prior to independence, in Ceylon at one stage, and in East Africa. A still different variant was the plural society of Malaya where, within the carefully preserved framework of the Malay Sultanates, the several racial communities lived largely separate lives with a varying political and legal status and with different school systems and languages. At the other end of the scale, assimilationist policies on the traditional French pattern may be as suspect to the nationalist as indirect rule or accepted pluralism since the assimilationist goal is the merger of colonial peoples into a nation of which the core is the mother country. . . .

Nationalism . . . has a chronology of its own derived not from the calendar but from the stages of the gradually spreading impact of the revolution which originated in Western Europe. It appears to have an essential role to play for peoples undergoing the kind of social and psychological transformation which that revolution imposes on them. One can plausibly argue that in the different but related stages of the cycle in which Asia and Africa are now engaged nationalism intrudes itself not only with an aura of inevitability but also as the bearer of positive goods.

Such a view carries with it no implication that everything ticketed with a nationalist label should be taken as desirable. The profoundly evil potentialities of nationalism have been amply demonstrated in the West by Fascism, Nazism, and many less globally disastrous movements. There is no reason to assume that its Asian and African variants are less likely to plunge into intolerable excesses. Japan's imperialism, the slaughter accompanying the partition of India, and the pretensions of Mossadegh, Nasser, and other Middle Eastern leaders are clues enough to the directions in which Asian nationalism can turn. Renan's idealized version of the nation as a soul and a spiritual principle is not wholly devoid of meaning, but it needs to be balanced by the harsh reality of national politics and prejudice and by taking into account the many millions whose poverty and ignorance exclude them from any effective share in the nation.

If we have no occasion to assume that nationalism is always right, we have equally little to take it as representing the ultimate good to which peoples should aspire. The double question which must be asked is as to the significance of nationalism for peoples at certain stages in their development and the extent to which it lays the indispensable foundations for building toward a more acceptable order than it can itself provide. The prospect of lingering for all eternity with nationalism would be appalling, but if it can be regarded as a steppingstone and if we could know with greater assurance where the steppingstones led, we might view its present evils with less apprehension—or, conceivably, with more.

To peoples emerging from imperial overlordship the major immediate contributions of nationalism are a sense of independent worth and self-respect and a new social solidarity to replace the traditional bonds. It is the sword and shield of those who are achieving independence. From being "natives" they rise to the honorable title of nationals. Through national self-assertion they achieve the spiritual satisfaction of demonstrating that they can make their own the forms on which the superior imperial powers pride themselves. They achieve also the more tangible satisfaction of overcoming that lack of social-political cohesion which earlier played so large a role in rendering them unable to resist the imperial pressure of consolidated nations.

For a dependent society to come to a sense of its own national existence is to make a substantial start along the road of equality with its alien rulers. The spokesmen for the imperial powers have habitually been concerned to insist that the peoples whom they govern have never constituted and do not now constitute nations. If the latter can be written off as no more than geographical expressions, owing such meager unity as they possess to alien rule, a large part of the justification for that rule is already established. The French, for example, have been much concerned to spread it on the record that the people of Algeria had no claim to being a nation at the time of the French take-over, even though that fact, assuming it to be proved up to the hilt, is irrelevant to their national status today. As the reverse side of the coin, to secure acceptance as a nation is to establish a people as having arrived in the modern world with a *prima facie* claim to all the benefits which may flow from self-determination. For Indian Moslems to win acknowledgement that they constituted a nation was regarded as an important step toward the achievement of Pakistan.

Colonialism has in many respects changed its spots of late, but the basic fact remains that, as a system, it involves the assertion of alien supremacy and the denial of the right and ability of peoples to manage their own affairs. Colonialism created not only the conditions which made nationalism possible, but also, as a complex of relationships subordinating "natives" to expatriate officials and employers, the conditions which made it an appropriate response for those who would regain their self-esteem. At least until the most recent times the white man who went out to any of the imperial domains assumed automatically the privileged position which the imperial order assigned him and which the people of the country were obligated to respect. Writing of Indochina, Paul Mus referred to the "colonial axiom" that the first of the Annamites should come after the last of the French. The assumption that colonial status is degrading was illuminated by the comment of the President of Burma, looking back to his days at Cambridge, that while Japanese, Chinese, and Siamese students were accepted as equals, "Indian and Burmese students were merely tolerated, if not treated with open contempt."

Where this principle is explicitly linked to race—as in South Africa's apartheid, the legislation and practices of Southern Rhodesia, or the white taunt in Kenya that the Kikuyu came down from the trees only fifty years ago—the humiliation which is inflicted runs so deep as to be almost beyond repair. What is involved is no longer an accidental or historically conditioned backwardness which may be overcome, but a charge of inherent inferiority against a race as a whole. To make matters worse this charge is often brought most vigorously by white settlers who have taken over the land and prerogatives of the people whom they condemn and who in this fashion seek to justify their position to themselves and to the world at large. The colonial peoples were not slow to point out that the racialism of empire ran very close to that of the Nazis which the imperial democracies were denouncing, and Nehru contended that the whole ideology of British rule in India was that of "the herrenvolk and the master race." . . .

The nation has been taken as the measure of the state, in Asia and Africa as in the West. Once that premise has been established the goal of policy inevitably becomes the promotion of the national interest, however that uncertain concept may come to be defined. One of the greatest of the unanswered and still unanswerable questions . . . is whether nations can supersede themselves, merging in some fashion in the pursuit of a larger common interest. The logic of the atomic age, unless it leads toward total destruction, leads irrefutably in the direction of an international society; but nationalism and logic have often parted company before this. A brilliant case can be made for the proposition, advocated by Lord Acton nearly a century ago, that the idea of nationality should be divorced from the state, making room for not one but many nations within the state, as there is now room for many religions. Who is prepared to make the first move to attack the menacing pretensions of nationalism, no longer compatible with survival, through abandonment of national sovereignty? And is there in fact an international society into which peoples seeking to break out of the narrow bounds of the nation can move?

Even given the most honorable intent on the part of Asian and African nationalist leaders to use independence to promote not only the national interest, but also the concerns of humanity as a whole, the climate of the period in which they have achieved freedom is scarcely one to inspire confidence in the international spirit. If the postwar world had seen a general sweep toward the consolidation of the community of mankind, the new nations might have welcomed an opportunity to take their equal place in a working global system. An organized international society which could guarantee peace, supervise the orderly liquidation of colonialism, and provide for the pooling of resources to promote economic and social progress would have an immense appeal for weak, unstable, and impoverished peoples. A divided world of hostile sovereign states holds out scant inducement, particularly when the surrender of national prerogatives carries with it the danger of renewed subordination to the imperial West or of satellite status in the Communist orbit.

Nations have arisen from the ashes of empire. Must they follow the ruinous course of their cantankerous predecessors upon the national stage?

7. COMMUNICATIONS

Lucian W. Pye and Daniel Lerner

LUCIAN W. PYE is Professor of Political Science and senior staff member of the Center for International Studies at Massachusetts Institute of Technology. He has also been Research Associate and Visiting Lecturer at Yale University, and has taught at Columbia University. He has been a consultant to the U.S. State Department, Chairman of the Committee on Comparative Politics of the Social Science Research Council, and Fellow of the Center for Advance Study in the Behavioral Sciences. His publications include *Politics, Personality and Nation Building* (1962), *Aspects of Political Development* (1966), *The Spirit of Chinese Politics* (1968), and he is co-author and co-editor of *Political Culture and Political Development* (1965).

DANIEL LERNER is Ford Professor of Sociology and International Communication at Massachusetts Institute of Technology and senior staff member of its Center for International Studies. He has taught at Columbia University, Stanford University, and universities in the Middle East, Europe, and Latin America. He has been a consultant to the U.S. State Department and the Ford Foundation as well as Director of the Institute of European Studies in Paris. His publications include *The Passing of Traditional Society* (1958 and 1964), *Sykewar: Psychological Warfare Against Germany* (1949 and 1971), and he is co-author with Harold Lasswell of *The Policy Sciences* (1951 and 1964) and *World Revolutionary Elites: Studies in Coercive Ideological Movements* (1951 and 1965).

MODELS OF TRADITIONAL, TRANSITIONAL, AND MODERN
COMMUNICATIONS SYSTEMS

The most striking characteristic of the communications process in traditional societies was that it was not organized as a distinct system sharply differentiated from other social processes. Traditional systems lacked professional communicators, and those who participated in the process did so on the basis of their social or political position in the community or merely according to their personal ties of association. Information usually flowed along the lines of the social hierarchy or according to the particularistic patterns of social relations in each community. Thus the process in traditional societies was not independent of either the ordering of social relationships or the content of the communication.

Since the communications process was generally so intimately related to the basic structure of the traditional society, the acts of evaluating, interpreting, and responding to all communications were usually strongly colored by considerations directly related to the status relationships between communicator and recipient. At present among many transitional people there is still a strong tendency to appraise the reliability of various media mainly on the basis of the strength of their personal relationship with the source of information.

A modern communications system involves two stages or levels. The first is that of the highly organized, explicitly structured mass media, and the second is that of the informal opinion leaders who communicate on a face-to-face basis, much as communicators did in traditional systems. The mass media part of the communications process is both industrialized and professionalized, and it is comparatively independent of both the governing and the basic social processes of the country. Both as an industry and as a profession the modern field of communications is self-consciously guided by a distinctive and universalistic set of standards. In particular the mass media system is operated under the assumption that objective and unbiased reporting of events is possible, and that politics can best be viewed from a neutral and non-partisan perspective. Thus even the partisan press tends to strive to appear to be objective.

A modern communications system involves, however, far more than just the mass media; the complex interrelationships between general and specialized informal opinion leaders, and between attentive and more passive publics, are integral parts of the whole communications system. Indeed, in modern industrial societies, with the ever-increasing ease of mechanical communications and physical travel and the increasingly effective organization of specialization and discipline, there tends to be—paradoxically—an increasing reliance upon direct word-of-mouth communication.

The critical feature of the modern communications system is that orderly relationships exist between the two levels so that the total process of communications has been aptly characterized as involving a "two-step flow." Political communications in particular do not rest solely upon the operations of the mass media; rather, there is a sensitive interaction between professional communicators and those in influential positions in the networks of personal and face-to-face communications channels. Above all, the interactions between the two levels take the form of establishing "feedback" mechanisms which produce adjustments in the content and the flow of different forms of messages. Those responsible for the mass media are constantly on the alert to discover how their communications are being received and "consumed" by those who control the informal patterns of communications. Similarly, those who give life to the informal patterns are constantly adjusting their actions to ways in which the mass media may be interpreting the temper of "public opinion" at any time.

In short, a modern communications system consists of a fusion of high technology and special professionalized processes of communications with informal, society-based, and non-specialized processes of person-to-person communications. This suggests to us that the measurement of modernization of the communications system should not be related solely or even primarily to the degree to which a society obtains an advanced technology, mass media system; instead, the real test of modernization is the extent to which there is effective "feedback" between the mass media systems and the informal, face-to-face systems. Modernization thus hinges upon the integration of the formal institutions of communications and the social processes of communications to the point that each must respond with sensitivity to the other.

With these considerations in mind let us now characterize in gross terms the essential characteristics of the transitional communications process. Structurally the key consideration is its bifurcated and fragmented nature, for it usually involves in varying degrees one system which is based upon modern technology, is urban-centered, and reaches the more Westernized segments of the population, and also a separate complex system which conforms in varying degrees to traditional systems in that it depends upon face-to-face relations and tends to follow the patterns of social and communal life. The essential characteristic is that the two levels and separate parts are not closely integrated but each represents a more or less autonomous communications system.

In the transitional society only in an erratic form does the urban-based communications process penetrate into the separate village-based systems. There is usually no systematic pattern of linkage in even a single country, and idiosyncratic considerations are often decisive in determining in any community the individual who plays the role of transmitting and interpreting the communications of the mass media to the participants of the local system. Differences in the particular social and economic status of these transmitters from community to community can have decisive consequences on how the different sub-systems are related to the mass media system.

In addition to this fundamental division between the urban and the elite level and the village or mass level, there is a further fragmentation in terms of the isolated sub-systems. Indeed, in most transitional societies villages in different parts of the country tend to have less communication with each other than they separately have with the urban centers. The pattern is like the spokes of a wheel all connecting to a hub, but without any outer rim or any direct connections among any of the spokes.

Most of the problems of political development can be thought of in terms of the ways in which such fragmented communications systems can become more effectively integrated into a national system while still preserving the integrity of the informal patterns of human association. Development thus involves the increasingly effective penetration of the mass media system into all the separate communal dimensions of the nation; while at the same time the informal systems must develop the capacity to interact with the mass media system, benefiting from the greater flow of communications but also maintaining a sense of community among their participants. . . . [T]he process of development is less dependent upon increased investment in the modernized, urbanized, or mass media system than it is upon the adjusting of the informal, rural systems to each other and to the mass media system. Indeed, excessive investment in the modern sector may create an even greater imbalance and thus exaggerate more than ever the bifurcated nature of the transitional system as a whole.

Although these structural differences appear to be the critical factors in differentiating the three types of communications systems, we must round out this brief characterization by suggesting some further differences which follow directly from these structural considerations.

There are, for example, certain fundamental differences in the volume, speed, and accuracy with which information is transmitted in the three systems. A modern communications system is capable of transmitting a massive flow of uniform messages to a wide audience. In contrast a traditional system handles only a very limited volume of messages, at very uneven rates of speed—some factual news might be spread very rapidly while more complete information might be disseminated at a much slower pace—and with great variety in repetition.

The sheer volume of communications possible in a mass media system means that much of the function of the informal, person-to-person level of communications in a modern system centers on screening out specialized information from the mass flow for the consumption of particular audiences. The role of opinion leaders is thus one of investing time and energy in "keeping up" with particular matters and insuring those who are dependent upon them that they are "fully informed" and "up to date" on the special subject. The tremendous volume of communications also means that single messages can easily be lost in the flood, and that the attention of a mass audience can be guaranteed only by repetition.

In a traditional system the prime problem besetting the active participant in the communications process was generally the inadequate volume of information to provide a complete picture. People turned to opinion leaders to learn what could be made out of the limited scraps of information received in the community. The skill of opinion leaders was not one of sorting out specialized information but of piecing together clues and elaborating, if not embroidering, upon the scant information shared possibly by all present. Thus the traditional system depended upon the role of the wise man and the imaginative story-teller who needed few words in order to sense truth and who could expand upon the limited flow of messages.

A transitional system, in combining features of both the modern and the traditional, usually does not have the necessary mechanism for controlling and keeping in proportion the volume, speed, and consistency of the flow of communications. The mass media sector of the communications process of the transitional societies generally relies heavily upon foreign and international systems of communication for the information it disseminates; but there are no ready criteria for selecting what should be retransmitted, and consequently there is a random element as to the relevance and appropriateness of what is communicated. An even more serious problem is the lack of specialized opinion leaders capable of sifting the messages of the mass media system and drawing attention to matters of special interest to particular audiences. Instead those in key positions in the face-to-face systems usually are more like the activists in the traditional systems, and hence their special skills lie in expanding upon limited information rather than in selecting from a voluminous flow of communication.

This difference in the skills stressed by informal opinion leaders in the modern and in the transitional systems tends to aggravate the consequences of the very unequal speed of communications at the two levels in the latter system. The mass media sector of the transitional system, with its inadequately staffed and poorly financed organizations, although it greatly exceeds the capacity of the more tradition-bound systems to retransmit their communications, may not be able to keep pace fully with the international flow of communications.

The limited rate at which the sub-systems can reflect accurately the flow of the mass media system creates one of the most basic tensions common to transitional societies. For it becomes apparent now that these societies do not have just the problem of relating or fusing elements of the international or world culture with parochial practices and sentiments, but they must usually operate with incomplete or inaccurate images of modernity and partly frustrated expressions of the parochial.

Toward a Communication Theory
of Modernization

HOW AND WHY THE MASS MEDIA SPREAD

If the mass media are to have some significant effect on modernization and democratic development—whether to facilitate or impede these desiderata—the first condition is that the mass media must spread. For, if the mass media do not spread, then we have no problem to discuss. We thus consider the question: what conditions determine whether the mass media spread?

One major condition is economic: the level of economic development in a country determines whether the mass media spread. All industrially developed countries produce mass media systems. No pre-industrial country produces mass media systems. Between these extremes lie the range of cases that interest us here, i.e., the developing nations. Here the general rule is that mass media spread in a direct and monotonic relationship with a rising level of industrial capacity. Where this rule applies, in general the spread of the mass media facilitates modernization. Where the rule does not apply, one may expect to find that the spreading mass media impede (or, perhaps more accurately, "deviate") modernization. Why does this simple rule have such general force as is here claimed?

The reasoning is clear if we consider information as a commodity. It is produced, distributed, and consumed like all other commodities. This brings information within the rule of the market. Notably, the supply-demand reciprocal comes into operation. This means that, to evaluate the functioning of a communication sub-system within a societal system, it is essential to consider—it may even be wise to begin with—the conditions that determine the efficient functioning of all economic processes: the capacity to produce and the capacity to consume.

We shall consider each of these briefly. Our discussion will draw its substance from the market economy model of the modern Western nations. It is in these countries, where the mass media developed in the private sector, that the mass media spread first historically, and where they remain today the most widespread in quantity of both production and consumption. Any account of this process that wishes to be relevant to happenings in the mass media around the world today must provide some reasonable explanation for the variant economic evolution of the mass media in the Communist countries and the developing countries. The Soviet system provides some especially interesting deviations from the rule of supply and demand, e.g., the political rule of enforced supply and acquiescent demand for a social commodity taken out of the economic market place. Events in the developing countries, such as India and Egypt, do not yet form a "system," but they do alert us to the possibility of new ways of handling information that differ significantly from the historic evolution in the modern West. We shall therefore try to frame our discussion in categories that *must* apply to the operation of mass media whether a country be capitalist, Communist, or neutralist.

Capacity to Produce. There must be a capacity to produce. No country —whether its ideology be Hamiltonian, Stalinist, or Gandhian—can produce information via mass media until it has an economic capacity to construct and maintain the physical plant of the mass media. I have made a simple checklist of the items needed to produce mass media products. This checklist is neither precise nor comprehensive. It is simply a reminder of what it has taken historically and what it takes today to produce information via the mass media. A glance will indicate how much more complex this list would become if one were considering the most efficient means of producing information according to strict considerations of economic optima. But such considerations lie far outside the present purview of developing countries. For these countries the simple checklist will do.

Capacity to Produce: A Checklist

1. PLANT: Buildings
                    Utilities (power, light, water)
                    Facilities (studios, workshops, offices)

2. EQUIPMENT: Books (linotype)
                    Newspapers (rotary)
                    Magazines (rotogravure)
                    Movies (film, camera)
                    Radio (amplifier, transmitter)
                    Television ("picture tube")
                    [Future standard equipment: satellites]

3. PERSONNEL: Copy producers (reporters, scripters, features)
                    Copy presenters (actors, printers, "layout")
                    Managerial corps (editor, publisher, producer, director)

The items required to produce information via the mass media are grouped under the three categories of plant, equipment, personnel. The three categories, as well as the items listed within them, are arranged in ascending order of complexity. They may even be construed as a scale upon which rising levels of economic capacity could be calibrated. Thus, if one thinks of the contemporary United States, it may seem too rudimentary to list the "plant." Yet efforts to spread the mass media in the developing countries have foundered, and continue to founder today, on just the three items listed in this category.

Even the item of buildings is a large hurdle and frequent stumbling-block. For one thing, buildings of adequate shape and size do not exist in most of the villages and towns and small cities of the developing countries. The mass media are perforce restricted to the capital cities for just this reason. But even such a capital city as Teheran . . . does not have enough buildings of the right shape and size to permit production or consumption of many full-length movies. The buildings in which the mass media operate must be provided with efficient utilities, such as power, light, water. How could a proper newspaper operate in Teheran without efficient telephonic communication, without regular telephone links to the great oil refineries at Abadan, to the summer and winter residences of the Shah, to other capitals of the world—not to mention the electronic equipment needed for receiving the huge volume of daily news files coming from the international press services? Yet which of us does not remember some amusing or frustrating incident connected with his use of the telephone in a rapidly developing country? Which of us has not witnessed the inhibiting, and sometimes paralyzing, restrictions placed upon the mass media in these countries by the inadequacy of their facilities? Of the thirty-six film companies in Teheran, only one had studios. This was the only company that had managed to produce a full-length feature film.

The varieties of equipment required by the mass media are manifold, complicated, and expensive. I have listed the principal media in the historic order of their evolution, which corresponds also to the complexity of the equipment they required at the time their major development occurred. Thus the book publishing industry was able to develop on the basis of the simple linotype machine. A further technological advance made possible the spread of the mass circulation daily newspaper, namely the rotary press. Illustrated magazines were a medium of elite communication because of their cost until the development of rotogravure machines made possible the cheap production of millions of copies of illustrated monthlies and weeklies. Similarly, the rapid development in our century of movies, radio, and television as industries hinged upon the capacity of American industry to produce at acceptable prices the mechanical and electronic equipment which are indispensable to the functioning of these mass media. The communication revolution of our time was technological before it became anything else. It is not implausible that in our century communication satellites will become standard equipment for the efficient functioning of mass media systems in many countries throughout the world.

The economic level of any country hinges also upon the quantity and quality of its skilled personnel. Particularly in the mass communication industries the capacity to produce hinges upon the availability of a corps of communicators, i.e., a substantial body of personnel trained in the array of special skills required for immediate production. Needed first of all are the skills that produce copy—whether it be for the news columns of a daily paper, a feature article in a weekly magazine, the script of a radio program, or the scenario of a movie or television show. Consider in passing the variety of features that fill the pages of every major daily newspaper. What a great variety of tastes, skills, and interests are needed to produce all this copy! Reflect for a moment that the man who has written a novel rarely turns out to be the man best equipped to adapt his own work for production as a movie. The man who does this may well be a person of much less creative talent but with superior specialized skill in "scripting." Consider the further array of skills needed to present copy, after it has been produced, to the consuming public. Actors do this for the spoken word, printers for the written word. But consider the extremely specialized skill required for that essential presentation function performed by the so-called "layout man." To make such large enterprises as a daily newspaper, a radio station, or a film company operate efficiently, a skilled managerial corps is also necessary. These are the editors and publishers, the producers and directors who are the kingpins of the mass communications industries. Without these many and varied persons the mass media have no capacity to produce.

If we simply reflect on the developing countries we know best in these terms, we promptly perceive that these conditions may well determine whether the mass media will spread. In reflecting further on the central question—whether the spread of the mass media will facilitate or impede modernization—we must take account of another condition: the capacity to consume.

Capacity to Consume. Three factors determine whether the capacity to consume media products spreads—and how fast—in any country: cash, literacy, motivation. There is a simple side to this matter. A person needs cash to buy a radio, a cinema ticket, a newspaper. If a newspaper costs as much as a loaf of bread, and if his ready cash is in a chronic state of short supply, then there is a diminishing probability that a person will consume newspapers. On the same simple level: only a literate person *can* read a book, paper, or magazine, and only a motivated person *wants* to read. The media flourish therefore in the measure that their society equips the individuals with cash, literacy, and motivation to consume their products.

There is a more complex sociology, however, that underlies each of these factors and their reciprocal interaction. It is no accident that the mass media developed in the monetized sector of every economy. The barter of country newspapers against farmers' produce or artisans' products was a brief and transitory phase—occasionally magnified in the sentimental memoirs of superannuated country editors. The media grew in the monetized sector because this is the distinctively modern sector of every economy. The media, as index and agent of modernization, *had* to grow in the sector where every other modern pattern of production and consumption was growing or else remain stunted.

The efficient operation of a money economy was made possible only by a great transformation in the thoughtways and life-ways of millions of people. Historically, in any society the "sense of cash" is an acquired trait. It has to be learned, often painfully, by a great many people before their society can negotiate the perilous passage from barter to exchange. Consider, for example, this sentence on the traditional Anatolian peasantry by Professor H. A. R. Gibb: "We may suppose the *re'aya* to have been animated hardly at all by any idea of gain, and to have worked their land with a minimum of effort and very little knowledge." [1]

Gain, effort, knowledge—these are huge categories of discourse. For any adequate comprehension of the personality transformation which accompanied the shift from barter to cash in contemporary Turkey we are obliged to take these large terms in their historical sense. What has been acquired in one generation among a population that had always been ignorant and indifferent is precisely the sense of gain, effort, knowledge which came over centuries to guide personal behavior in the modern participant society of the West.

Cash is an essential solvent in modern life, and the achievement of rising per capita income distribution is a major objective of modern societies. Here the political and sociological problems of the developing countries become intertwined with their economic problems. Economies long caught in the vicious circle of poverty cannot easily break through into the modern industrial system of expanding production of goods and services. This fact reflects no inherent and inevitable distaste for the good things of life among developing peoples. It reflects rather the difficult communication process—which in the West occurred over several centuries—of stimulating desires and providing means for satisfying them where neither desires nor facilities have previously existed. Westerners engaged in economic development problems have only recently recognized that, once a start is made, the reciprocity between desires and facilities tends to operate in the new nations as elsewhere.

Consumption of media products is thus an economic function, but it performs simultaneously several other functions that are sociological, psychological, and political. Literacy is a technical requirement for media consumption. But literacy, once acquired, becomes a prime mover in the modernization of every aspect of life. Literacy is indeed the basic personal

[1] Hamilton A. R. Gibb and H. Bowen, *Islamic Society and the West*, London, Oxford University Press, 1950, Vol. I, Part I, p. 244.

skill that underlies the whole modernizing sequence. With literacy people acquire more than the simple skill of reading. Professor Becker concludes that the written word first equipped men with a "transpersonal memory"; Professor Innis writes that historically "man's activities and powers were roughly extended in proportion to the increased use of written records." The very act of achieving distance and control over a formal language gives people access to the world of vicarious experience and trains them to use the complicated mechanism of empathy which is needed to cope with this world. It supplies media consumers, who stimulate media production, thereby activating the reciprocal relationship whose consequences for modernization we have noted. This is why media participation, in every country we have studied, exhibits a centripetal tendency. Those who read newspapers also tend to be the heaviest consumers of movies, broadcasts, and all other media products. Throughout the Middle East illiterate respondents said of their literate compatriots: "They live in another world." Thus literacy becomes the sociological pivot in the activation of psychic mobility, the publicly shared skill which binds modern man's varied daily round into a consistent participant life-style.

Literacy is in this sense also a precondition for motivation. People who can read usually do read—as, indeed, they consume more of all the audio-visual products of the media (the well-known "centripetal effect") and participate more fully in all the modernizing activities of their society. What is required to motivate the isolated and illiterate peasants and tribesmen who compose the bulk of the world's population is to provide them with clues as to what the better things of life might be. Needed there is a massive growth of imaginativeness about alternatives to their present life-ways, and a simultaneous growth of institutional means for handling these alternative life-ways. There is no suggestion here that all people should learn to admire precisely the same things as people in the Western society. It is suggested, much more simply, that before any enduring transformation of the vicious circle of poverty can be started, people will have to learn about the life-ways evolved in other societies. What they subsequently accept, adapt, or reject is a matter which each man will in due course decide for himself. Whether he will have the capacity to reach a rational decision hinges, in turn, upon the fullness of his participation in the modernizing process as it works through every sector of his personal and social life. The final test comes in the arena of political participation.

Mass Media and Political Democracy. Democratic governance comes late historically and typically appears as a crowning institution of the participant society. In countries which have achieved stable growth at a high level of modernity the literate individual tends to be the newspaper reader, the cash customer, and the voter.

The media teach people participation of this sort by depicting for them new and strange situations and by familiarizing them with a range of opinions among which they can choose. Some people learn better than others, the variation reflecting their differential skill in empathy. For empathy, in the several aspects it exhibits, is the basic communication skill required of modern men. Empathy endows a person with the capacity to imagine himself as proprietor of a bigger grocery store in a city, to wear nice clothes and live in a nice house, to be interested in "what is going on in the world" and to "get out of his hole." With the spread of curiosity and imagination among a previously quietistic population come the human skills needed for social growth and economic development.

The connection between mass media and political democracy is especially close. Both audiences and constituencies are composed of participant individuals. People participate in the public life of their country mainly by having opinions about many matters which in the isolation of traditional society did not concern them. Participant persons have opinions on a variety of issues and situations which they may never have experienced directly—such as what the government should do about irrigation, how the Algerian revolt could be settled, whether money should be sent to Jordan or armies to Israel, and so on. By having and expressing opinions on such matters a person participates in the network of public communication as well as in political decision.

The mechanism which links public opinion so intimately with political democracy is reciprocal expectation. The governed develop the habit of having opinions, and expressing them, because they expect to be heeded by their governors. The governors, who had been shaped by this expectation and share it, in turn expect the expression of *vox populi* on current issues of public policy. In this idealized formulation of the relationship, then, the spread of mass media cannot impede but can only facilitate democratic development.

But ideal types do not always match perfectly with their empirical instances. In the developed democracy of the United States, for example, the capacity to produce information via mass media is virtually unlimited. The capacity to consume media products—thanks to an abundant supply and widespread distribution of cash, literacy, motivation—is unparalleled anywhere in human history. The production-consumption reciprocal has operated efficiently on a very high level over many decades. Yet as American society presented the world with its most developed model of modernity, certain flaws in the operation of the system became apparent. I do not speak of the Great Crash of 1929—which exhibited a merely technical flaw in management of the economic sub-system. I speak of a much deeper flaw in the participant system as a whole, i.e., the emergence of non-voting as a political phenomenon. A generation ago Harold Gosnell called our attention to this danger. In recent years an alarmed David

Riesman has generalized this phenomenon to the larger menace of political apathy. If Americans were really suffering from widespread apathy about their public life, then a cornerstone of our media-opinion system would be crumbling—namely, in our terms, the cornerstone of motivation. (We note in passing that in the developed democracy of France only a short while ago leading thinkers and scholars convened for solemn discussion of political apathy in France—of all places!)

If one danger to developed democracies comes from literate non-voters, the parallel danger to developing democracies comes from the reverse configuration, i.e., *non-literate voters!* Can universal suffrage operate efficiently in a country like India or Egypt which is 90 per cent illiterate? Can the wise Jeffersonian concept of a literacy test for voters be completely ignored nowadays because we have radio? President Nasser has proffered a counter-doctrine for the developing countries, to wit: "It is true that most of our people are still illiterate. But politically that counts far less than it did twenty years ago. . . . Radio has changed everything. . . . Today people in the most remote villages hear of what is happening everywhere and form their opinions. Leaders cannot govern as they once did. We live in a new world." [2]

But has radio really changed everything? When illiterate "people in the most remote villages hear of what is happening everywhere," what do they really hear? They hear, usually via the communal receiver at the village square in the presence of the local elite, the news and views selected for their ears by Egyptian State Broadcasting (ESB). Their receivers bring no alternative news from other radio stations. Being illiterate, they can receive no alternative news and views from newspapers and magazines and books published anywhere.

In terms of personal achievement almost nothing happens to these "people in the most remote villages" by way of Radio Cairo: broadcasting now supplies them with the kind of rote learning each acquired by memorizing the Koran (which he could not read) in childhood. But in terms of personal aspiration nearly everything happened to these people when radio came to their remote villages. For the first time in their experience—both the experience of centuries inherited through their parents and their own lives—these isolated villagers were invited (and by none less than their rulers!) to participate in the public affairs of their nation.

The invitation carried with it, however, none of the enabling legislation needed to make radio-listening an integrative agent of modernization. In a modern society the radio listener is also the cash customer and the voter. In the remote villages of Egypt, when the government inserted radio into

[2] Gamal Abdul Nasser, *Egypt's Liberation.* Washington, D.C., Public Affairs Press, 1955.

the community, nothing else changed in the daily round of life—except the structure of expectations. This is the typical situation that over the past decade has been producing the revolution of rising frustrations. The mass media have been used to stimulate people in some sense. It does so by raising their levels of aspiration—for the good things of the world, for a better life. No adequate provision is made, however, for raising the levels of achievement. Thus people are encouraged to want more than they can possibly get, aspirations rapidly outrun achievements, and frustrations spread. This is how the vicious circle of poverty operates in the psychological dimension.

The impact of this psychic disequilibrium—its force as a positive impediment to modernization—has been disclosed by Major Salah Salem, the youthful Minister of National Guidance who tried to run the Egyptian mass media during the contest for power between Naguib and Nasser. Major Salem, finding his problems of national guidance insoluble, finally solved them by voluntarily locking himself in jail. There he prepared a memoir of his own frustration in the impossible task of converting an inert and isolated peasantry into an informed and participant citizenry by the mass media alone. Major Salem concludes: "Personally I am convinced that the public was wrong." [3]

In similar vein, Nasser has written retrospectively: "Before July 23rd I had imagined that the whole nation was ready and prepared, waiting for nothing but a vanguard to lead the charge. . . . I thought this role would never take more than a few hours . . .—but how different is the reality from the dream! The masses that came were disunited, divided groups of stragglers. . . . There was a confirmed individual egotism. The word 'I' was on every tongue. It was the solution to every difficulty, the cure for every ill." [4]

These judgments by leaders who were frustrated in their aspiration for quick and easy modernization reveal why transitional Egypt . . . has been so deeply frustrated. Can "the people," in Salem's sense, ever really be "wrong"? Can a social revolution ever really be accomplished in "a few hours"—or its failure attributed, in Nasser's sense, to "egotism"? Or is it, rather, that these young enthusiasts had never learned Lasswell's lesson—that political life is largely a question of "who gets what"? When people get involved in politics, it is natural that they should expect to get more of whatever it is they want. Instead of rebuffing such aspirations as egotism, the statesman of an enlarging polity and modernizing society will rather seek to expand opportunities for people to get what they want. He

[3] This memoir is quoted in D. Lerner, *The Passing of Traditional Society,* pp. 244–245.
[4] Gamal Abdul Nasser, *op. cit.*

will seek above all to maintain a tolerable balance between levels of aspiration and achievement. In guiding the society out of the vicious circle toward a growth cycle his conception of the role of public communication is likely to be crucial.

8. EDUCATION

James S. Coleman

JAMES SMOOT COLEMAN is Director of the Institute for Development Studies at the University of Nairobi, Kenya, and Representative in East Africa of The Rockefeller Foundation. He has been Professor of Political Science and Director of the African Studies Center at the University of California, Los Angeles, as well as President of the African Studies Association of the United States, Vice President of the International Congress of Africanists, and a member of the Committee on Comparative Politics of the Social Science Research Council. He has written *Nigeria: Background to Nationalism* (1958), and is co-editor and co-author of *The Politics of the Developing Areas* (1960), *Political Parties and National Integration in Tropical Africa* (1964), and *Education and Political Development* (1965).

The introduction of a modern educational system in colonial areas had significant political consequences. It was the single most important factor in the rise and spread of nationalist sentiment and activity. From the modern educational system emerged an indigenous elite which demanded the transfer of political power to itself on the basis of the political values of the Western liberal tradition or the ethical imperatives of Christianity, both of which had been learned in the schools. The educational system was also the medium for the development of a common territorial (national) language which alone made possible effective political communication and the political mobilizaton of a mass following. Designed essentially to serve only evangelizing or imperial purposes, Western education became a prime contributor to the emergence of new independent nations. Intended not to be a structure for political recruitment, it in fact called forth and activated some of the most upwardly mobile and aggressively ambitious elements of the population—elements most determined to acquire political power, most confident in the rightness of their claim, and most convinced of their capacity to govern. The serendipital effects of colonial education are among the great ironies of the historic encounter between the West and the non-West.

Western education not only hastened the collapse of colonial rule; it also left a legacy that continues to have relevance in many of the developing areas. At least two elements in this legacy should be noted. One is the instrumentalist attitude toward education which developed as a consequence of the high valuation it acquired under colonial conditions. European colonial rule was rationalized and justified in terms of the special grace that education purportedly bestowed upon the alien governing class, a class composed mainly of persons with higher education. Upward mobility into the more prestigious and remunerative roles available to the indigenous inhabitants in the modern sector of colonial society was usually determined by educational achievement alone. Education was also highly valued, and its legitimation of elite status was espoused, because so substantial a number of the upwardly mobile elements in the emerging indigenous elite in colonial society came from the lower strata of traditional societies. Members of this elite obviously had strong vested interests in the primacy of achievement criteria in recruitment to high occupational and political status. These and other factors furthered the belief that there was a close connection between educational achievement and elite status. The resultant instrumentalist conception of education has tended to persist in the post-colonial period. . . .

A second aspect of the colonial legacy is the uneven acquisition of education by different ethnic or status groups, or in different regions of a country, during the colonial era. This unevenness in the impact of education was sometimes owing to colonial policies favoring or "protecting" one group or section against another. At other times it reflected the differential adaptive capacity, or receptivity, to education on the part of indigenous cultural groups. In many instances it was solely the consequence of the fortuity of the impingement of modernizing influences. Whatever the cause of the unevenness, at the time of independence gross imbalances frequently characterized the representation of ethnic groups or sections of the country in party leadership, the bureaucracy, the army, the police force, and other authoritative spheres of the polity. The struggle to counter or correct or to maintain such imbalances is often at the heart of post-colonial politics in the new states.

The attainment of independence and the transfer of power provided the opportunity for indigenous successor elites to make fundamental changes in educational systems. At least three types of change have been sought. Characteristically there has been a marked expansion in educational facilities, in the proportion of the national budget allocated to education, and in the number of students enrolled at all levels. A second pronounced tendency has been the secularization of both the structure and the content of education as manifested in the state's assumption of primary responsibility for the school system and the consequent atrophying and eclipse of traditional and religious educational institutions. Third, there has been pressure for a revision of the educational curriculum in the direction of "practicality," "indigenization," and "politicization."

The high valuation education acquired in the terminal stages of colonial rule resulted in strong political pressure for an expansion in educational opportunity. Among the commonalty there was a widespread conviction that only education could bring higher status and a better standard of living. Moreover, political elites tended to assume that increased educational opportunity was the sine qua non of their own continued popular support. Added to these influences has been the feeling that expanded education is the prime requisite not only for economic development, but also for the badge of modernity which will extinguish the stigma of backwardness, and secure for peoples in the developing areas, individually and collectively, full acceptance in the modern world community.

The consequences of this great expansion in the educational system have been varied. An immediate result has been (or predictably will be, depending on the rate of economic growth and the expansion of occupational roles in the modern sector of the societies) the devaluation of education as the principal channel for upward mobility into political elite status. . . .

Rapid educational expansion may also have disunifying consequences which, in the short run, may outweigh the integrative expectations on which such expansion has been predicated. . . . [T]he expansion of schools in Indonesia has shifted the central focus of secondary education from the urban centers of the island of Java to the new outlying schools. During the colonial period the very limited extent of educational development and the centrality of institutions of higher education contributed immeasurably to elite integration in many instances. The existence of a single institution of higher learning in a country or region, particularly when it was a boarding school (as most of them were), provided an institutional setting for the homogenization, to a degree, of values and perspectives of diverse peoples drawn from an extremely heterogeneous milieu. . . . The characteristic result of the expansion of an educational system, however, is proliferation into an ever-increasing number of separate units. In culturally fragmented societies, where primordial ties tend to remain transcendent, expansion and proliferation of the system will at least perpetuate, and very likely intensify and exacerbate, local parochialisms. This accentuation of fragmentation is particularly to be expected where the central government's control over the educational system is weak and fragile. . . .

The third consequence of educational expansion is, of course, the aggravation of the problems of unemployed school leavers and second-generation aspirants. . . . Of variable internal political significance in the developing countries, these problems are bound to be most acute in countries that have experienced a rapid expansion of education, that have enjoyed only limited economic growth, and that have been burdened with fragile and unresponsive governments.

Politically dysfunctional situations of this type within one developing country frequently create or aggravate similar situations in other developing countries, because one of the first actions taken, or encouraged, by a government faced with mounting pressure from its own unemployed educated nationals is "localization." As used here, this term refers to the process of displacement of non-local by local persons in all but the most menial jobs. The circumstances associated with localization campaigns are largely the product of the uneven spread of Western education during the colonial period. Certain groups, regions or countries became exporters of educated manpower to meet the needs of Western colonial enterprise in other areas. Jamaica, the former colony of Sierra Leone, southern Togo and Dahomey, eastern Nigeria, Uganda, Nyasaland, Egypt, Lebanon, and India, among others, sent educated persons to other less educationally developed areas during the colonial period. The post-colonial expansion of educational facilities in the less developed host countries has inevitably produced ever more "local" job aspirants asserting a higher and more rightful claim as "sons of the soil." Thus a process that commenced with the nationalist demand for the displacement of alien European colonists by non-Europeans in the power structure inexorably persists to its logical end of total localization, leaving in its wake a succession of displaced elements. Some become pariahs in the host country; others return to their country or region of origin, where they further aggravate an already acute problem of unemployment among educated persons. The process can be politically explosive in many developing countries in the years of sorting-out following independence.

The second post-colonial phenomenon of concern to us here is the pressure for the secularization of both the structure and the content of education. This process characteristically involves the assertion of the supremacy, if not the monopoly, of the state over the educational system, at the expense of religious schools or traditional educational institutions. It also reflects the triumph of secular values and the primacy of the technical and utilitarian imperatives of modernization, and, where foreign missionary societies are involved, becomes an assertion of nationalism. The impulse for secularization varies according to the character and the strength of traditional educational systems, the degree of penetration and control of the educational system by foreign missionary enterprise, and the strength of the commitment to secularism or ideological purity on the part of the new state builders. In Indonesia, . . . the weakness or the hesitation of the central government, coupled with the decentralized character of the educational system, has moderated or dissipated the impulse toward secularization. In Egypt, however, . . . the Nasser regime has established its control over both private Egyptian schools and foreign schools. In Guinea the strong commitment of the governing elite to a national education system has resulted in the progressive assertion of state control over mission-run schools, which under colonialism included most of the country's educational institutions. In mid-1961 the government finally ordered the closing of all such schools. The purpose has been not only to extinguish foreign influences, but also to consolidate a purely secular state-run educational system in the interest of a more effective political socialization of the new generation of Guinean citizens.

Drastic action like that taken in Guinea, particularly in developing countries where missionary societies have provided most of the teachers, can have profound short-run staffing and financial implications of no little political relevance. The state-church educational struggle will be most acute in sub-Saharan Africa where Christian missions have carried the main burden of education. The problem will not everywhere be solved so neatly, and with such finality, as it has been in Guinea. A similar effort at radical secularization in the Eastern Region of Nigeria or in Uganda, where Catholics are politically powerful, for example, would produce political strife of possibly serious proportions.

In areas where traditional indigenous educational institutions have a longer history, and are more integrally a part of the local culture, the drive for secularization by modernizing elites has been pursued more cautiously. In . . . Tunisia, for example, . . . the mosque-university has become an integral part of the national educational system.

When a traditional educational system that has acquired high visibility and great respect has at its apex an ancient institution of renown such as Al-Azhar in Egypt, a dual pattern tends to evolve. . . . [T]here are limits to the adaptability of such an institution to a modern national educational system. The cultural gap between the educational patterns in the different spheres of the dual system inevitably means that the graduates of the traditional institution have a competitive disadvantage in the modern sector of society. In sub-Saharan Africa, however, the problem of integrating traditional indigenous educational patterns with modern secular structures has been and will continue to be much less of a problem. . . .

The third general post-colonial trend in educational development is curriculum revision. At least three aspects of the efforts to change the content of formal instruction are relevant: the move toward greater "practicality" in subject matter, the pressure for "indigenization," and "politicization." These trends, like educational expansion and secularization, are a reflection of both utilitarianism and nationalism. They show a determination to harness the educational system to the task of economic and social modernization and to the creation of a new viable political community of allegiant citizens.

The move toward greater "practicality" in the curriculum, . . . is also evident in many other developing areas. The impetus for change comes from a variety of sources; from governing elites alarmed over the ever-increasing number of unemployable graduates with literary or legal training; from those concerned over the high cost and the political undesirability of filling manpower shortages in the technical fields with foreigners; from nationalist leaders and development planners, who see the urgent need for a tighter fit between the content of instruction and the manpower needs and occupational structure of a developing society; from educators who increasingly sense the need for a curriculum stressing applied science and technology; and from the students themselves, who perceive that a more technical and practical education offers brighter career prospects.

There are, nevertheless, obstacles and even resistance to the shift in emphasis. . . . [L]egal degrees continue to have high prestige as a legacy from the past. The resistance to change also exists among some African intellectuals, who, writes Sir Eric Ashby, "confuse such changes with a lowering of standards. They are accordingly suspicious of any divergence from the British pattern." [1]

Several factors will operate to overcome such survivals from the colonial period. One is the emergence of a new occupational structure in which practical and technical education will provide the most visible means for higher status and upward mobility. Another is prospective changes in the curricula of European institutions of higher learning, which have heretofore served as models for most of the developing countries. A third factor is the multilateralization of external educational assistance as a result of a conscious shift from a single-dependency relationship with the former metropolitan country (or the country whose institutions were emulated) to a multiple-dependency relationship with many countries having radically different educational traditions. The major foreign countries that have been added to the widened spectrum of post-colonial overseas educational dependence are the United States and the Soviet Union, countries in which the tradition of technical and practical education has always held a commanding position.

Students from developing countries who undertake training in institutions abroad will also enjoy an increasing diversity of foreign educational experiences. In the past the enormous resistance to any alteration or adaptation of the imported educational system came from its product,

[1] Sir Eric Ashby, *African Universities and African Nationalism,* Cambridge, Harvard University Press, 1964, p. 61.

the indigenous educated elites. Their own sense of self-esteem, as well as their perception of how others esteemed them, was based upon the maintenance of the purity and the primacy of the system that had endowed them with actual or presumptive high status. As new generations of persons return from abroad with more varied educational experiences, and with degrees from a variety of foreign educational systems, standards of evaluation and prestige ranking will be keenly debated. Those derived from the colonial period will be increasingly challenged. What sort of amalgam, if any, will finally emerge is still unclear. It is unlikely that the unbalanced legal, humanistic, and literary form of education will continue to prevail.

The pressure for "indigenization"[2] of the content of education, the second type of curriculum revision, is in some respects nothing more than characteristic nationalist assertiveness, frequently tinged with a heavy dose of romanticism. It also reflects an understandable effort to correct the neglect or underemphasis of local history and culture which everywhere resulted from the uncritical importation of the school curriculum of the imperial country. The injection of local or national content into the curriculum helps to develop a sense of national identity; it also enhances the students' understanding of their own human and natural environment. . . . Educational institutions everywhere must teach not only what is of universal validity, but also "what is of parochial value, either because it is practical or because it cultivates the parochial [or national] cultural tradition."

Post-colonial political elites have shown surprising restraint on the issue of indigenization of the school curriculum. Pressure for radical changes in curriculum content has been strong among university students. . . . It is most marked, however, in the revolutionary-centralizing regimes compulsively preoccupied with what David Apter calls "political religion."[3] Among the new states, Guinea, Ghana, Mali, Algeria, Egypt, and Indonesia represent an orientation toward this type of regime. Other new states like Nigeria and Tunisia—in fact, most states recently removed from a colonial experience—tend to be more relaxed, less ideological, and more inclined to pragmatism in defining their relationships with the external world and in adapting imported institutions. . . .

One would expect that the politicization of educational content, the third form of curriculum revision examined here, would be actively sought by modernizing elites endeavoring to create new political com-

---

[2] "Indigenization" is a neologism used here to refer to the generic process of replacing foreign with indigenous content, symbols, meaning, or personnel. It subsumes such common terms as "Africanization," "Indianization," "Arabization," and the like.

[3] David E. Apter, "Political Religion in the New Nations," in Clifford Geertz, ed., *Old Societies and New States,* New York, Free Press of Glencoe, 1963, pp. 57–104.

munities and national identities. The remarkable fact is that in only a few instances have schools been made agencies for manifest political socialization by governing elites. Indeed, only the revolutionary-centralizing states—which have what David Apter calls "mobilization systems"—have taken explicit steps to politicize the school curriculum. One of the more eloquent proponents of this orientation is President Sékou Touré of Guinea. A key feature of the revised curriculum in the schools of independent Guinea is instruction in party history and doctrine. Touré has repeatedly criticized teachers for objecting to "teaching politics" in the schools, "as if," he adds, "the facts of politics were not the condensation of economic, social, and cultural facts!"

How can one explain the fact that, except for such states as Guinea and Indonesia, the developing countries have not pursued the politicization of school curricula more vigorously? Most of the explanations are explicit or implicit in the previous discussion. Where there continues to be a marked dependence for teaching staff upon the former metropolitan country, overt ideological indoctrination in the schools would obviously be difficult, if not impossible. Moreover, in many instances, indigenous members of the teaching staff tend to be either to the left or to the right of the government of the day; they are, therefore, unreliable agents for political indoctrination in the ideological line of the regime. Furthermore, despite a strong conviction that a national ideology is necessary, efforts thus far made by governing elites to develop an indigenous political ideology have been generally unimpressive. The reasons lie partly in the nature of the historical situation these elites confront and partly in the culturally fragmented societies they rule. In addition to these disabilities, the ruling elites in most new states also lack the necessary organizational capacity, and the supporting cadres which, among other things, would make possible more effective politicization in the schools. . . .

9. ELITES

Harry J. Benda

HARRY J. BENDA is Professor of History and Fellow of Timothy Dwight College at Yale University. He has also taught at the University of Rochester, has held a Guggenheim Fellowship, and has been Assistant Editor of the *Journal of Asian Studies.* He has written *The Crescent and the Rising Sun: Indonesian Islam under Japanese Occupation of Java* (1958), and *A History of Modern Southeast Asia: Colonialism, Nationalism, and Decolonization* (1969).

To avoid confusion, we should distinguish between two kinds of non-western intellectuals, *viz.* the "old" and the "new" intellectual. The first bears a distinct resemblance to the intellectual of the pre-industrial west, especially—though neither invariably nor exclusively—to the "sacral" intellectual of mediaeval times. For purposes of our present analysis, this group is of relatively minor importance, since it does not furnish the new political élites of contemporary non-western nation states. This is not to deny that it has played, and in some significant ways continues to play, important political roles. But for one thing, the "old" intellectuals' role, like that of their western counterparts, has almost invariably been limited to an ancillary function, a political task delegated to them, so to speak, by more or less powerful classes in their societies. Not infrequently these intellectuals (in west and non-west) were actually members of the ruling classes themselves and did not exercise independent political power *qua* intellectuals (priests, scholars, etc.) as such. Admittedly there were at all times also members of this "old" intelligentsia—such as Buddhist monks and Muslim *ulama*—who here and there allied themselves with the "outs" rather than the "ins," and who thus attained political significance by resisting the indigenous *status quo* and, in modern times, western colonialism. On the whole, however, the "old" intellectuals of the non-western world have suffered, and are suffering, a decline in their prestige, great as it may still be in areas hitherto untouched by modernization, especially the countryside, where the "new" intelligentsia's influence is only slowly penetrating.

These "new" intellectuals are a recent phenomenon, for they are for the greater part the product of western education during the past few decades. But though western-trained and therefore in several respects kin of their western counterparts, they also differ from the western intellectuals in some very significant respects. In the first place it is not literacy *per se* but westernization that stamps the non-westerner as the "new" intellectual. To the traditional tasks of manipulating the tools of communication have now been added the tasks of what Toynbee has aptly called the "human transformer." He, so Toynbee says, has "learned the tricks of the intrusive civilization . . . so far as may be necessary to enable their own community, through [his] agency, just to hold its own in a social environment in which life is ceasing to be lived in accordance with the local tradition." [1] Since, then, the criteria of westernization and "transforming" are their hallmarks, non-western intelligentsias will tend to include wider categories than has been the case of western intelligentsias. Westernization—thinking and acting in western, rather than tradi-

---

[1] Arnold J. Toynbee, *A Study of History*, Abridgement of Volumes I–VI by D. C. Somervell, New York, 1947, p. 394.

tionally indigenous ways—can extend to types of social activity that in the west have not, as a rule, formed part of intellectual activity as such.

The most common, and historically also most significant, representative of this category is the new military group, the "Young Turks" so to speak, of the non-western world. Nor is this at all surprising, since one of the prime contacts between west and non-west during the past century-and-a-half has been military in nature. As a result, the desire to attain equality with the west has often found expression in terms of military equality, and officers were often the first social group to receive western training. Thus very frequently military westernizers, or westernized officers, have played a leading—at times a preponderant—role as independent political leaders in non-western countries. What distinguishes them as prototypes from traditional military rulers or dictators is, first, the fact that they are consciously using the means of coercive, military power for the attainment of essentially non-military, ideologically conceived social ends. And, second, unlike *e.g.* the military *juntas* of Latin America, the twentieth century military leaders in Asia and the Middle East are almost invariably social revolutionaries whose coming to power signals the end of the *status quo* and the eclipse of the traditional ruling classes. In some isolated instances of the twentieth century, non-western military leaders can be found who combine these ideological ends with the qualities of charismatic leadership. The Peróns, the Nassers, and the Castros are thus yet another phenomenon of the "new" non-western intelligentsia.

Second, to a degree unparalleled in the west, non-western intellectuals are very frequently an isolated social group in indigenous society. This is largely due to the fact that this "new" intelligentsia is not, as in the west, a product of organic social growth, but rather a product of alien education more or less precariously grafted on indigenous non-western societies. Unlike the "old," predominantly sacral, intellectuals most of whom represented or spoke for the powers-that-were, and who thus performed the ancillary political roles usually assigned to intellectuals throughout the world, non-western intelligentsias do not, sociologically speaking, as a rule represent anyone but themselves. It is the exception rather than the rule that the young aristocrat, the landowner's son or for that matter even the scion of a newly-established bourgeois class, once he has acquired a western education of any kind, becomes the defender and spokesman of the class of his social origin. In turn, it is equally the exception rather than the rule that these "new" intellectuals will be supported by traditional social classes with a vested socio-economic interest in non-western societies.

In short, non-western intelligentsias, insofar as they are politically active —and, as will be seen, most of them are so to a far higher degree than in the west—tend to be social revolutionaries whose ideological aims as often as not militate against the *status quo*. Since, by definition, most of these aims are western-derived and transplanted to a social environment inherently still far more conservative than is true of the more advanced industrial societies of the west, the task of social engineering becomes far more radical, and its proponents, the only group with a vested ideological interest in change, may find themselves driven to the use of radical reforms in order to hasten the approximation between reality and ideal.

There is, third, an additional reason for the relatively high incidence of radicalism among non-western intelligentsias, and it is connected both with their numbers and employability. As for size, it is on the whole relatively smaller than in industrialized western societies, for the number of persons able to afford western education, at home but particularly abroad, is more limited, and democratization of education has—with the exception of Japan—not yet paralleled that in the west. Yet, in spite of the smallness of non-western intelligentsias, the supply by far exceeds social demand. This unhappy phenomenon of the overproduction and underemployment of intellectuals is in part doubtless conditioned by the social, psychological and ideological traditions of most non-western societies.

Since education, in these predominantly pre-industrial communities, still enjoys great traditional prestige, western education has automatically attracted large numbers of non-westerners; but in spite of the fact that the process of modernization and industrialization would indicate the need for technical, vocational and scientific training, the aristocratic or gentry bias common to pre-industrial societies has, in fact, led non-western students to bypass these fields in favour of humanistic and legal studies. Thus, while a crying shortage exists almost everywhere in Asia, the Middle East, Africa and even Latin America for physicians, engineers and scientists, the bulk of non-western intellectuals can be found in the humanities and the law, both of which appear to promise status satisfaction in traditional terms. In fact, it is predominantly graduates in these fields that compose the present-day political élites of so many non-western states.

The absorptive capacity for this kind of intellectual is, however, severely limited in non-western societies. As a result, intellectual unemployment—a phenomenon by no means unknown in some western countries—has social and political consequences of great importance, for non-western intelligentsias are by and large politicized to a degree unknown in the west. Particularly in areas recently freed from western colonial control, where national liberation has invariably led to a rapid expansion of western-style education, the steady growth of a largely unemployable "intellectual proletariat" presents a very real political threat to stability and social peace. There, the "new" intellectual-rulers are thus, paradoxically enough, threatened by their own kind.

Finally, there is a fourth factor of great importance, that of ideological causation. In opposing the *status quo* of traditional non-western societies, most of the "new" intellectuals also tend to oppose the *status quo* of a world which either directly or indirectly can be held responsible for the internal social and political conditions that form the prime target of the intelligentsia's attack. Thus "feudalism" as well as colonialism—rule by entrenched native classes or rule by foreigners—can be blamed on the political, military and economic preponderance of the western world. It is, therefore, not surprising that socialist and communist teachings have found far more fertile soil among non-western intellectuals than among their western counterparts. If it is symptomatic that the first statues ever erected for Marx and Engels stand on Russian soil, it would be equally fitting to find statues, say of Harold Laski gracing the main squares of New Delhi, Colombo, Rangoon, Accra, and even Baghdad.

Indeed, it is not too surprising that modern socialism has so profoundly attracted intellectuals all over the world. In the most highly industrialized countries of the west, it is, in fact, among intellectuals, rather than among the proletariat itself, that this social philosophy has found its most numerous adherents. This is very likely due to the fact that socialism, especially Marxism, is the most recent, and perhaps also the most coherent and intellectually most respectable version of the philosopher king, the social engineer ruling in the interest of abstract social justice *par excellence.* An intelligentsia thus not only has a vested intellectual interest in socialism, it also has a vested social and political interest in it. In spite of the Marxian theory of the class struggle as the major social determinant of history, in spite even of the quasi-humility at times exhibited by Marx and his later followers in terms of their willingness to be "guided by," and "learn from," the proletariat, programmatic, "scientific" socialism has always, as Lenin himself bluntly stated, been the product of a bourgeois intelligentsia. It is the "vanguard" of the proletariat, not the proletariat itself, that is cast for the crucial role of governing, and for quite obvious reasons: in proclaiming the rule of social justice, the socialist intellectual is proclaiming rule by his own kind.

But whereas in the west the Marxist intellectual's political aspirations have as a rule encountered great difficulties, at least in working-class movements dominated by, or at least highly dependent upon, union leaders, the non-western socialist intellectual can in the absence of a sizable proletariat (as well as of other organized socio-economic forces) actually become ruler in his own right. Socialism, in addition to providing the desired combination of anti-western—*i.e.,* anti-capitalistic—westernization also provides the non-western intellectual with a justification for rule by the intelligentsia. In embracing it, he feels *ipso facto* justified in looking askance at political competition from other segments of society, such as "old" intellectuals, aristocracies, and landowners, but also nascent capitalistic middle classes. Planning in the name of socialism means planning with the intelligentsia as planners, irrespective of whether they be the military intellectuals of Nasser's stamp or the "pure" intellectuals of the Nehru variety.

Up to this point we have drawn no distinction between the military and the civilian, or "pure," intellectual, yet this distinction is of great analytic significance. It is by no means a matter of historic accident whether a non-western country, insofar as it has become westernized and undergone change, is ruled by either one or the other prototype. The existence of a military group of young officers in itself depends on the political status of a country; it depends, that is to say, on the fact of political (though not necessarily economic) independence. It is, therefore, only in non-colonial countries that westernization has been primarily channelled through military leaders. Kemal Ataturk, Yüan Shih-k'ai and the Satsuma and Choshu *samurai* are good examples, as are the many military régimes in Latin America and the newly emerging élite groups in the Middle East.

Wherever, then, the impact of the west did not lead to outright political domination, wherever a non-western society was given a chance of adjusting to the demands of the modern era by internal adaptation without suffering direct political control from the outside, there the officer has almost invariably emerged as the modern political non-western leader. Since he as a rule possesses a monopoly of physical power, he can fairly easily grasp control in a society where he represents the most powerful —even if numerically weak—social group with a vested interest in modernization and change.

Westernization as well as the *status quo* prevailing in these countries, have, as we said, combined to stamp many, if not most of these younger military leaders with an ideological orientation not usually found among the professional soldiers in the west, or for that matter among the older generation of officers in independent non-western states. While this orientation is at times fairly close to the socialism so prevalent among non-western intelligentsias in general, while as a rule little love is lost between them and either the aristocracies, clergies or the nascent capitalist classes in their lands, their political goals tend to centre around the creation of strong, "socially just" régimes rather than around the creation of parliamentary régimes. In their distrust of the professional politician, including the "civilian" intelligentsia, non-western military leaders like the Japanese *samurai* of the nineteenth century and Colonel Nasser of today bear a recognizable similarity to the military prototype of modern societies in the west. Under a military régime "pure" intellectuals play a subordinate role as political leaders, if indeed they are at all tolerated by their military colleagues. In some of the contemporary non-western military dictatorships the intellectual as an independent political actor is politically as ineffectual as he was in, say, Meiji Japan. He has the choice between playing auxiliary to the new powers-that-be and being doomed to political impotence.

If the military intelligentsia has emerged as the most universal revolutionary phenomenon in the non-colonial countries of the non-western world, the "pure" intellectual has made his appearance as political ruler in many areas recently freed from western colonialism. This is an interesting phenomenon, for, unlike the military, the "pure" intellectual does not *a priori* command the means of physical coercion that have, throughout history, made military power so significant a factor. It is, indeed, a phenomenon rooted in modern western colonialism itself. The absence of an indigenous military élite proper is one of the most significant sociological aspects of colonialism of all times. Since military power rests with the alien ruling class, this occupation is closed to the indigenous population. Nineteenth century colonialism had other stultifying effects on social growth as well, particularly in preventing or retarding the development of a sizable bourgeoisie within the populations of many areas. This is particularly true of the plural societies of South-East Asia and parts of Africa, in which the introduction of capitalist economies has tended to benefit foreign rather than indigenous entrepreneurs.

It is this stunted social growth that turned the western-trained intellectuals—the doctors, the lawyers, the engineers, the professors and the students—into the only sizable group with a vested interest in political change. Unlike their military counterparts in non-colonial areas, however, the intellectuals of colonial Asia and Africa remained politically impotent as long as colonialism lasted, *i.e.,* they had no instruments for physically seizing power, and had to content themselves with the weapons of ideological warfare, political organization and nationalist protest within the limits set by their alien overlords. As the westernized leaders of nationalism and anti-colonialism, these non-western intelligentsias formed a numerically very small, and in most cases also very weak, élite group. In some few areas, like British India, where indigenous entrepreneurs had gained a measure of economic strength, they have supported the intelligentsia in order to bolster their position *vis-à-vis* foreign competition. In most cases, however, the nationalist leadership did not have such support at its disposal. Smarting under the constant vigilance of colonial masters, it was vociferous rather than politically entrenched. It is doubtless true that these intellectuals—as westernized intelligentsias throughout the non-western world—have sought identification with the rural mass of the population and the "nation" at large, but this identification rests, as we will presently discuss, on slender roots. Partly this is due to the very westernization of these urban élite groups and partly to the fact that in virtually all colonies access to the peasantry was rendered extremely difficult, if not impossible, by the colonial authorities. Only in British India again did the urban intelligentsia—largely through Gandhi—succeed in forging a link with the peasantry.

Thus, whereas military leaders were able to grasp political control in non-colonial areas whenever the opportunity arose from the internal power constellation—as *e.g.* in China after 1911, in Japan after 1867, in Turkey in 1918, in Thailand in 1931, etc.—the "pure" intellectuals had to wait for external liberation from colonial rule to step into the political arena as actual rulers in their own right. It is not coincidental that the Japanese occupation of South-East Asia performed this act of liberation for the intellectuals of Burma and Indonesia, and that the train of post-war liquidations of colonial possessions has paved the way for the intelligentsia elsewhere, as in India, Ghana, Tunisia and to some extent also in Malaya. In the social and political vacuum created by modern colonialism, the western-trained intellectual was, at the crucial hour, the only politically and ideologically trained élite group on whom political power could devolve.

But if there is historic logic in the emergence of "civilian" intellectuals as rulers in post-colonial non-western areas today, continuation of this fairly unique phenomenon is fairly problematical. The demise of colonialism itself has brought with it the breaking down of the artificial barriers to social growth that were, as we said, one of its most significant sociological aspects. In the newly independent countries of Asia and Africa the "pure" intellectual is now free to search for non-intellectual avenues to social status and prestige, and some of them—Aung San of Burma is an excellent example—have rapidly turned towards a military career. In this sense, colonial countries are socially "coming of age," and are demonstrating the adaptability of non-western intelligentsias to new social conditions, an adaptability previously exhibited by Leon Trotsky and some members of the Chinese communist intelligentsia in a non-colonial setting.

Second, quite apart from this incidental transformation of individual "pure" intellectuals, independence, and in particular the revolutionary struggle against colonialism—in South-East Asia, conscious Japanese policies—has given rise to a distinct group of military leaders, who socially, educationally and often also ideologically stand apart from the western-trained academic intellectuals of the colonial era. Having played a significant role in the liberation of their countries and having gained access to military power, they have also created a political following, both among their subordinates and, quite often, among the public at large. The military, in short, have become a competing élite which has increasingly come to challenge the "civilian" intelligentsia's monopoly of political power in formerly colonial non-western countries.

As the struggle between Sun Yat-sen and Yüan Shih-k'ai symbolically showed, the contest between "pure" intellectuals and military leaders is, because of the latter's physical superiority, fraught with grave dangers to the civilian leadership. But the new military élites, it must be remembered, are for the greater part not simply war lords or "strong men" only.

To a large extent, they, too, make ideological appeals—if nothing else, appealing for national unity in the face of disunited civilian leadership—that render them truly formidable political opponents. . . .

The apparent ease with which civilian régimes are being replaced by military ones points to the inherent weakness and instability of rule by "pure" intellectuals. The causes of these are not far to seek. In the first place, the "pure" intellectual, however well versed he may have been in the politics of opposition to colonialism, very rarely possesses actual administrative experience that could make him an effective and efficient statesman. Second, the democratic or parliamentary institutions imported by western-trained intellectuals are as a rule operating in a social and political vacuum, with no organizational framework connecting the new edifice at the centre with the country at large. It is true that many non-western intellectuals are stressing the intrinsically democratic nature of traditional village government in their countries; but it may be doubted whether this "village democracy"—whatever its merits—can serve the purpose of providing an adequate underpinning for a modern, viable constitutional state.

Finally, the political parties functioning under most non-western parliamentary systems do not as a rule represent organized social forces so much as factions centred around personalities. The temporary unity exhibited before the attainment of independence thus tends to wane once nationhood has been achieved, and to give way to fierce factional struggles. It is these struggles, accompanied by lack of central purpose and achievement, that leave the intellectual in a precarious position, and thus render the appeal of the military so forceful.

The substitution of a military for a civilian régime does not necessarily involve more than a change within the intelligentsia, and thus a structural change in the façade of government. The short-cut solution of the military *coup* does no more than eradicate the often anaemic institutional forms of a western-style political system; it does not substitute more viable forms in their stead. If the "pure" intellectuals encounter almost insuperable obstacles in realizing their goals, the military leadership, moving into the *terra incognita* of politics, may find it at least equally difficult to translate their long-term aspirations into reality.

If the difficulties besetting non-western intelligentsias as ruling classes of both types appear formidable, they are in many areas partly offset, or at least obscured, by the "countervailing" power of *charisma* embodied in individual members of both the civilian and the military, such as Nehru, Nasser, Nkrumah, Sukarno and Castro, to mention but a few outstanding examples. The simultaneous appearance of charismatic leadership in Asia, Africa, the Middle East and Latin America is perhaps one of the most important phenomena accompanying the political readjustments in the contemporary non-western world. It is the charismatic leader who by force of sheer personality can apparently bridge the gap between the westernized élites and the rural population, and who can serve as the symbolic link between the ruler and the ruled.

It is a moot point whether the presence of such leadership alone can suffice to guarantee a measure of political stability or to extract the cooperation required to set sustained modernization and economic improvement in motion. It is similarly a moot point whether an intelligentsia, bereft of its charismatic leader, will produce adequate cohesion to continue in power. At any rate, there can be little doubt that the charismatic leader is already a deviant from the standard pattern of the western-educated intelligentsia, whether civilian or military: insofar as the charismatic appeal is politically important in the non-western world it is so not because of these leaders' western training and ideological orientation, but perhaps in spite of them. In the eyes of the general population, the charismatic leader may well be *malgré lui*, the reincarnation of the "old," sacral intellectual rather than the modernizer and westernizer he claims to be. . . .

It is not unlikely that intelligentsias represent a[n] . . . intermediate stage in the non-western political evolution. But it is probable that their displacement is not a matter of the immediate future, even though, as we have seen, there exists an apparently growing trend for power to devolve upon the military within these non-western intelligentsias. Members of older social groups, such as landowners or sacral intellectuals—as *e.g.* the Muslim Brotherhood in Egypt, the Hindu Mahasabha in India, or the Darul Islam in Indonesia—though they may here and there exert significant political influence, seem as a rule to be lacking in strength or social dynamism to constitute a real threat to the new order. The urban bourgeoisie is numerically and often also economically too weak to challenge the new intelligentsia-rulers. And, finally, the revolutions are of too recent date to have laid the groundwork for the growth of other social groups able and willing to form a viable opposition, in terms of economic strength at least.

For quite some time to come, non-western intelligentsias may therefore be expected to retain their virtual monopoly of political power. To a large extent this continuity seems to be assured by the fact that the national polities over which they rule are of recent date, and, indeed, of the intelligentsias' own making. Essentially, these are modern governmental edifices superimposed on societies which, as yet, do not nourish them by established channels of political communication. The political process in non-western societies is thus, to a far greater extent than is true of most western societies, a superstructure without viable underpinning. This state of affairs, for sure, cannot but be transitional. But as long as it lasts, intelligentsias are very likely to remain the prime political actors in many non-western countries. Political changes are likely to take place within these élites rather than to affect their predominance as ruling classes.

10. BUREAUCRACY

Fred W. Riggs

FRED W. RIGGS is Professor of Government and Director of the Social Science Research Institute at the University of Hawaii. He has taught at Indiana University, the University of the Philippines, and Yale University. He has published *Thailand: The Modernization of a Bureaucratic Polity* (1966), *Administration in Developing Countries* (1964), *The Ecology of Public Administration* (1961), and *Formosa under Chinese Nationalist Rule* (1952).

A phenomenon of the utmost significance in transitional societies is the lack of balance between political policy-making institutions and bureaucratic policy-implementing structures. The relative weakness of political organs means that the political function tends to be appropriated, in considerable measure, by bureaucrats. Intra-bureaucratic struggles become a primary form of politics. But when the political arena is shifted to bureaucracies—a shift marked by the growing power of military officers in conflict with civilian officials—the consequences are usually ominous for political stability, economic growth, administrative effectiveness, and democratic values. It seems important, therefore, to give serious attention to the relation between political and administrative development, to the question of how balanced growth takes place. . . .

If we make a quick survey of the transitional societies today, we will be impressed by the weakness of their extra-bureaucratic political institutions in contrast with the burgeoning growth of their bureaucracies. In every country a great expansion of governmental agencies and a proliferation of functions has taken place, especially in the new nations that were recently under colonial rule. By contrast, parliamentary bodies have, in the main, proved ineffectual and, even in the countries like India and the Philippines where they have been most vigorous, their role in basic decision making has been questioned.

Elections have often been conducted in such a way as to give but a poor reflection of the popular will; the courts have not generally shown themselves to be bulwarks of the rule of law; and chief executives have more often than not shown themselves to be arbitrary and authoritarian, relying on their charismatic leadership qualities or a party machine rather than on formal political institutions as the basis of power. Under these conditions it is not surprising that bureaucrats themselves have often had to play a crucial part in determining what would, or perhaps *would not*, be done. . . .

In the governmental sphere . . . development in public administration, bureaucratic change, takes place more readily than counterpart changes in politics: technics change more easily than techniques. The reasons are apparent. The initial demand for Western institutions in many non-Western countries was in the military sphere, for defense against an intrusive imperial power. To develop the means of defense, rulers employed foreign military advisers and sent students to European military academies. The costs of modern arms were high, and so in national finance, in taxation, especially in customs, and state monopolies like salt, in budgeting and accounting, transformations were carried out. Defense needs also created a demand for effective control over outlying areas of a traditional realm, and so led to a reorganization of territorial administration, the creation of a Ministry of Interior, recruitment of a career service of district officers, prefects, governors, and a central secretariat to control their operations.

While this proliferation and expansion of bureaucratic machinery was taking place in most of the non-Western countries, no corresponding development of the non-bureaucratic political system occurred. In the independent countries, political leadership was still provided by traditional rulers—as in Siam, Iran, Ethiopia, Japan—although in the Japanese case perhaps the greatest success was achieved in establishing new political institutions, a central legislature, political parties, and a cabinet system. This success is, of course, directly relevant to the phenomenal Japanese achievement of industrialization and the greater effectiveness of its governmental institutions as compared to those of other non-Western countries. Even here, however, bureaucratic elements, especially from the armed forces, tended to exercise disproportionate influence in the political structures, notably in the period leading to the Second World War.

In the countries under colonial rule the proposition is even more patently true—at least until recently. Here the colonial administration itself created a bureaucratic apparatus not subject to political control within the dependent territory, so that administrative institutions proliferated while political structures remained embryonic and largely extra-legal, hence unable to relate themselves effectively to control over the bureaucracy. . . .

In the contemporary era of large-scale technical assistance under international and bi-national programs, we see a continued infusion of external pressure and assistance in the expansion and proliferation of bureaucratic organs, with relatively little attention to the growth of strictly political institutions. The reasons are quite evident. Administration is regarded as a technical matter (technics) subject to foreign, "expert" advice, whereas politics is so closely linked with fundamental values and social mores (techniques) that aid would be construed as "intervention."

Moreover, the demand for economic development and modernization impinges directly on agricultural, industrial, public health, and educational spheres in which external assistance is fed directly to segments of the bureaucracy, and only weakly mediated through central political institutions. The foreign experts and advisers, for their part, while competent to deal with technical matters in a variety of program fields, and even the related administrative questions, would scarcely claim any competence to assist in the establishment of new political institutions.

The question naturally arises: what is the relationship between this burgeoning of bureaucratic institutions and the course of political development? The relationship may be examined from two sides: the effect of political weakness on administrative effectiveness, and the consequences of bureaucratic expansion for the political system. . . .

My general thesis is that premature or too rapid expansion of the bureaucracy when the political system lags behind tends to inhibit the development of effective politics. A corollary thesis holds that separate political institutions have a better chance to grow if bureaucratic institutions are relatively weak.

11. POLITICAL PARTIES

Manfred Halpern

MANFRED HALPERN is Professor of Politics and Faculty Associate of the Center of International Studies at Princeton University. Before joining Princeton in 1958, he was associated with the U.S. State Department as Senior Analyst in the North Africa Division and special assistant to the Chief of the Division of Research for the Near East, South Asia, and Africa. He has written *The*

Dialectics of Transformation in Politics, Personality, and Society (1972), *The Politics of Social Change in the Middle East and North Africa* (1963), and has co-authored *Communism and Revolution: The Strategic Uses of Political Violence* (1964), *The Role of the Military in Underdeveloped Countries* (1962), *International Aspects of Civil Strife* (1963), and *Revolution* (1966).

. . . In the modern age, when all strata of society are being affected by political issues, and the terms of all issues are new, the need has become all the more acute for institutions that can effectively initiate diverse groups into a common state and society: for example, Arabs, Kurds, Sunni Moslems, Shia Moslems, Nestorian Christians, Syrian Orthodox Christians, Armenian Orthodox Christians, Yazidis, Sabaeans, Baghdadis, army officers, Diwaniyah tribesmen, Istiqlal party members, unskilled workers—which is merely an incomplete way of saying all Iraqis. Schools can provide basic knowledge and teach prospective citizens how to think, and so prepare for participant politics, mass media can inform and influence their audience, but they cannot become vehicles of organization; armies leave civilians outside their ranks; parliaments demand intense political activity by a small number of individuals; elections restrict political opportunity to a few occasions. No other existing institution . . . is capable of instilling a sense of citizenship and organizing public participation in political decisions as effectively as political parties. Only a party can be in daily contact with the constituency, teach, propagandize, or put pressure upon that constituency to adopt new ideas and patterns of action. Only a party can stimulate involvement in campaigns for literacy and higher production no less than particular political issues, and gather new talents and thus regularize recruitment into the new elite.

Political parties have peculiar advantages as instruments of social change. . . . [I]nsofar as they are not novel disguises for restricted traditional cliques, but rather truly voluntary associations operating in a public realm, they cease being organically related to the old social structure and so can move themselves and others beyond the established order.

Only parties can link leaders and masses in almost daily contact. The problem of contact is all the more acute because it arises in the modern age in paradoxical form: the involvement of the masses in politics sharpens the authority of leaders and of personal forms of authority—for none is as readily comprehensible and reassuring—yet never has personal political contact been as difficult to achieve as in a mass society. A political party offers an opportunity for binding together four forces which can resolve this paradox and create a viable political culture: charisma, ideology, organization, and accountability to an increasingly larger constituency. There is no escape from discussing these separately and in sequence, but they are effective only in combination—both because they reinforce each other and also act as checks and balances against each other.

THE HARNESSING OF CHARISMA

In times of social crisis, when customary institutions and values are threatened, losing potency, and can no longer attract implicit assent, men often search for charismatic leaders. They put their trust in the seemingly magically heroic personality, relying upon his policies above all because they accept the man. In periods of social change, the charismatic leader may often serve as the model of the new human being required by the newly evolving pattern of life, and succeed in encouraging, by his very example, a rapid transformation of existing attitudes. It may well be fortunate that at a moment when almost everything is changing or in doubt, and experienced, knowledgeable men are still scarce, people find it possible at least to unite behind an inspiring leader. Pakistan's political development was doubtless greatly handicapped by the death of several of its most inspired leaders soon after the country achieved independence, and by the country's inability quickly to discover successors of equal charismatic appeal.

This special gift of seeming grace in leaders, however, appears as readily in fanatics and adventurers as it does in saints and politicians. Unless bound to countervailing forces, charismatic leaders can destroy individual judgment, indeed, individuals and institutions. To perpetuate a new sense of direction requires more powerful magic than the luck that may attend a particular personality. The problem of Middle Eastern governments in the modern age is to routinize charisma by attaching it to secular institutions, at least until these are accepted as legitimate. Charisma by its very nature cannot assure stability but can only originate the foundations upon which stability may be established.

Part of the leaders' charisma needs to become routinized in bureaucracy —a set of offices that is not really institutionalized until it can survive the rise and fall of political leaders and political parties. Bureaucracies, however, are in touch with citizens only as they execute orders. Only parties can organize enthusiasm on the basis of a solidarity of interests with citizens outside the government. The routinization of charisma in political parties becomes possible as the leader makes consistent use of that organization, speaks in its name, and lends it his mantle. In the Middle East, leaders and parties who successfully win national independence together have several signal advantages in this respect. To both leader and party a charisma will then already adhere, validated for both by heroic triumph in behalf of the community and its homeland. Both will already be experienced in maintaining an organization under conditions of adversity. Both, upon victory, are likely to possess a relatively unresented monopoly of control to give them confidence and time for routinization. That even they sometimes fail to establish enduring institutions may well be due to weaknesses of organization, ideology, and accountability to a larger constituency. It is to the problems of organization that we turn next.

THE NOVELTIES OF VOLUNTARY POLITICAL ASSOCIATION

The political party is still a novel instrument of collaboration in the Middle East. It is a voluntary organization in a region that hitherto had known only organizations based on kinship, religion, force, economic survival, or on coalitions of personal interests. Organizing a party of autonomous strangers to deal with public affairs is a new and unfamiliar art. Following upon the establishment of a number of secret political societies in the second half of the nineteenth century, the first important cadre parties began to emerge in the Middle East only in the first decade of the twentieth century. The Young Turks Associations were united in 1908; the National Party was founded in Egypt by Mustafa Kemal in 1907. The first mass party in the Middle East was the Egyptian Wafd, formed in the fall of 1918 by Sa'ad Zaghlul—but by the late 1930's it had lost its contact with the masses.

Few men join political parties until traditional social and political units become uncertain sources of concrete satisfactions, of useful, and above all hallowed ideas, and of solidarity. For a Middle Easterner to become a member of any party is thus to pay dues to a new age. Organizers and members may not be altogether at ease with each other. Organizers are likely to be almost entirely drawn from the salaried new middle class. If they confine their recruitment to other members of that class, they will leave the majority of the population to potential political rivals. They will also fail to establish a single political culture, and hence fail as agents of modernization. It is also difficult to organize well when the organizer entered a new age only a few years ahead of most members. The middle class is still so new that it is just beginning in most countries to overcome the cultural barriers between urban and rural inhabitants, between those literate in the ideas of a new world and those literate in tradition, or illiterate in both.

It is not easy to attract stable support at a time of rapid transfiguration of the individual, of the relevance of his accustomed group loyalties, and of the truth of his values. In this uncertainty, membership in "devotee parties" such as the Moslem Brotherhood or the communist party (which, through its front organizations, is adjusted to exploit various degrees of faith) offers a certainty and solidarity—a sacred movement—more akin to ties of kinship and religion than parties that are secular and pragmatic.

There is not only the task of recruiting but also the problem of restricting membership. While a party must mobilize more than one class to become a mass party, it is not in its interest, as Nasser learned to his chagrin in Egypt, to enlist the entire nation. If everyone is in the party, why should anyone bother to be in it? A conflict of strategies therefore arises and is seldom consciously resolved. If the party contains a multitude that lack discipline and understanding of issues, it will be ineffective. A comprehensive nationalist party may not be eager to purge itself lest it encourage the growth of rivals; yet if it accepts all who favor "nationalism" and "anti-imperialism," what will serve to inspire the party by distinguishing it from all other patriotic inhabitants?

THE USES AND ABUSES OF IDEOLOGY

Truisms do not constitute programs. Parties in the Middle East will not be capable of inducting their followers into a new political culture or of guiding change effectively unless they become ideological parties. This sounds at first glance like a recipe for profound mischief. Daniel Bell comments: "What gives ideology its force is its passion. . . . A social movement can rouse people when it can do three things: simplify ideas, establish a claim to truth, and, in the union of the two, demand a commitment to action." [1] Similarly, Professor Shils observes: "It has been the belief of those who practice politics ideologically that they alone have the truth about the right ordering of life—of life as a whole, and not just of political life." [2] By assuming that "politics should be conducted from the viewpoint of a coherent, comprehensive set of beliefs which must override every other consideration," ideologists make impossible the pursuit of "civil politics" based on the "virtue of the citizen who shares responsibility in his own self-government" with the understanding that no virtue is final and that every virtue costs something in terms of other virtues. [3]

A passion for dogmas that will once and for all fix loyalties and shape decisions has often been the bent of ideological politics. Much political doctrine in this part of the world, as elsewhere, consists of basic symbols of sentiment and identification whose function it is to arouse shared emotions of enthusiasm, faith, and loyalty, and plausibly to explain situations which leaders have not been able to predict or control in a fashion that can sustain morale. For some time to come such emotionally inciting and arational doctrines may well remain an inescapable aspect of Middle Eastern mass politics. Whenever they are allowed to become the core of political ideologies, they can easily produce a mood that becomes a substitute for constructive action, as in ultra-nationalism, or engender a spirit of dogmatic rigidity in the midst of rapid change, as in neo-Islamic

[1] Daniel Bell, "The End of Ideology in the West," *Columbia University Forum,* Winter 1960, pp. 4–7.
[2] Edward Shils, "Ideology and Civility," *The Twentieth Century,* July 1959, p. 3.
[3] *Ibid.,* pp. 1, 4, and 6.

totalitarianism, or be used to justify, as in communism, the sacrifice of all other values for dogma's sake.

Yet there is a distinction to be made which is not merely analytical but reflects concrete differences in actual Middle Eastern practice. There is another aspect of ideology—the explicitly formulated framework of means and ends, the rational, experimental, and programmatic element in political ideas. The practice of, among others, Turkey's Ataturk and Tunisia's Bourguiba demonstrates that the two aspects of ideology—the rational and the passionate—can both be utilized politically, but in a style and combination which minimizes the corruption of reason.

Ataturk sought deliberately to stir and stimulate passion in politics. The political tasks which his society faced were enormous and the sacrifices and efforts involved were unlikely to be contributed merely as the result of cool calculation. The principles of Ataturk's revolution—nationalism, secularism, populism, etatism—attracted the deep emotional and intellectual commitment of many. But these principles never became political myths to be both believed and admired without question. They were strong and clear enough to set broad limits (for example, nationalism was to be non-expansive, secularism was opposed to archaic religious practices but not to religious faith). As the fruits of decades of earnest and, at least within the emerging new middle class, open discussion, they remained flexible and never received final codification as a comprehensive and coherent doctrine.

Ataturk felt no compulsion to arrogate to the newly emergent secular state a sacred and totalitarian task—to create a new faith. As a result, he became neither the prisoner of his own doctrine nor the executioner for its sake. He remained free to learn, experiment, and change. Growing discussion and participation among politically alert Turks became possible at least without being permanently confined to an authorized political grammar and vocabulary. Passion in Turkish politics was being harnessed primarily to buttress Ataturk's charismatic position and to support each individual, concrete act of policy. Passion attached itself less intensely to the less-crystallized, and indeed still-evolving symbols of the revolution and its ideology. Hence Ataturk remained free, within broad limits, constantly and with an open mind to weigh strategies and costs in transforming his society.

An ideology that passionately fuses political myth and political requirements can devour even its adherents. A party that offers merely a set of political planks may not possess enough that is relevant to an age in which not only political power but the sense, spirit, and survival of the whole society are at stake.

There are Middle Eastern parties whose program, implicitly or explicitly, expresses the aims of a vested interest group, or of a traditional class, or else the perpetuation and opportunistic exploitation of existing popular preconceptions. None of these will save a party, or a country, for long. Egypt, for most of the years between 1907 and 1952, was alternately controlled by parties offering one of these three kinds of program, and so failed to deal with social change. None of these parties—however large some grew during this period—have survived. In Iraq, most parties organized during the Mandate period gradually died after the achievement of independence in 1932. They had differed only on how independence was to be won, and most of them had little desire to come to grips with internal changes thereafter.

If a political party accepts the task of becoming one of the principal agents of social transformation, its success depends upon the adoption of an ideology in tune with rapid change—a framework of values, methods, and direction concerned with all issues of modernization, and therefore without a final comprehensiveness, a final coherence, or a final intensity. Such an ideology, given the Middle East's scarcity of expert analysts and practitioners in problems of social, political, and economic change, is seldom likely to be the intellectual creation of a single man. In practice it is more likely to emerge as the product of continual and intense discussion and bargaining among leading members of the new middle class. Organization and accountability to a larger constituency must accompany the tempting powers of charisma and ideology if the vital encounter with political realities is to be maintained.

In today's Middle East, however, there is a tendency to infuse ideology with too much passion and also, obversely, to ignore the task of clarifying political doctrines intellectually. The daily, unexpected exigencies of power that confront any elite, whatever the class from which it springs and the ideology it cherishes, are bound to muffle the clarity and consistency of thought and expression of party leadership. One particular obstacle to ideological clarification looms large—the dominant role of nationalism among ideologies.When independence is gained, as it is in most states of the Middle East, by a single party uniting many different political and social views under one nationalist banner, there is often a reluctance to split such a large and comprehensive political vehicle by refining its ideological orientation. Every politician everywhere in the modern age prefers to speak in the name of all the "people." In an area of great scarcities and inequalities, and in an era of a plurality of rapidly, but unevenly, changing values, populism can be a mask for almost any program, or else a nostalgic emotionalism for no program but immediate satisfaction. An ideology concerned not only with nationalism but also with social reform cannot help identifying domestic enemies.

As long as landowners dominate the state and exploit the majority of its people, for example, there will be no opportunity for important reforms. As long as education remains under religious control, only the past will be memorized. As long as extremist movements such as the Moslem

Brotherhood and the communist party are not decisively kept out of power, the freedom to choose future courses may come to an end. Bribery and nepotism may be endemic, but it takes political courage to name names. A call for sacrifices to be made for future investments will find many unwilling to subject themselves to an equality of wants. Thus, however prudently and shrewdly a party may proceed in transforming society, it cannot avoid making domestic enemies. And however reluctant it may be to publish this fact by formalizing its ideology, a party's leadership will find it difficult to win and keep the kind of following it requires unless its path and purpose are made clear.

ACCOUNTABILITY IN ONE-PARTY REGIMES

A party that perceives itself as an agent of modernization may act to establish a one-party state on the grounds that only a single party can make sure that it is a truly national organization. A plurality of parties at this stage of development is likely to give scope to movements representing only particularistic economic, religious, ethnic, or regional interests, and hence prevent agreement on long-range planning; only a single party can sustain a determined course of economic development for a sufficiently long time to secure the foundations of national unity and prosperity; only a strong, single, national party can keep the army subordinate to civilian administration and the bureaucracy alert and efficient, only a single, well-organized party can marshal public opinion, which is by no means any longer feeble in the Middle East, or protect itself against coups by a score or less who can otherwise still overthrow Middle Eastern governments; only a party with a clear monopoly of control can undertake those far-reaching reforms in the social, economic, and political structure which are needed to remove the barriers to democracy.

Nowhere in the Middle East where single-party states have emerged, as in Egypt or Tunisia, is the situation a regression from democracy simply because no effective constitutional democracy had preceded such regimes. In contrast to the totalitarian neo-Islamic and communist parties, no one-party regime now in power in the Middle East justifies its right to govern alone in terms of dogmatic assumptions concerning the laws of historical development.

The arguments for taking an authoritarian road in the Middle East may be strong—but what are the odds that a political party so oriented will actually move in the direction of more democracy rather than more authoritarianism? . . . One optimistic note may be sounded, however. . . . If a party chooses to face the problems of modernization and social change, and hence accepts the task of creating a new political culture, it will find that one requisite for its success is the institutionalization of accountability to an increasingly larger constituency.

If a party is to be effective as an agent of modernization, it will need to attract as its nucleus a cadre of politically sensitive and skilled men, not merely party hacks awaiting favors. It will need to listen to experts and, for the very survival of their craft, allow them to debate, even if it does not always accept their advice. If a regime intends to be effective in creating a new political culture, it will also need to reach out for mass support, and teach new standards and patterns of political behavior. Such efforts will inevitably involve more flow of ideas and demands from the top to the bottom than the reverse, and much distortion and propaganda will accompany that flow. However, if contact is to be maintained, the leadership will have to know what conceptions, expectations, and criticisms are in fact current among the masses so that their own communications relate to real emotions and concerns. If the local party branches meet regularly, much autonomous discussion of political issues is bound to be generated. This dialogue will be uneven, but, in contrast to earlier political relationships, almost constant. It is quite unlikely, given the rapidity of social change and the varieties of its expressions in the Middle East, that any leader should ever be so omnipotent as to manipulate this dialogue entirely to his own satisfaction.

These points must not be exaggerated. Manipulation of cadre and ideas alike is becoming, if anything, a more refined art, distorting the process of political accounting to the constituency in many countries, not only in the Middle East. To turn skepticism into cynicism, however, is to miss certain potentialities. From a recognition of these requisites under single-party regimes, grew . . . the parliaments of Tunisia and Egypt, and the multi-party system of Turkey.

12. LANDLORDS IN A DEMOCRACY: THE ADAPTABILITY OF A TRADITIONAL ELITE

Wolfram Eberhard

WOLFRAM EBERHARD is Professor of Sociology at the University of California at Berkeley. He has also taught at Peking, Ankara, Heidelberg, Frankfurt, Munich, and Taipei (Taiwan). In 1934–35 Professor Eberhard did field-work in mainland China; 1951–52, in Turkey; 1956–58, in Pakistan; 1958, in Burma; 1960, in Korea, Japan, and Afghanistan; and 1960–70, seven study trips to Taiwan. He has also held a Guggenheim Memorial Foundation fellowship. His publications include: *Minstrel Tales from Southeastern Turkey, Sin and Guilt in Traditional China* (1967), *Settlement and Social Change in Asia* (1967), and *The Local Cultures of South and East China* (1968).

Landlordism is a typical trait of non-mechanized agricultural societies and it occurs in almost all studies dealing with Asian societies. Two points seem to characterize many of these studies: (1) it is assumed that landlordism is an old institution and as such more or less unchanging; (2) it is difficult to get objective data other than simple statistics. For many countries we have fairly reliable statistical material, such as, for instance, that eighty per cent of all farm land is in the hands of five per cent of the farm population. This information may point to the existence of landlordism, but neither proves, nor describes it. Where landlordism exists, the landlords are usually unwilling to give pertinent information about their activities to outsiders, and local social scientists, even if they can get the data, are hesitant to publish them. At the time when landlordism is abolished, many reports appear, for instance in Communist China. But nobody would accept, for example, accusations made before a people's court as scientific source materials. I am glad, therefore, to be able to present a case of landlordism in modern Turkey, more precisely in the district Kadirli, province of Adana, in South Turkey. For this case the documentation is ample and reliable, because it occurred at a time of reasonable freedom of press, permitting publication of political material, while at the same time existing laws precluded the publication of slanders. I hope to show that landlordism is not necessarily old, but that it can spring up and function under numerous conditions, even under a democratic form of government, and that it can originate from different roots. I suspect that there is often, in Turkey as well as in other parts of Asia, though not always, a relation between landlordism and wet rice cultivation. I believe that further inquiry into these connections may lead some day to a revision of K. A. Wittfogel's theory of Oriental Despotism which is based upon the concept of hydraulic societies.

The data for this study are taken partly from my own observations in the area, but mainly from more than two hundred newspaper reports published in Turkey between 1961 and 1962.[1] This, of course, implies some limitations and weaknesses of the study; newspaper reporters do not always study the facts objectively and do not always report them completely.

Southern Turkey, the area between Adana and Gaziantep, and extending into present-day Syria was since at least seven hundred years the winter camp of nomadic Turkish tribes which spent the summers in the

[1] I want to express my thanks to my Turkish friends who have helped me in the collection of these materials, but who want to remain unnamed.

high mountains of the Taurus, the Anti-Taurus, or on the high plateau of Anatolia. They usually left the coastal plains around March and returned in late October, so that it did not matter if during their absence some farmers used their winter pasturages for agriculture. The farmers liked the pasturages, because the animals had fertilized the soil. Upon their return, the nomads found on the harvested fields, which after the fall of the first rains got a new coat of fresh grass and weeds, enough winter fodder for their animals.

Some tribes, however, took to a more stable way of life by settling along the Taurus foothills. Here they had a pleasant summer climate, but had also two other advantages: first, they could graze their animals in the swampy riverine plains which were unfit for agriculture but densely overgrown by reeds and grass; and, secondly, they could dominate the trade routes which connected Anatolia and the Balkan peninsula with Arabia and the East. Domination of trade routes could mean that they themselves engaged in trade by using their animals for transportation, or that they robbed or "taxed" caravans which had to pass through the area between the mountains and the swamps. Thus, small "states" developed in the foothill area. They continued to exist until the nineteenth century, although nominally the area was a part of the Ottoman empire. They were loosely attached to the empire in a way which can be called "feudalistic."

Around 1860, the concept of what constituted a "state" had changed so much in the Ottoman empire that the independent lords of these "states" came to be regarded as bandits and that military action was used to bring the area under direct control of the Ottoman government. The main action in the Kadirli area took place in 1865, when armies under Dervish Pasha defeated the lord of Kozan and environment. From 1866 on, the defeated tribes, still under the traditional authority of their chiefs, were given land and forced to settle permanently, i.e., to give up nomadism and banditry. In the absence of a land cadaster the land given to each tribe was described only in general terms. As a matter of fact, a precise description and the writing of land titles was not really necessary, since the area was only very sparsely inhabited and a part of the traditional area of the tribes. Further, as the grant was made to the tribes, the tribal leaders began to regard the land as their property, and tribal people began to be regarded as tenants of the leaders. This development was most outspoken in the more eastern parts of our area, around Antep, Urfa, and Syria. In the area of Kadirli, which is very close to Kozan, the former "feudal" state, the tribes were given mostly swamp land which apparently in the first period was very poor in quality. Each family tried its best to make a living as farmers. However, the leaders of former tribal sub-groups, called "oba," retained their traditional prestige and were called "agha." This title was "like a kind of title of nobility," it had nothing to do with wealth.

These leaders, aghas, began to engage in several lines of activity to improve their conditions. First, it became obvious that the swamps could not immediately be used for farming. The memory of the jungle-like character of the land was still very strong all between Adana, Ceyhan, Osmaniye, Kozan when we visited the area in 1951. In order to use the land, which here is almost completely flat, clearing of brush and reeds and digging of irrigation and drainage canals had to be done. For this work, the aghas could draw upon the labor of "their people," the former tribal people, when the old loyalties were still strong enough. Or they could attract landless people from other areas, in our case Arabic-speaking *fellahin* from Syria. With this labor supply, they dug canals and created first wheat, later rice fields. Rice cultivation on a large basis came into this area only in the 1920's. Even disregarding the price differences between rice and wheat, on the average one acre of irrigated rice brings about twice as much (as unhusked rice) as an irrigated wheat field, and four times as much as a dry wheat field. Moreover, rice can stand a fairly high alkaline and salt content in the soil. As after twenty years of irrigation in many areas of Turkey, if special precautions are not used, the alkaline or salt content tends to become too high for wheat; this is another incentive to shift from wheat to rice. Only, rice means much more labor investment than wheat.

The irrigation and drainage canals, whether they were on land which the aghas regarded as their own or on land claimed by others, were regarded as the private property of the entrepreneurs, i.e., the aghas, who proceeded to sell the water to those who wanted to have a share. These conditions still exist and they make rice cultivation very difficult for a small farmer. If he has so little land that he can cultivate it all by himself, he will most likely have no private access to water. As the farmer has no cash reserves, he cannot "buy" the water which is sold at competitive prices. In one case in Kozan, even a wealthy farmer with 200 *dönüm* land could no longer buy the irrigation water which at the time cost him TL 65,000. Thus, either he cultivated without irrigation wheat, barley and cotton with his own tools; or he went into an agreement with the owner of the water: the owner of the water took over the fields for a year, and the farmer worked as a tenant on his own fields, gaining a share of the profits which came out of the sale of the rice by the owner of the water. As in the Kozan area rice cultivation was at the time permitted only once every four years, the farmer had to make such an agreement once every four years, if he wanted to participate in the relatively high profits from rice. If a farmer owns more land than he can cultivate by his own labor, and with water rights, wants to plant rice, he has to invest TL 100 per *dönüm* in order to earn roughly TL 600 at harvest time, and, normally, he cannot finance such a relatively high initial investment in spring, months before the harvest. Out of this situation, in combination with the bonds of traditional tribal loyalty, the well-known features of tenancy came into existence. The aghas succeeded in clearing more and more land into which they put canals. This land they regarded as their own and gave to tenants who often were descendants of the same tribe. In a case in Kozan, a farmer rented from an agha 160 *dönüm* land on the basis of an oral contract. Implements, water rights, plow animals, all belonged to the agha. The tenant worked on the rice fields and received twenty-five per cent of the harvest, while the agha took seventy-five per cent. If the work was more than the tenant himself could do, he had to hire additional labor and must pay twenty-five per cent of the labor cost. It was up to the agha to decide whether he would sell the total harvest and pay the tenant's share in cash or whether he would let the tenant sell his share, depending on what the agha felt was best for him.

A second line of activity of the aghas after the tribe had settled, was collaboration with bandits. As we pointed out, at the time before 1865, the tribal lords had had their armed men who engaged in trade or banditry. After the settlement, all tribal people who had violated one of the laws of the Ottoman state to which they were now subjected, fled into the mountains. The new mountain villages, settled by tribal people, were too poor to sustain bandits, so that the bandits renewed their ties with the former tribal leaders, the aghas. The aghas have been using them to get extra income, as in the past, from smuggling weapons, but also flint for lighters which was a state monopoly in Turkey, etc. They have been using them also to cut lumber illegally in violation of the new laws protecting the forests, and to sell this lumber after having brought it secretly into the plains. The last big action against bandits in our area occurred in 1932, although cases of banditry in 1935, 1940, 1953 and 1958 were reported. In the 1932 action the involvement of the aghas was so clearly established that some local agha families were exiled to Diyarbakir. The bandit of 1958 was seized in the house of an agha, and his downfall was the consequence of a fight between the two agha families whom he served. He already exhibited the more modern type, insofar as he was used as a tool for illegal activities not only in the villages, but even in the capital of Turkey. He may be viewed as a counterpart of the well-known type of *goonda* in Pakistan and India, the outlaw who is sustained, often in the house of the landlord, by a landlord and who does the "dirty" jobs for him: intimidation of farmers and tenants, pressure upon officials, etc. In our area, in which the tribal past is still so near, tribal loyalties are still strong, so that the outlaw serves "his" agha from "his" tribe, just as a tenant works with "his" agha and cannot afford to

change "his" agha for another one, since this would result in fights between the aghas in which the tenant would suffer more than the aghas.

The introduction of a democratic system has greatly contributed to the
growth of agha-landlordism in our area. Landlordism was hardly of importance here before 1923. In the following period, it was Atatürk's ideal
to rule the country with a one-party system and through a parliament
in which the educated élite of the country was to be represented. In fact,
by clever manipulations, he succeeded in getting a Turkish parliament
which, before the Second World War, had the highest percentage of
intellectual deputies ever contained in any parliament. To be sure, there
were already some landlords in the first parliaments, for political reasons
and because there were landlord sons among the intellectual élite. But
with the creation of a two- and later a multi-party system (after 1946),
the parliament became more and more an assembly of landlords, and as
the cabinet had to be selected from the ranks of the deputies, the government had the same fate. On the other hand, the situation at the beginning of Atatürk's reforms and throughout the time of the one-party system led to the growth of a new élite out of the urban classes, including
non-landlord small-town people. This new élite was imbued with the
nationalist and socialist ideas of the Atatürk regime and, naturally, was
opposed to the traditionalist tribal tendencies of the landlords who
regarded themselves as the legitimate leaders of the countryside.

CULTIVATION OF STATE LAND

The main lines of the specific development in the Kadirli area between
1930 and 1960 were as follows. The new regime, using modern legal
ideas, regarded as state property those lands for which there were no land
titles, and it made grants or sales of state land to various groups of people.
Thus, for instance, nomads usually did not have any title at all to their
pasturages, and, therefore, it happened quite often that the government
gave their winter pasturages to farmers who then either tried to keep the
nomads out or requested payment of rent.[2]

Furthermore, after 1920 most of the aghas in this area had taken unoc-
cupied land under cultivation; such lands were either former property
of Armenians who had been killed, or expelled or had left the area
voluntarily after the end of World War I, or they had been swamps
which had been drained. To give a few examples:

1. Agha A had 77 *dönüm* registered land, but used 1000 *dönüm* state land.
2. Agha B had 200 *dönüm* registered land, but used 4800 *dönüm* state
   land.

[2] This problem was discussed in an earlier article, "Nomads and Farmers in
Southeastern Turkey," *Oriens* 6, 1953, pp. 32–49.

3. Agha C had 350 *dönüm* registered land, but used 1000 *dönüm* state land.

It may be assumed that nobody protested against the use of formerly uncultivable land, since this certainly meant a development of the area. On the other hand, the government had to solve a problem of settlement of refugees. When Turkey lost territory to Russia at the end of World War I; when Turkey concluded treaties of exchange of populations with Greece, Bulgaria, Jugoslavia, etc. (1927), many refugees, mostly former farmers, were promised recompensation in form of land grants, to be given from state land. Thus, about 650 *dönüm* state land farmed for the son of agha C, had been given to settlers already in 1927; in 1950, 219 *dönüm* of land used by agha A and 665 *dönüm* used by agha B were adjudicated to settlers. The landlords attempted to fight these decisions through political pressure or they took their cases to the courts. As no clear land deeds existed, the courts had a difficult time deciding whether the landlord or the state was the real owner of the land under dispute. As a landlord in 1960 had a net gain of TL 500 per year per *dönüm* under rice cultivation, it is in his interest to protract the court suit as long as possible, so that he can have the profits of the land as long as possible. It can easily be seen that the sums involved here have been considerable, reaching millions of Turkish pounds each year. As many agha families now have members of their families trained as lawyers, they can be assured of the best legal help even if their claims are untenable.

WATER USE

The whole area of Kadirli was infested with malaria which became worse with the introduction of rice cultivation after the settlement of the tribes. The government attempted to control the disease by sending doctors into the area. It is reported that the landlords first attempted to bribe the doctor, later threatened him and finally had him transferred to another area because they were afraid that the malaria campaign would mean an interference with rice cultivation, which indeed it did. Later, the government succeeded in setting up rules regulating the rice cultivation. Each farmer who wanted to plant rice had to get a new permit every year, and one of the conditions for a permit was the proof that the fields could be properly irrigated. Each landlord, therefore, needed to have control of water and irrigation canals. As the official land survey was not up to date, landlords could get rice permits on the basis of maps which showed non-existing canals or by claiming to have water although in reality their canals were dry. Because of such conditions fights would break out and still break out over the use of canals and water. To protect their "rights" the landlords tend to hire strong-men (i.e.

former bandits, see above). Consequently, a very high number of criminal cases have resulted from water disputes. An agha can also "rent" or "buy" water rights. If a canal belonged to the state, the water was sold by auction, just as state land could be rented to tenants by auction. In these auctions the aghas intimidated the small farmers by making use of their traditional tribal prestige, aided by a tacit understanding between aghas and government administration, and as a result the aghas got the use of water and land at prices far below normal. Thus, they could increase their economic power more easily than others.

In some cases, even the ownership of canals was open to question. The Savrun river, the main water source for the Kadirli area, has two branches. One branch seemed to belong without dispute to the aghas, while the other branch with its canals apparently belonged to the city of Kadirli. But already before 1923 the aghas had stopped the flow of water to the city and, regarding the system as their own, they began to sell the water. When an administrator took the water away from the aghas, serious reactions began.

OTHER ECOMOMIC FACTORS

The data which I have for the modern Kadirli landlords contain only one other field of economic activity, namely the ownership of grain mills. Already, in earlier times, water-driven mills belonged normally to land-lords, because of the cost of investment and the necessity of having water rights to operate the mill. As the possibility to build mills was limited and farmers had to have their grain milled or unhusked, mill owners had a kind of monopoly, although the milling fees were set by tradition. Several landlords in Kadirli have mills; one of them is the owner of the largest modern rice mill in Southern Turkey. From other areas we know that landlords try to organize or to control the wholesale of local farm products, especially in the case of rice and cotton; their organization may even extend into foreign countries, if the amounts of products are large enough to warrant speculative activities in the world markets. Our docu-ments also contain no information on indebtedness of tenant or free farmers to the landlords, a typical trait in most countries, but, as far as I can judge, not important in Turkey today. . . .

REORGANIZATION OF FAMILY RELATIONS

The normal pattern of marriage in our area, and especially among the élite, was cousin-marriage.[3] Until 1950, other marriages were unusual, although they occurred occasionally at all times as "political marriages." With the development of democratic institutions, especially the party

[3] Father's-brother's daughter; if she is not available (too young, too old, or if there is none), Mother's-brother's daughter.

system, the relations between agha families seem to have changed. Evidently, it became more necessary to create solid ties between *different* groups of agha families because fights, common as they are among all nomadic tribes or tribes with an aristocratic tradition, have to be fought now not only locally but at the same time in the cities, at the courts, in the provincial capital and assemblies, in the national parliament, in the party organizations, and in the government administration. Exercising real power today requires the cooperation of many more people than before. Thus, we see that in the meantime different agha families have created marriage alliances among each other. . . .

POLITICAL POWER

As in Syria before the last changes, the tribal élite succeeded in getting into the party system by simply using their traditional influence over the tribesmen under their control. Aghas who had old feuds, tended to join opposing parties and continued their fights on a new basis. When tribal loyalties were not sufficient, the aghas could use means of influencing the vote of their tribe members by, for instance, promising to help them to get land if they promised to vote for them or by promising to help them in law suits. From other situations we know that landlords would bring their "strongmen" into the villages who would impress upon the villagers by their mere presence the fact that they had to vote for the right man. The way through one of the parties may mean at first chairmanship in the local or the provincial organization, but it could also mean to become a deputy with a seat in the national parliament in the capital, Ankara. From there, the way to a minister's chair was open. A second way to attain and to retain local power was by aiming control of all the new local organizations of more technical character, such as securing chairmanship of the Chamber of Agriculture, getting on the Rice Committee which controls the granting of rice certificates for cultivation of rice, becoming a member of the Provincial Committee, or city mayor, or to work as a lawyer. In 1962, five of the sixteen deputies to the Parliament and senators of the Adana province were men from agha families in Kadirli. It is important to note that no agha of our area has been a teacher, banker or local administrator, such as forestry official, district governor (*kaymakam*) or police chief. These men, today, are typical products of the Atatürk era: they tend to come from middle-class, mostly urban families and are, emotionally, often quite outspoken against the agha system. Representing the modernistic, bureaucratic ideology, combined with modern special training, these men stand in "natural" contrast to the aghas and their system. The controversy between both groups has exhibited several strategic approaches from the side of the agha. One of the methods designed to check the power of these appointed bureaucrats has been to impress upon the tribal and dependent people that they could never hope to get anywhere by appealing to the government. The representatives of the government have been depicted as corrupt and lazy, and also as powerless. The people were encouraged to rely upon the agha who would help them either directly and quickly on the local scene or by his personal influence upon the government. One of the ways to impress the commoners with agha power has been, for instance, to let the villagers know, sometimes weeks before the event, that a local official was to be transferred or demoted, with the clear implication that he received this fate because he had displeased the aghas.

A second method designed to check the power of the administrators has been to plant trusted men into office jobs in the lower, untrained, levels of the local administration. These men would try to push non-conformists out and then to control the chief administrator who, not being a local man, depended upon this subordinate for local information. These men could also cause important documents to disappear if these documents were dangerous for the landlords.

The third way to check the power of the local government administration has been to treat the chief administrator, upon his first arrival, extremely lavishly with gifts, celebrations, parties, including dinner and drinking parties, even girl parties in the big cities. Photographs taken at such occasions, as well as other information, collected in the meantime, have been used if the administrator remained cool towards the aghas. The next step might consist of producing little incidents designed to frighten the administrator or his wife, or in direct threats, or in the spread of rumors in the towns and villages.

The next step, if the administrator has not yet resigned of his own free will, might well be to accuse him of criminal acts or irregularities in the office, first at the provincial level, then at the central government. The accusations might be trivial and poorly substantiated, but they might be more serious accusations such as condemning private property without paying indemnity or diverting government funds to private organizations, or illegally receiving money or other illegal enrichment.

If all this does not help, personal influence might be used in the capital to remove the man. While normally transfers of officials are announced some time before they have to leave their job, and while they never have to leave before the travel money is transmitted, in such cases the transfer might be made extremely fast.[4] Normally, transfers are not made in

4 In one case, the order asking the district governor to leave his district arrived on March 22 (*Yeni Adana*, March 22, 1962); on the following Sunday his successor was already in town at 7:00 A.M. with all his furniture, ready to move into the governor's house and office (*Türk Sözü*, March 27, 1962; *Yeni Adana*, March 27, 1962). The new governor had received orders by telegram and had received travel money (*Yeni Adana*, March 27, 1962), while the old governor received his travel

winter but in May, because even today travel in Turkey during the winter is often quite difficult. Normally, these abnormal transfers have been to places along the Russian or Iranian border, i.e., to a backward part of the country where life is difficult; however, they were done in a way to satisfy the letter of a law covering such cases.[5]

The power of the landlords of Kadirli can be shown by the fact that in general in Turkey a district governor (*kaymakam*) remains in one place for two years, while in Kadirli the average stay was four months eight days; until Spring, 1962, Kadirli had thirty-seven district governors in fifteen years, two more replacements happened soon after. To remove a district governor before May is of special importance for the local élite. In March, everybody who wants to plant rice in the coming season, has to file his intention with the chairman of the Rice Commission. The chairman is the district governor. He issues the permits in April or May, and irrigation occurs from June to October. If the district governor leaves before April, the new man will have to issue the permits. But, being a newcomer, he has no way of checking into the legality or appropriateness of the applications.

The new conditions, of course, provide the opposing urban élite with some ways of defense. As long as the prime minister or the president or both are not landlords themselves, recourse to them may be effective. This is an extremely important point. It seems that in the long run in Turkey, generally recognized leaders can only be men who are not tied to the aghas, because the aghas, far from constituting a unified class or clique, are divided into many local factions. Any agha as state leader would have the support of only some agha groups and no permanent support from other agha groups or other sectors of the population. The present (1964) crisis in Turkey seems to be that forthcoming elections may favor a new party, but this party has not been able to put up a generally acceptable leader of high prestige who is not connected with one of the agha groups. It was this very situation which repeatedly led to the emergence of military men (Atatürk, Inönü, Gürsel) as political leaders, because the military has been relatively free from agha infiltration.

Another modern way for the urban élite to oppose landlordism has been to present relevant cases in parliament. As we said, the aghas are not all united in one party. Each clique of them selects the party which is opposed to their enemies. Besides, each party contains elements of the urban population who are unfriendly towards the aghas. As a result,

---

money only on March 31 (*Cumhuriyet*, March 31, 1962) and less than half of the customary sum.

[5] According to this law, district governors have to serve two years in districts near the Russian or Iranian borders (*Yeni Adana*, March 27, 1962).

discussion of such matters in parliament may lead to quite lively, if not violent activities.[6] Whether or not the new élite is successful depends upon the power situation of the moment.

Finally, as the most modern ways of attempting opposition, there have been delegations from villages and towns going to the capital in the attempt to influence the powerful men in the government; there have been posters in the towns; there has been mobilization of university student organizations, as well as strikes.

This example from Kadirli, mainly the development during the years from 1960 to 1962, is perhaps the best documented case of the functioning of modern landlordism in the Near East, although the newspapers reported other cases at the same time, with their own peculiarities. Yet, I think that much of what is reported here has its direct parallels in other parts of Turkey, of Iran, Afghanistan, Pakistan, and even China before 1948. There seems to be a pattern of landlordism which has direct connections with the requirements for rice cultivation (heavy investment of capital and/or labor). It might emerge at any time in history. In Kadirli it emerged as recently as thirty years ago. The system is effective and may become even more effective when democratic institutions are introduced thanks to the landlord's adaptation to modern conditions.

[6] Violent discussions and fist fights in parliament occurred in connection with the case of the district governor of Kadirli (*Yeni Gün,* April 17, 1962; *Kudret,* April 17, 1962; *Hür Vatan,* April 17, 1962).

WHAT PATH TO MODERNIZATION?
FIRST AND SECOND WORLD
PERSPECTIVES

PART Three presents a variety of views of the third world from the perspectives of both the first and second. The first two selections represent opposing sides of a continuing debate: can the developing nations afford the luxury of pluralistic competitive democracy, or are they condemned to the possibly more efficient but harsher methods of authoritarian dictatorship? William McCord argues that the democratic alternative is not only preferable, but that the case for authoritarianism has not been and cannot be proven. I. Robert Sinai, on the other hand, feels that the tasks confronting the third world are so overwhelming that the deliberate, slow-moving political processes of democracy will prove utterly inadequate.

John H. Kautsky presents a view of the underdeveloped countries as seen from the perspective of the Kremlin. Kautsky deals with both theory (or Communist party doctrine) and tactics (or the realities of Soviet foreign policy). He makes the arresting observation that communism is not the formula for radical reform of the industrialized West that Karl Marx had originally intended. Rather, it has become a specific prescription for modernization and industrialization of underdeveloped countries, one which, moreover, proclaims the same goals as the nationalist elites of these countries.

Finally, Richard Lowenthal examines the political forms that have appeared in the developing nations. He concludes that these nations have assimilated some aspects of both the first and second worlds of development while rejecting others. They seem to have adopted some of the ideology of the first world—specifically, nationalism and socialism—and some of the political practices of the second world—specifically, centralized planning for economic development. (This characterization has to be qualified, for the Leninist analysis of imperialism has been widely accepted throughout the countries of Asia, Africa, and Latin America, as Irving L. Horowitz notes.) Lowenthal sees a unique political format evolving in the developing nations. He suggests that this new type of political system be styled as revolutionary "regimes of development." Moreover, Lowenthal argues that these regimes cannot escape the dilemma of "bread" vs. "freedom." Every developing country must choose the amount of freedom it is willing to give up for the sake of rapid modernization.

13. THE CASE FOR PLURALISM

William M. McCord

WILLIAM MAXWELL MC CORD is Professor of Sociology at Syracuse University. He has also taught at Harvard, Stanford, and Rice Universities. He has been a consultant to the President's Commission on Crime and the Commission on Civil Unrest, as well as the National Institutes of Mental Health. His publications include *Origins of Alcoholism* and *Mississippi: The Long, Hot Summer* (1965).

History has granted the new nations, particularly those which have most recently won independence, an almost unique opportunity. Their leaders may start a new body politic. They may create economic and political institutions which the world has never known. Like the Founding Fathers in America, Mao, Sukarno, Nehru, Nasser, and other new leaders have had enormous, although not unlimited, latitude to build societies which offer food, freedom, and hope to their people.

Unfortunately, many of these charismatic heroes have chosen to follow a path already well trodden in the past: by the Wang Mangs, Caesars, Bismarcks, Hitlers, and, indeed, the old colonialists. The ideologists of the most recent wave of authoritarians affix fancy labels to old techniques. Today, dictatorship hides under such appellations as a "people's," "guided," or "tutelary" democracy. Slogans, however, cannot conceal the facts. As they have for thousands of years, generals, redeemers, emperors, or "chairmen"—all-too-mortal in their decisions—enforce their will over the people with coercion and indoctrination. And as ever, the frustrations of human existence provide a sufficient number of true believers who think that *this* time the millennium has arrived and all will turn out for the best.

Current trends offer scant justification for such hopes. The recent histories of Indonesia, Ghana, and China can give little, if any, substantiation to the claims put forth by contemporary authoritarians in emerging nations or by their sympathizers in the West. . . .

First, is it true that the exigencies of economic development require the establishment of a central state armed with dictatorial powers? Does such an authoritarian regime give more hope than a liberal polity to those societies launched into the storms of development?

China's experience, at least until 1960, appeared on the surface to lend credence to authoritarian presumptions, for it seemed apparent that dictatorial rule had finally freed the Chinese from starvation. If Mao and his men do not repeat the mistakes of the "Great Leap Forward"—or worse, commit the majestic errors which Perón did in his attempt to industrialize Argentina forcefully—one can hope that the richly fertile economy of China will fulfill its promise. Nonetheless, to generalize from China to the majority of emerging nations, to argue that they should all adopt totalitarian methods, would be a superficial and dangerous assertion.

It must be remembered that the Chinese people, like those of Meiji Japan, had long submitted themselves to the discipline and terror of dictatorship. To their advantage, the Communist elite had at its disposal a society already cowed by centuries of despotism. Most emerging peoples, in contrast, have a proud tradition of liberty (partially derived from the Western Enlightenment, most of it inherited from prior centuries of self-government). Would an Ibo in Nigeria, lacking even a concept of chieftaincy, accommodate himself to a "God-Emperor"? Would the village republics of India permanently surrender sovereignty to a single, overarching ruler? Would Bolivian tin miners let their union become simply one more organ of an all-powerful party? I doubt it, *if* they had any informed role in the decision. A political system has to adhere more or less closely to a nation's dominant culture, if it is to survive permanently. China and a few other countries have never tasted the sweetness of freedom, but for most of the world, indigenous political and social relationships do not conform to a totalitarian model.

We must raise a further question about China's economic advances: Did totalitarian methods, "the elimination of freedom of thought for the few," really play a significant role in China's material progress? Conventionally, most commentators assume that China's improvement could not have been accomplished without the extermination of millions of "counterrevolutionaries." Yet . . . most objective scholars attribute China's success to specific, flexibly applied *economic* policies—a high rate of investment, mobilization of rural masses as the spearhead of advance, an emphasis on small-scale industry, education, and agriculture—all measures which do not, in and of themselves, require totalitarianism. Indeed, China's strictly economic policies for attaining growth resemble those of nineteenth-century, democratic Denmark as much as those of Stalin's Russia. The Chinese achieved a faster rate of growth (until 1960) than did the Danish, but after all, China had many economic advantages: more abundant resources, foreign aid, virgin land, larger markets, experience with industrialization, and close collaboration with another large nation. The question cannot be answered dogmatically, but there seems a real possibility that China's growth should be attributed to sensible economic policies which could be followed with almost equal ease by a free nation as by a terrorist regime.

Even in China's case, therefore, we must be highly cautious in assuming that any direct relationship exists between economic growth and the use of authoritarian methods. . . .

A comparison of Indonesia and the Philippines redounds to the advantage of a democratic approach; the more popular pairing of India and China purports to show the superiority of an authoritarian solution.

Such comparisons suggest that *the success of a drive for economic growth depends not on the degree of political coercion involved but rather on the unique culture of the nation and on particular economic policies followed by the government in power.* An authoritarian regime, as in China, may possibly aid in stimulating economic advance; it may, as in Indonesia, cause a potentially irrevocable depression. A democratic polity may make economic mistakes, but they seldom have the permanent effect of errors committed by a dictatorship.

At the very minimum, an unbiased observer has to conclude that authoritarianism provides no panacea for poverty. Even if they ignore the human sacrifices involved, leaders in emerging nations should hesitate to adopt strong-arm methods. . . .

In the drive for development, all signs point to the sovereignty of politics. At their core, attempts to change the wretched condition of transitional men rest on political choices. How to accumulate capital and yet resist the tempting path of compulsion? How to preserve traditional culture but still change a feudal social structure? How to build a growing economy and yet avoid the exploitation which accompanied the expansion of industry in the past? This is the apex of the problem, for political —or, if you will, ethical—decisions determine the answer to such questions.

In responding to the stresses which afflict their societies, leaders in developing countries have divided into two political camps. Ranged on one side stand the authoritarians who are willing to use any practical means, including force, to achieve their ends. Authoritarian ideologies, while presented in varied garbs, assert certain common goals:

The authoritarian wishes national independence, freedom for the State or People—but not for the individual. Sékou Touré of Guinea has stated this view with blunt openness, "We have chosen the freedom, the right, the power, the sovereignty of the people, and not of the individual." The survival and power of the group comes first; no domain of the individual's life should remain—on principle or in fact—outside the purview of the state.

The authoritarian believes that only a single party can create a sense of nationhood and unity which he regards as necessary during a period of modernization. Autonomous organizations or political parties, each articulating its own goals, are dispensable. Through some mystic identification, the authoritarian contends, Leader, Party, and People can become one. The unified party supposedly serves as the vanguard of progress and discourages disunity, factionalism, and subversion during a time of great tensions.

The authoritarian demands that development should occur through "socialist" methods. He believes that only socialism, usually conceived as heavy industrialization, can eradicate the poverty, disease, and illiteracy characteristic of pauper nations.

For the authoritarian, all human resources must be mobilized in the service of Party and Productivity. While robed in new garments, the authoritarian of today can find ample, if unsavory, company in the past. His arguments have been advanced from the Pharaohs' epoch to that of Goebbels. Witness Frederick the Great, in his defense of a "modernizing" Germany: "At the moment when the State cries out that its very life is at stake, social selfishness must cease and party hatred be hushed. The individual must forget his egoism, and feel that he is a member of the whole body."

The world has never lacked those who defend their own power, privileges, and perquisites in the name of a brave cause or those who have claimed that history will absolve them for any action they commit. The Cause, the Party, or God have almost always overridden the quiet cries of an unknown individual, caught in the movement of history.

Yet, with whatever effect—and sometimes it has been noble—a band of questioners have wondered whether the particular emperor wore any clothes. In the face of many temptations, these men still fight a battle for freedom in the developing countries. They can be found under a variety of labels: liberal, democratic socialist, even conservative. Yet, they share certain assumptions about the nature of man and society. This pluralistic political credo entails these commitments:

The pluralist affirms the potential creativity, rationality, and dignity of the individual. He rejects the supremacy of the State or People, as these abstractions are expressed in the arbitrary decisions of an uncontrollable leadership.

The pluralist views with suspicion any group which claims to have discovered "the true faith," for he believes that the road to progress is barred by dogma. He therefore rejects the pronouncements of those arrogant "shepherds" who assume that fate has elected them to herd the masses. He remembers Demosthenes' advice that "there is one safeguard known generally to the wise, which is an advantage and security to all, but especially to democrats as against despots. What is it? Distrust!"

The pluralist wishes to create political and judicial institutions which will assure freedom from arbitrary arrest, freedom to criticize authority, freedom of movement, and freedom to organize a representative opposition to those in power. He rejects the fashionable argument that the social context of new nations alters the essential nature of these liberties, for he contends that freedom's defense, in today's West Africa as in ancient Greece, requires a vigilant watchfulness expressed in a network of institutions reinforced by the rule of law.

The pluralist finds unconvincing the argument that a one-party bureaucracy can somehow be cleansed by the vigilance of the people. He recognizes that, regardless of the historical situation, the victim feels the same when he fears an informer, when he knows that his judge is a political stooge, when he is kept in ignorance by a muzzled press, or when he languishes in jail for political crimes. The pluralist believes that no discourse about "new" forms of freedom can convince a political prisoner in Ghana, China, or Indonesia that he really has his liberty.

The pluralist knows well that a society cannot release itself from fear until the curse of starvation has ended. He adheres to Lord Acton's dictum that "the theory of liberty demands strong efforts to help the poor. Not merely for safety, for humanity, for religion, but for liberty." The pluralist, therefore, wishes to abolish privilege, end economic serfdom, and extend equality of opportunity to all. He does not, however, necessarily identify human happiness with a growth in national income or the spread of industrialization. He understands that industrialization has not always extended the scope of individual freedom, and he knows that the most wealthy nations have the highest rates of mental disorder, alcoholism, and suicide—unmistakable signs that even a cornucopia of material goods cannot make up for a loss of personal dignity and security. In consequence, the pluralist believes that economic growth should be measured in terms of the degree to which it ends suffering, enhances individual dignity, and widens the possibility of free choice.

It is of vital importance to assert once again these principles of liberty and to recognize that men live not by bread alone. But for the embattled leaders in emerging nations—faced with the anarchy of the Congo, or the irresponsible union movement in Bolivia, or the reactionary power of a caste system—mere expostulation does not go far enough. In building a better society, as Africanist Immanuel Wallerstein has commented, "the only useful question to ask, in the old-fashioned American pragmatic tradition, is how you get from here to there."

Unlike the authoritarian, who has the propaganda advantage of claiming ready-made solutions to all problems, the pluralist has to content himself with accepting the uncertainties of responsibility. But the pluralist can depend on certain principles which history has validated:

The methods which leaders use affect them and their societies. If stampeded by cruel methods which destroy their dignity, self-reliance, and indigenous democratic institutions, the ruled lose their capacity for freedom and may, as in Indonesia, lose their prosperity, too. In particular, leaders must realize that an increase in wealth will not spontaneously produce a politically free society. History has yet to provide an example of a nation which, through the use of Draconian methods, achieved both literacy and prosperity, as well as liberty of conscience and a rule of law. As philosopher John Plamenatz has perceptively warned the new nations:

> The recipe, *first* raise productivity and material well-being and abolish illiteracy, doing whatever needs to be done to these ends, and *afterwards* set about establishing freedom and democracy, is bad . . . history gives us no example of a nation that first grew prosperous and acquired a strong centralized government and then afterwards became free and democratic. It is not true of the Greeks or the Romans or the Dutch or the English or the Swiss or the Americans; of any of the people who have cared most for freedom or democracy, or have enjoyed them the most securely.

Those who desire both bread and freedom for their people should not be beguiled by the promise that authoritarian rule is merely a transitory stage. From the beginning, leaders must use methods which are consonant with the goal of creating a free society.

To create a politically open society, the leadership must work to maintain or build a plural social structure—depositories of power independent of the group which controls the government. A rule of law, the right to criticize, the right of privacy—all the majestic liberties first created in the West—depend upon a complex, interdependent social structure which no government thinking of its own survival would dare to attack. Only a balance of economic power between various segments of a community can serve to preserve liberty. In particular terms, this means that the government should give all possible encouragement to trade unions and entrepreneurs, to rural co-operatives and village councils, to small industries and a free landholding peasantry. These independent units should be nourished both because of the economic reasons which we have previously discussed and because they serve as the surest defense of liberty.

A corollary of this position is, of course, that the central state should, as far as possible, avoid any movement toward total collectivization of property. History has issued a clear warning concerning the relationship of state authority and economic collectivization. As political scientist Massimo Salvadori has observed:

> Since the beginning of civilization there have been numerous collectivist societies. Not a single one has enjoyed free institutions. Miracles can happen; but it is wiser to believe in miracles (especially economic and political miracles) after they have happened and not before.

In a developing country the government must play a very wide role indeed, not only in maintaining justice and order but also in planning and co-ordinating the economy, building an infra-structure, and breaking up concentrations of power in feudal hands. Nevertheless the government should try most of all to plan consciously for a devolution, rather than a concentration, of economic power.

A paradox which confronts pluralists in almost all countries is that, while seeking to encourage a diversity of pressure groups, they must also imbue their peoples with a "public philosophy" and a sense of nationhood. The leadership must encourage interest groups within their society to listen, negotiate, and compromise with each other in the name of the "national good." It would seem that only the vehicle of nationalism can transform warring tribes, castes, regions, economic or ethnic groups into united countries. Yet, the dangers of narrowly conceived nationalism are all-too-obvious. The nationalist credo has served as an excuse for despotism, a hindrance to international economic co-operation, an incitement to wars large and small, and, in this era of global history, it carries the ultimate threat of atomic extermination.

The task is, therefore, a delicate one, calling for unusually talented and enlightened leadership. . . .

The task of those who desire to create a free and abundant society in the "Third World" is by no means easy: they must decentralize power but maintain stability and a sense of nationhood; they must create a basic consensus without suppressing dissent; they must maintain a pluralistic social structure but undermine the power of traditionalist groups who seek to hold back progress; they must put their faith in the villagers and respect the people's potentiality, while realizing that tutelage from above may long be required; they must comprehend that now, as in Europe of 1848, the decisions taken by individual leaders at points of crisis will critically affect their nation's destiny—and they cannot fall back on the comforting sense that history is on their side. They find themselves involved in a series of paradoxes which inspire fear, if not despair, in the stoutest of hearts.

But regard the authoritarian alternative: a single party controlling all aspects of life; an elite arbitrarily and often mistakenly directing the economy; detentions without trial; a *Gleichschaltung* program of ranging everything from unions to the family under the guidance of a party bureaucracy; a "Redeemer" who promises, but often fails to deliver, economic welfare; a regime which treats men as part of an experiment in animal husbandry. Is this the way to a good life for mankind? Is this some new constitutional form, or merely tyranny adorned with different slogans? Those of good will, those of historical perspective, those who respect individuals rather than abstract masses will, I am convinced, choose the more ambiguous but eventually more rewarding path of building a plural society.

14. THE CASE FOR AUTHORITARIANISM

I. Robert Sinai

I. ROBERT SINAI is Visiting Research Associate Professor in Political Science and History at Long Island University. He also taught at the New School for Social Research in New York City. He has been an official of the Histadruth Trade Union Federation of Israel, and an information officer in the Israeli Foreign Office. He represented the Israel Labor Party at the Secretariat of the Asian Socialist Conference in Rangoon, Burma. He has written *The Challenge of Modernization* (1964) and *In Search of the Modern World* (1967).

It has become a commonplace of world politics to describe the changes that have taken place in the Afro-Asian countries as a revolution. The international atmosphere is absolutely clogged with slogans, speeches and books extolling the "Great Revolution" that has supposedly been brought about in all these populous territories. Some glibly announce that these countries are already involved in a "Revolution of Rising Expectations." President Kennedy has spoken of the "Revolution of the Rising Peoples." Liberals, socialists and conservatives alike mobilise all the stale clichés of a simple-minded but heart-warming "progressivism" in support of the "Afro-Asian Revolution" and thoughtlessly bend to the "Wind of Change," without really understanding what kind of wind it is and where it is blowing and what has been changed or what will have to be changed.

But the distressing fact about all the changes that have taken place in the Afro-Asian lands is that they do not in any way add up to a revolution. No revolution has, as yet, taken place anywhere. There has been a political change-over, political power has been transferred to new ruling elites, new flags have been designed and unfurled, the number of nations represented at the United Nations has gone up by leaps and bounds, but neither the men who now rule nor their societies have been revolutionised. They have neither acquired new virtues nor removed old vices. The present-day regimes are mere synthetic substitutes for the genuine revolutions that will still have to be made. What we are witnessing in reality is a colourful masquerade, a sort of superior political orgy, superficially exciting but essentially undermining, and leading only to a process of dissolution.

All these countries have achieved their independence not because they were ready for it, or had adequately prepared themselves for all its consequences, but only because two destructive and fratricidal European wars have demolished the material, political and moral foundations of Europe's world authority, and because the growth of liberal and democratic ideas within the Western community has made the business of dominating others both unpopular and unrewarding. The decline of colonialism in the West is due much more to the spread of liberal and socialist ideas among their peoples than to any increase in Afro-Asian strength. The importance of these countries, moreover, does not stem from their inherent capacities but only from Western weakness and gullibility and from its disturbing loss of confidence in itself and in its civilisation. The Afro-Asian camp has been exalted because the West has systematically been degrading itself.

All these countries are, in fact, faced with three main tasks:

(1) to produce a new elite of reformers and innovators, ready and willing to assume the hardships and risks of modernisation, and nerved with the courage to overhaul their societies and to change the ethos of their civilisation. (Within this innovating political elite, the entrepreneur, the captain of industry, the bold economic pioneer, will have to occupy a place of the highest importance);

(2) to develop a new ideology with the power to bring about a cultural revolution; to make people work-minded and development-minded, to sweep away the countless barriers to disciplined, rational effort, resulting from traditional habits and superstitions, and to achieve what the Reformation and the Enlightenment combined attained over the centuries in the West;

(3) to organise the state in such a manner as to impose collective savings far beyond the limit of what individuals would be likely to save

if left to their own devices and to invest these forced savings in an all-round development programme.

It should be quite obvious by now that this new elite, if and when it arises, will find it impossible to carry out all these tasks in a liberal democracy, because to implement them requires the concentration of a great deal of economic and social power in the state, the taking of a great many unpopular decisions and an attack on the people's most cherished beliefs and traditions. The economic tasks of development, moreover, cannot be realised by the methods of a liberal economy. The country is backward precisely because one of the basic conditions for a liberal economy—a private class of entrepreneurs—is absent. Capital can only be accumulated out of the abstinence and deprivation of the poor and economic development requires the taking of decisions which will hurt many vested interests. This cannot be done within a democratic framework. Democracy unfortunately is not a panacea for every situation, is not suitable for every country and is not even desired by every people. And at some stages in human development, a form of absolutism is needed to clear the ground of the accumulated debris of centuries and to impose unwelcome but necessary changes upon the "unenlightened" people. Before any kind of economic transformation can take place, however, there must be the indispensable non-economic conditions for the take-off. What all these countries need above all, therefore, is the emergence of a new elite, capable of assuming all the burdens and risks of leadership and ready in the very depths of their hearts and minds to break with the enervating customs of their traditional societies and to accept the immense sacrifices necessary for taking their peoples through all the unsettling but liberating upheavals and innovations which the West had to go through before it could become modern and dynamic and prosperous and democratic.

The new elite that will develop, if at all (at the present moment there is no sign of it apart from the communists), will consist of exceedingly unattractive specimens. Whether we like it or not, this will be an elite of "hedgehogs," consisting of men who, in the words of Isaiah Berlin, will "know one big thing," and very little else, and who will relate everything, every aspect of their lives and thoughts, to a single, central vision. They will be narrow-minded fanatics, half-educated, crude and primitive, without sophistication or wide interests, full of an unscrupulous self-confidence and organised and tempered by one idea—how to modernise and strengthen their societies and drive their peoples by "forced marches" into the modern world.

This new group will at first be stern and harsh and will cast aside the pretence of ruling by democratic means. Their political thinking will be determined by two pressing essentials: the need to turn their society up-side down and inside out and the need for discipline and order. They will accept the fact that rapid change is more desirable than the partial gradual change of traditional institutions and wisdom. Instead of patch-ing, grafting, clipping and altering this or that branch of the national society, and thereby only creating new discrepancies and discordances, the new, purposeful elites will seek to transform the whole pattern in one sweep, break with the familiar past and develop a more or less consistent set of new habits. They will, therefore, organise an authoritarian (if not totalitarian) state and will be quite ready to sweep away the last vestiges of the traditional order, to jolt the people out of their ruts, and to attack their most ancient beliefs and practices. The rights of the individual will be overruled, traditional safeguards will be rejected, and no class or interest will be permitted to stand in the way of modernisation. This group will be as hard as nails, organised for governing, and they will be the inflexible servants of an idea. It will be moulded by the slogans of an oversimplified ideology, and sprung out of the most energetic and virile sections of the "intelligentsia" and the "people." In spite of its many de-fects, in spite of its many ugly features, it will have the necessary strength of character and self-confidence to destroy most of the tra-ditional obstacles to modernisation.

Before this new elite, however, can even begin to wrestle with the pon-derous and sluggish social forces with which it will have to contend, it will have to absorb the spirit generated both by the Reformation and En-lightenment. Without assimilating these Western values, emotions, virtues and drives, no development of any sort will be possible. And unless these new qualities are transmitted to the society as a whole, in the course of a prolonged process of change and innovation, these countries cannot be-come rational enough to confront their problems. To build a new civilisa-tion, irrespective of the speed of its development, is an arduous work that must, in the very nature of things, stretch over centuries and can never really be finished. But as a beginning, a new ideology has to be devel-oped, forceful enough not only to effect a revolution in their traditional scale of ethical values, but powerful enough to create a new type of character. It can only live in a series of individuals who are capable of intellectually and morally incorporating it in themselves. It must not only stand for new ideals of social conduct but also have the strength to fashion and fertilise souls. It must, in short, be capable of injecting a germ of such powerful potency into the society that it will at once be able to act as a stimulant to sustained and energetic enterprise and as an acid dissolving many of the obstructing customary relationships. And this potent germ of innovation will have to affect every department of life and it will have to penetrate every nook and cranny of the country. Starting with the top layers of the society themselves (and there everything will have to begin) it will have to seep down to the civil servant in his office, to the student in his classroom, to the worker in his factory or small workshop, to the peasant and agricultural labourer in his village, field and cottage. And from this first circle this new spirit of life and movement will have to be communicated through all the spheres of the nation. But before such a new momentum can draw the society together and drive it forward, millions of people in every walk of life are unfortunately going to experience the dislocations, the pains and ferment produced by that leaven of change which they have for so long tried to resist. But if they want to enter this new age of increased opportunities and benefits and of new problems, troubles and anxieties, they will have to pay the high price that it demands. No society can become richer without emphasising hard work and thrift, without developing a high propensity to innovate and without revealing a high level of willingness to accept and initiate change. And the hard work will not only have to be done by the working classes of the society, but the example will have to be set by the elite itself. The poor countries have remained poor for so long because their values have not emphasised becoming rich and because they have given too high a place to stability, tradition and the other-worldly values of religion.

Now this new ideology which they will have to develop can assume different forms although it will have to serve the same central purpose: to break decisively the powerful and unreformed forces of religion and tradition and to clear the ground for the building of more rational societies. In its search for this new ideology, it can either try to go back to the past, though it is irretrievable, or determine to leap forward into the bravest and most dazzling future, though it is unrealisable. It can invent a completely novel idea or seize hold of an ancient superstition. It can aim at creating something new or at restoring in a new and modern form something that existed many centuries ago. This ideology can be naive or sophisticated; it can extol the beauties of nature or the superior virtues of urban life. But it must have one supreme and indispensable quality: it must call for a sharp break with the nation's predominant traditions and call into question its most cherished beliefs. It must create a new type of man, strong and ruthless enough to revolutionise himself and his society. Unless it has the force to make people change themselves and to break with all those traditions that have clogged their minds and frustrated their energies, it can never serve as that instrument of liberation which is needed.

15. THE COMMUNIST PERSPECTIVE

John H. Kautsky

JOHN H. KAUTSKY is Professor of Political Science at Washington University in St. Louis. He has held research fellowships from the Rockefeller and the National Science Foundations and research positions at Harvard University and the Massachusetts Institute of Technology. He is the author of *Moscow and the Communist Party of India* (1956), *Communism and the Politics of Development* (1968), *The Politics of Development: Conflict and Change* (1971), a forthcoming book on *The Politics of Traditional Societies*, and is editor and co-author of *Political Change in Underdeveloped Countries* (1962).

The Russian Revolution and the regime it brought to power were no historical accident, as they have so often been called in an effort to explain the appearance of a "socialist" government in an underdeveloped country. Historical accidents are, in fact, generally resorted to as explanations exactly where no adequate explanations of a phenomenon are available. No such explanations of the Russian Revolution and the Communist regime could be available as long as they were sought through the exclusive application of Western European models, including the Marxian one. Perhaps we can help replace accident by regularity and mystery by understanding, which is, after all, the function of science, by fitting the Russian Revolution into the broad historical pattern of the nationalist revolutions in underdeveloped countries.

THREE DECADES OF PROLETARIANISM

For at least thirty years after the Russian Revolution, the Communists suffered from their inability to make as complete a break with Marxism in their thought as they had in their actions. Far from maintaining the "unity of theory and practice" to which they professed to adhere, they could not, in their theory and propaganda, as they did in their practice, entirely replace the party of the proletariat with the party of the intellectuals, the class struggle and the revolution of the proletariat with the nationalist movement and the industrialization of the underdeveloped countries. Had they been able to see themselves for what they were, in fact, more and more becoming, the Communists could have presented themselves to their fellow intellectuals in other underdeveloped countries as the first ones to succeed in attaining their common goal—rapid industrialization and elimination of the aristocracy and Western domination.

Instead, they thought of themselves as the vanguard of an industrial proletariat and, therefore, of their revolution as an example to the West. The result was that they fell between two stools. In the West, where there was a proletariat, the appeal of Communism failed because its real achievement was irrelevant in already highly industrialized countries. In the underdeveloped countries, where its achievements were highly relevant, its appeal failed because it obscured that relevance by insisting on the proletarian and hence Western nature of Communism. For this reason Communist propaganda could do little or nothing to overcome Communism's general lack of progress before World War II. . . .

The Communists' stubborn insistence on appearing as the representatives of a largely non-existent class fighting battles against virtually non-existent capitalists was, no doubt, an important factor in their amazing failure to make headway even in those underdeveloped countries where the growth of a nationalist movement indicated the existence of a very real revolutionary potential. Thus, in India, where the nationalist Congress had 500,000 members by 1936, the Communist Party, during 1934, after 15 years of organizing efforts, increased its membership from 20 to 150! By 1939, the Congress passed the 5 million mark, while the Communist Party had a mere 5000 members by 1942. Only in China, of all the underdeveloped countries, did the Communists make some significant advances before World War II and there they did so to the extent that they broke with the general "proletarian" pattern of Communism, when their failure in the cities forced them to adopt Mao Tse-tung's strategy of reliance on the peasantry.

NEO-MAOISM AND NATIONALISM

The cold war between the United States and the Soviet Union compelled international Communism to develop a new strategy, which was destined finally to bring the policies and propaganda of Communist parties throughout the world, and particularly in its underdeveloped parts, into line with the modernizing nationalist role which Communism had played in the Soviet Union. It was a strategy which, in short, turned Communism from a professedly proletarian into a frankly nationalist movement. This new strategy was first developed by Mao Tse-tung during World War II in his battle against the Japanese. It is for this reason that I have called it the neo-Maoist strategy, but it was adopted by Moscow and the Communist parties, in response to Soviet foreign policy needs, beginning about 1947. . . .

The neo-Maoist strategy was an attempt to appeal to all classes at a time when an alliance with most major parties, including most nationalist movements, was impossible. Under it, the Communists' main enemy was identified as neither capitalism nor Fascism, but as "imperialism," a term that has become virtually synonymous with the United States in the Communist vocabulary. Whether the opposition to foreign imperialism and its alleged native allies, such as the nationalists, was to be peaceful or violent was a matter of flexible tactics rather than worldwide strategy, but it was always to be based on what the Chinese Communists have called the bloc of four classes. That bloc consisted of the proletariat, the peasantry, the petty-bourgeoisie (which is the rather inappropriate Marxist-Western term the Communists apply to the old middle class, and to some extent also to the intellectuals), and, most notably, the antiimperialist capitalists. That this latter group may, in fact, hardly exist in underdeveloped countries does not reduce the importance of its explicit inclusion by the Communists in the neo-Maoist front, for it is at this point that the wholly novel character of their new strategy becomes apparent.

Neo-Maoism did not differ much from the old "right" strategy in establishing a broad front of the four classes (to which have since been added aristocratic elements). But since the former party-allies were not available any more, the Communist appeal to all these groups now had to be directed "from below." This meant that the Communist party now had to claim to represent the true interests not only of the "exploited" classes, as it had always done, but also of their "exploiters." For the first time, Communist parties could transcend the limits imposed on them by their former "proletarianism"; they freed themselves from the proletarian myth after being prisoners to it for thirty years. . . .

The relative success of Communism in the postwar period as compared to the prewar era has been due to a number of factors in addition to its adoption of the neo-Maoist strategy. Thus, colonialism was weakened both by the war itself and by changes that had taken place in the colonies as well as in the colonial powers. Communism's prestige and power had grown as a result of the Soviet Union's victory in the war and its occupation of Eastern Europe and North Korea, and of the role Communist parties played in the anti-German and anti-Japanese resistance movements. Perhaps most important, the achievements of Soviet industrialization have been far more dramatic and obvious recently than they were before World War II. Neo-Maoism, however, made it possible for the Communists to exploit fully the attractiveness of these achievements to underdeveloped countries.

With a strategy openly appealing to, in their own often-used phrase, "all classes," the Communists in underdeveloped countries were no longer tied to a non-existent or very weak proletarian base or obliged to attack the native capitalists, if any, or, for that matter, any other native groups except those closely connected with "imperialist" interests. They could thus seek support from any group to whom their anti-colonialist program appealed. The main domestic plank of this program was the promise of rapid modernization and industrialization on the Soviet and Chinese Communist model. For the first time, the appeal of the Soviet Union having achieved the goals of intellectuals in underdeveloped countries—elimination of aristocratic rule and quick industrialization without dependence on Western capital—could be fully brought home to these intellectuals. In industrialized countries, it is difficult to appreciate the power of this appeal and the depth and urgency of the intellectuals' concern with the problem of modernization. To them the appeal is hardly weakened by knowledge of the sacrifices which the Communist path to modernization imposed on millions in the Soviet Union and China. In countries where mass starvation was a common occurrence and millions are still undernourished, sick, and illiterate, and where there is no tradition of individualism and civil liberties, such sacrifices do not weigh very heavily as against the hope of future improvements. Nor do the intellectuals expect to bear these sacrifices themselves; what makes the Soviet and Chinese examples so attractive is also the fact that it put intellectuals in control, with seemingly untold opportunities to gain power and prestige.

In fact, Russia in 1917 was not, like many underdeveloped countries today, overpopulated, nor did her industrialization really proceed without Western aid: it began with the foreign capital accumulated under Tsarism and continued with the support of Western credits, machinery, and technicians until the end of World War II, after which the industrial plant and specialists of the newly conquered European satellites were heavily relied upon for some time. But all this is little understood in underdeveloped countries and does not seem to reduce significantly the relevance of the Soviet—and not at all that of the Chinese—example to the intellectuals in these countries. The fact remains that the Communist revolutions in Russia and in China, like their own nationalist movements, confronted the problems of backwardness at home and weakness and dependence in international affairs, and they have already in large measure attained the goals which to the intellectuals in most underdeveloped countries are still chiefly unfulfilled aspirations. This is an appeal that the Western societies, which have been industrialized and powerful so much longer, and have acquired their industry and their power under such different circumstances, inherently have difficulty in matching.

If . . . nationalists in underdeveloped countries are intellectuals appealing to all strata of the population in their drive for industrialization and against colonialism, and Communists in underdeveloped countries are, as we have now seen, intellectuals appealing to all strata of the population in their drive for industrialization and against colonialism, then Communists are nationalists. This conclusion sums up the vital change that the neo-Maoist strategy brought to international Communism beginning in the late 1940's. To be sure, since complete and sudden breaks in ideological development are impossible, the Communists still conceal this change from themselves and from others by their continued habit of seeking doctrinal support for their practice in quotations from Marx and Engels and by their continuing affinity for the vocabulary of the nineteenth-century Western socialist movement. But though words lag behind action or, to use Marxist terminology, the ideological super-structure is transformed more slowly than the material base, even in Communist propaganda and theoretical writings, the "people's masses" and "all peace-loving people"—and, most broadly, simply "the peoples"—are more and more replacing the "proletariat" and the "working class," fighting now not the "class struggle" for "class interests" and for the "socialist revolution," but in the "national interest" for "national independence." . . .

THE CONVERGENCE OF COMMUNISM AND NATIONALISM

With the adoption of neo-Maoism, Communist parties had been turned into nationalist parties with respect to their ideology and policies, but they and the Soviet Union were still opposed to the older nationalist movements in underdeveloped countries. In the early 1950's, however, even before Stalin's death, a change in Soviet and subsequently in Communist party policy became apparent.

The realization evidently grew among Soviet policy makers that their anti-American objectives could be served at least as well by the non-Communist nationalist movements and governments as by the Communist parties in underdeveloped countries. This had become true not so much as a result of changes in the policies of these non-Communist nationalist movements as of the gradual ripening of changes in Communism itself. Communist goals had now become limited to those that can be effectively served by nationalism—chiefly the elimination of American political, military, economic, and cultural influence wherever possible.

Soviet reliance on non-Communist nationalists to help carry out Soviet objectives would have been quite impossible when the Communists still thought of themselves as champions of the lower classes, and of their goal as a social revolution. Then the nationalist movements were contemptuously referred to as "bourgeois-nationalist." A generation after the Revolution, the dream of world-wide social revolution, which had conditioned even some short-run policies of Lenin and Trotsky and probably affected the long-run calculations of Stalin, had receded so far into the background as not to influence Soviet policy any longer. Statements by Soviet leaders that world Communism is their ultimate goal are of the same significance as similar statements with regard to worldwide justice and liberty made by other government leaders. They are no doubt believed by those who make them and they serve as important symbols to mobilize the loyalties and exertions of their followers, but they cannot account for any particular foreign policy decision. . . .

Once world Communism had, in effect, been dropped as a Soviet policy objective and replaced by the much more realistic one of expansion of the power of the Soviet Union and of those who govern it, Khrushchev could recognize the existence of a third, neutralist, "camp" in addition to Zhdanov's two. In an evolution not entirely dissimilar from that of American foreign policy, which also at one time tended to regard neutralism as "immoral," Moscow came to accept and even to see advantages to itself in the existence of governments that were, if not pro-Soviet in their policies, at any rate frequently anti-American. During the 1950's, the Soviet Union acted more and more as the champion of the neutralist countries and supplied some of their regimes with increasingly significant amounts of economic and technical aid, all, of course, in an attempt to swing these governments to its side. Its side, however, could no longer be defined as that of Communism, if by Communism we mean either an ideology or a social system, whether of Marx, of Lenin, or even of the present-day Soviet Union. Rather, its side is now simply that of the Soviet Union in the international power conflict, in which the neutralist governments can lend support to the Soviet Union by denying to the United States and its allies military bases, raw materials, markets, and diplomatic support, and by extending similar advantages to the Soviet Union.

Soviet backing of neutralist regimes, therefore, is generally in no way dependent on the adoption by such regimes of policies favorable to the lower classes, such as land reform or support for trade unions, or even of policies favorable to the local Communist parties. Many nationalist movements do, for reasons of their own . . . , pursue such policies, but regardless of that fact, there is today hardly a nationalist movement left anywhere, either in the government or in the opposition, with which Soviet foreign policymakers do not consider cooperation to be possible and profitable. Some of the few underdeveloped countries that are still so backward as to have virtually no movement of nationalist intellectuals— Ethiopia, Yemen, Afghanistan, and Nepal—are among the chief beneficiaries of Soviet foreign aid, again regardless of the fact that their governments are what traditional Communists would have considered the most reactionary regimes in the world today.[1]

The change in Soviet foreign policy deeply affected the role of the Communist parties in underdeveloped countries. As the nationalist move-

---

[1] The government of Yemen was, after this was written, seized by some military "nationalist intellectuals" who have enjoyed Soviet support just like the government of the Imam they overthrew.

ments and governments changed, in the Soviet view, from stooges of Western imperialism to peace-loving defenders of national independence, Moscow expected the Communist parties to give up their opposition, which they had, with very few exceptions, maintained in the late 1940's. . . .

At the 20th Party Congress of 1956, Khrushchev asserted that "in all the forms of transition to socialism, an absolute and decisive requirement is political leadership of the working class, headed by its vanguard. The transition to socialism is impossible without this." However, in the very same year, this old established Communist doctrine, which provides much of the *raison d'être* of Communist parties, was beginning to be modified in Moscow with respect to underdeveloped countries.

The doctrine of proletarian leadership and—what amounts to the same thing in Communist thinking—Communist party leadership in all conflicts in which Communists have been engaged has occupied such a central place in Communist ideology that it has not been openly thrown overboard all at once. Soviet leaders and writers keep repeating it, as Khrushchev did at the 20th Congress, to provide symbolic reassurance to their followers. They may continue to do so also in response to the pressure of the Chinese Communists to whom, for reasons to be indicated, insistence on Communist party leadership is a matter of great importance. The Communist parties all over the world, too, frequently cling to the concept, motivated not merely by doctrinal orthodoxy and habit but, more obviously, by the desire for self-preservation.

The repetition of old formulae cannot conceal the marked shift in Soviet behavior, however. It is most clearly visible in the changing foreign policies of the Soviet Union during the 1950's which increasingly rely on the non-Communist nationalist leaders and movements more heavily than on the Communist parties to support the Soviet Union in its conflict with the United States, i.e., to assume the leadership in the "struggle against imperialism." . . .

The Soviet Union's present policy of reliance on the nationalist movements was strongly defended by E. Zhukov, a leading Soviet expert on underdeveloped countries, in an important article in August 1960:

> It is known that at the head of the majority of new national states of Asia and Africa stand bourgeois political leaders who usually take a position under a nationalistic flag. However, this cannot belittle the progressive historical importance of the breakthrough that has taken place on the imperialist front. The working class is the most consistent enemy of imperialism. Nevertheless Lenin considered it natural that *at the beginning* of any national movement the bour-

geoisie plays the role of its hegemonic force (leader) and urged that in the struggle for the self-determination of nations support be given to the most revolutionary elements of the bourgeois-democratic national-liberation movements. . . . An arrogant slighting of anti-imperialist actions when in certain historical conditions nonproletarian elements appear on the forestage, is a most dangerous form of sectarianism that leads to self-isolation.[2]

To be sure, both to maintain their own claims to orthodoxy and as a reaction to Chinese pressure, Soviet Communists acknowledge leadership by the national bourgeoisie only "at the beginning" or "in the present stage" of the national liberation movement. They even invented a new name for this stage, that of "national democracy," which is regarded as a transition to the ultimate attainment of "socialism." That ultimate goal of socialism, however, is in their view too distant to influence Soviet policy decisions in the present, and it is thus the "transitional" stage that is decisive.

The important innovation in the policy recommended to the Communist parties of underdeveloped countries by the Soviet Union since 1956 is the willingness to put the nationalist movements (labelled "bourgeois" or, in Cuba, "petty-bourgeois") in the position of leaders and the Communist parties in that of followers, whether it be in the march toward "socialism" or the march toward "national liberation" (a distinction which is in any case probably becoming more and more shadowy in the minds of Soviet leaders). That the idea of the bourgeoisie leading the proletariat toward socialism is a startlingly new one by all traditional Communist standards needs no emphasis or elucidation. However, the acceptance of the bourgeoisie in the leading role of the "national liberation" movement, too, is a decisive break with the policy advocated by Communists until the mid-fifties. . . .

The arrogant sectarians whom Zhukov attacked—or counterattacked—are the Chinese Communists. In cooperating with the nationalist governments of some underdeveloped countries, they had never gone as far as Moscow has since 1956 to subordinate the Communist parties to the nationalists, and beginning about 1957 or 1958 they returned more and more to the original neo-Maoist strategy of opposition to the nationalist governments.

Whatever the reasons for the reversal of the Chinese attitude toward

[2] Ye. Zhukov, "Significant Factor of Our Times. On Some Questions of the Present-Day National-Liberation Movement," *Pravda*, August 26, 1960, pp. 3–4; condensed translation in *The Current Digest of the Soviet Press*, XII, No. 34 (September 21, 1960), 18–19. Italics in the original.

the nationalist-neutralist governments, the divergence of Chinese from Soviet policy on this point is clear. However, just as the Soviet Communists' repetition of the doctrine of proletarian leadership obscures their actual policies, so the constant use by the Chinese Communists of the Marxian symbols of the class struggle and the dictatorship of the proletariat serves to distort the actual issues in the conflict between Moscow and Peking. That conflict does not turn on the relationship between the proletariat as a class and the bourgeoisie as a class. Both sides are quite agreed on the necessity of Communist cooperation with the national bourgeoisie in the conflict with "imperialism"—though it now suits Peking more than Moscow to stress the vacillating character of the bourgeoisie in its alliance with the proletariat. The difference lies elsewhere: The Chinese Communists want Communist parties in underdeveloped countries to cooperate with the bourgeoisie *against* the nationalist governments and even encourage Communist-led "armed struggle" against them, while the Soviet Communists want Communist parties to cooperate *with* these nationalist governments (whom they identify with the national bourgeoisie). What is at stake, then, is the relationship between the Communist parties (often labelled "the proletariat") and the nationalist governments.

The Chinese Communists evidently no longer trust the anti-imperialism of these governments.

> . . . [T]hese states can never expect to effect the transition to socialism, nor indeed can they thoroughly fulfill the task of the nationalist, democratic revolution. It should be added that even the national independence they have won is by no means secure. . . . [The bourgeois nationalists] may even pave the way for the emergence of bureaucratic capitalism, which is an ally of imperialism and feudalism. . . . In the final analysis, they can never escape from the control and bondage of imperialism.[3]

To be sure, where the "anti-imperialist" character of a nationalist movement was beyond doubt, because it was in open conflict with one of the Western powers, the Chinese Communists have supported it, sometimes sooner and more vigorously than the Soviet Communists, as when they recognized the FLN as the government of Algeria at a time when Khrushchev still hoped for improved relations with de Gaulle.

Generally, however, the Chinese Communists insist that the Communist parties in underdeveloped countries must remain independent of the

---

[3] Wang Chia-hsiang in *Red Flag* on the 10th (1959) anniversary of the People's Republic, as quoted in Donald S. Zagoria, "Sino-Soviet Friction in Underdeveloped Areas," *Problems of Communism*, X, No. 2 (March–April 1961), p. 8.

nationalist movements, must lead their own united front against these movements, and must themselves eventually seize power—and they imply strongly that this can ordinarily be done only by means of "armed struggle." As against Soviet suggestions that Communist parties follow the leadership of non-Communist nationalists, Liu Shao-chi, in 1959 insisted on "the firm grasping of hegemony in the democratic revolution by the proletariat through the Communist party." [4] The Chinese continue to summarize "the experience gained and the road taken by the Chinese revolution" as "under the leadership of the working class (through the Communist Party) and based upon the alliance of the workers and peasants, to unite all the forces that can be united, wage armed struggles and establish the people's democratic dictatorship; then to achieve socialism and communism." [5] And as against Soviet emphasis on the nationalist movements, the Chinese emphasize the importance of the Party: "Lenin considered it of prime importance for the proletariat to establish its own genuinely revolutionary political party which completely breaks with opportunism, that is, a Communist Party, if the proletarian revolution is to be carried through and the proletarian dictatorship established and consolidated." [6]

To Moscow's suggestion that the non-Communist nationalist movements may be leading the way to socialism, Peking replies sharply: "The modern revisionists and certain representatives of the bourgeoisie try to make people believe that it is possible to achieve socialism without a revolutionary party of the proletariat and without the . . . correct [united front] policies of the revolutionary party of the proletariat. . . . This is sheer nonsense and pure deception." And in answer to Moscow's praise of Nehru's socialism, Peking sneeringly says that a "motley variety of so-called 'socialisms' have emerged from among the exploiting classes in certain countries. . . . They only put up the signboard of 'socialism' but actually practice capitalism." [7]

[4] Liu Shao-chi, *The Victory of Marxism-Leninism in China* (Peking: Foreign Languages Press, 1959), quoted in Zagoria, "Sino-Soviet Friction in Underdeveloped Areas," *op. cit.,* p. 4.

[5] Li Wei-han, "The United Front—A Magic Weapon of the Chinese People for Winning Victory," *Peking Review,* IV, No. 23 (June 9, 1961), 13–16, and No. 24 (June 16, 1961), 17–21, at p. 21.

[6] "Long Live Leninism," *Red Flag,* No. 8 (April 16, 1960), reprinted in G. F. Hudson, Richard Lowenthal and Roderick MacFarquhar, *The Sino-Soviet Dispute* (New York: Frederick A. Praeger, 1961), pp. 82–112, at p. 84.

[7] *Ibid.,* p. 109.

16. THE CASE FOR REVOLUTIONARY "REGIMES OF DEVELOPMENT"

Richard Lowenthal

RICHARD LOWENTHAL is Professor of International Relations at the Free University of West Berlin. He is the author of *World Communism, The Disintegration of a Secular Faith* (1964) and of various contributions to scholarly works and periodicals on the comparative politics of Communist regimes and of Communist and national revolutions. His most recent major essay entitled "Development vs. Utopia in Communist Policy" appeared in Chalmers Johnson (ed.), *Change in Communist Systems* (1970).

. . . *[T]he effort to use political means for catching up with the technical, economic, and cultural development of modern societies begins regularly with the assumption of power by a new regime—with a revolutionary act.* It is revolutionary, not necessarily in the sense of a violent overthrow of the constitutional order but in the sense of a clearly marked break in the continuity of the elites running the state, of the principles by which they legitimize their rule, and of the tasks they set themselves. Whether the break is constituted by emancipation from a colonial regime or from indirect forms of dependence or by the overthrow of an indigenous, traditionalist form of government, the victory of a "regime of development" is the precondition for a comprehensive attempt to tackle the tasks [of modernization]. . . .

The question of the prospects of different forms of government in the developing countries, to which this essay is devoted, may . . . be . . . phrased as follows: How effective have various forms of government proved in accomplishing the tasks of a "regime of development," or what specific advantages and weaknesses have they shown if viewed in relation to those tasks? Here we must begin with a word of warning. *In the developing countries, systems of government that are identical or closely similar in their constitutional forms may serve as a framework for the rule of totally different social groups pursuing diametrically opposite aims;* hence the political scientist must beware of confusing the effects due to the ruling group's positive or negative attitude to the goals of development with the effects due to the form of government as such.

The practically relevant range of possible regimes of development is thus confined to governments of revolutionary origin claiming to represent the will of the people. It extends from a development-oriented democracy of the Indian type at one extreme via the various forms of one-party predominance, military dictatorship, and one-party dictatorship, to the ideological dictatorship of a Communist Party regime at the other extreme. We now turn to a comparison of the favorable and unfavorable effects of the forms of government within that range on the process of development.

In any such comparison, the first thing that strikes the eye is the tested efficiency of the Communist model. In its Stalinist form, Soviet Communism has proved itself as a gigantic engine of development. Indeed, in surveying the basic measures taken by the Soviet government in the course of forty-five years of "socialist construction," we find that they have been concentrated precisely on the tasks we have just enumerated: the forced accumulation of capital by the state; the planning of investment by the state; the mobilization of the masses for the development goals set by the state and for loyalty toward the regime by a political movement embracing every stratum of the population; and the use of this movement for re-educating the masses in a cultural revolution by struggle against superstition and illiteracy, for disciplined work according to plan. No wonder the modernistic, nationalist intelligentsia of all the developing countries is fascinated by the Soviet model!

Yet the same groups of nationalist intellectuals are also becoming increasingly aware of the extraordinarily high price the Soviet government and the peoples of Russia have paid for this achievement—a price that was only partly inherent in the task of development but was raised far beyond necessity by Communist ideological dogma. The dogma of irreconcilable hostility to the "capitalist" world has barred any form of Western development aid to the Communist countries and forces them to squeeze the needed capital funds exclusively from the bones and muscles of their own peoples. The same dogma requires that absolute priority be given to the buildup of heavy industry in order to achieve complete military independence from the "enemy" as quickly as possible: this needlessly prolongs the period during which the efforts and sacrifices of industrialization bear no fruit for the people's standard of living. The dogma that declares state planning to be incompatible with private ownership of means of production results in the needless rejection of the collaboration of the all too few industrial entrepreneurs available in the developing countries, hence in needless delay in the training of the necessary number of qualified technical and economic cadres. The dogma that declares planning to be incompatible with a market economy—so far revised only by Yugoslavia among Communist states—leads to the senseless attempt—particularly absurd in the conditions prevailing in underdeveloped countries—to have every detail of production centrally regulated by an immense bureaucratic machinery, hence to inflated costs, to graft, to interruptions of supply, poor quality of output, and continuous discrepancies between the type of goods produced and that demanded. Most crucial of all, the dogma of agricultural collectivization, originally imposed on the peasants as a means to enforce delivery of their produce at state-fixed prices, has caused agriculture miserably to lag behind industrial development in all those Communist countries that still cling to it, again unnecessarily depressing the standard of living.

To this considerable economic cost of the Communist road of development a political price must be added. A Communist dictatorship is not, after all, content to proclaim the realistic goal of modernizing its own country—an aim limited in space as well as time; it justifies itself by the utopian goal of the worldwide victory of the Communist order, the achievement of a classless terminal stage of history. The worldwide aim implies indefinite continuation of an unbridgeable conflict with the non-Communist world; the classless Utopia requires indefinite preservation of the party dictatorship at home, which can only "wither away" once the unattainable terminal stage has been reached. The choice of the Communist road of development thus has to be paid for by the rise of an *ideological* dictatorship that tends to cling to power by maintaining a state of permanent external and internal tension even after the original task of modernization has been completed.

It is becoming increasingly evident even for the nationalist intelligentsia of the developing countries that *the specific advantages of the Soviet model are due to the comprehensive tackling of the tasks of development proper and to the organized concentration of economic and political power, while the specific disadvantages are due to the dogmatic narrowness of Communist ideology.* Hence the tendency, manifested by other "regimes of development" with growing frequency, to copy the organizational forms of central investment planning, and even of the one-party state, but to reject Communist ideology in favor of an eclectic combination of nationalist and socialist ideas with native traditions while deliberately limiting their practical program to the modernization of their country.

Among the "regimes of development," the opposite extreme to Communist ideological dictatorship is represented by Indian democracy. Its achievements, if measured by the short time of its existence, the level of poverty on which it started and the intensity of population pressure, are no less impressive. Its methods of combining internal accumulation with the acceptance of economic aid from both power blocs, central planning of investment with a market economy giving scope to private enterprise, promotion of the voluntary formation of agricultural cooperatives with the fostering of peasant initiative, and the authority of a leadership tested in the struggle for independence with democratic freedom for opposition and public criticism under the rule of law, are also studied and admired in many other developing countries; but they are rarely imitated. This is due first of all to the fact that the working of the Indian political system is linked to conditions that are absent in most developing countries. . . .

But even where a combination of favorable conditions allows a democratic regime of development to function as in India, the important advantages which this form of government assures for the personal freedom as well as for the long-term political education of the citizens have to be balanced against the social cost of having measures necessary for development slowed down by the opposition of vested interests. The implementation of land reform and of important elements of the economic plan, particularly in the field of taxation, are impaired by the resistance of the representatives of landowning and capitalist interests inside the Congress Party and particularly inside the provincial ministries and administrative offices staffed by this party. Moreover, the appearance of such obstacles is not accidental but inherent in a democracy operating under the rule of law: A process of state-directed development requires that powerful interests that are linked to the old order or to its remnants must be hurt, and the resistance of such interests may of course be broken more speedily by the methods of revolutionary dictatorship than by methods involving respect for minority rights, for strictly democratic procedures of decision-making, and for a division of powers assuring the rule of law.

. . . [E]ven in such old, highly developed industrial countries as the United States and Great Britain, recurrent dangers of political stagnation, of a paralysis of decision, arise from the nature of a pluralistic democracy under the rule of law—dangers that must each time be overcome by special impulses, such as the pressure of a major crisis or unusual qualities of leadership. Where the need for modernization is as urgent as in the developing countries, the problem is even more serious. It may indeed be stated that *within a certain range, there exists for these countries a dilemma of choice between the extent of pluralistic freedom they can afford and the pace of development they can achieve.* It is not a dilemma of absolutes which would force them to choose between the extremes of total dictatorship or total stagnation, but a continuous line of alternatives where *every degree of increased freedom has to be paid for by some slowing down of development, every degree of acceleration by some loss of freedom.* In the nature of the process of state-directed development this seems inevitable.

Because this is the case, the large majority of genuine "regimes of development" has so far shown a preference for forms of government that lie between the extremes of pluralistic democracy under the rule of law and the totalitarian ideological dictatorship of the Communists. Here we intend first to distinguish the main types of these intermediate forms of government, and then to point to their common features.

Closest to Indian democracy is the system of *nondictatorial one-party hegemony*. It combines a democratic constitution—usually of the presidential, more rarely of the parliamentary type—with a situation in which the formation of opposition groups is not hampered by legislation or police action, but where the incomparable authority of the governing party, based on its leadership in the national revolution, leaves no effective chance for the development of political alternatives. Such regimes, like the rule of the Partido Revolucionario Institucional in Mexico, of the Neo-Destour in Tunisia, or of the Union Populaire Senegalaise in Senegal, seem to differ only in degree from the Indian type, yet the difference is substantial. The Indian opposition parties . . . are real factors in Indian politics: They are strong enough to give the Congress a serious battle at election times, to exert effective pressure on government policy, and to force the formation of various types of coalition governments in a number of provinces. By contrast, the opposition groups in the countries just mentioned are too weak to play an effective political role in that sense; the importance of their admission lies primarily in keeping a safety valve open for free criticism, and indirectly in giving a chance for the democratic struggle of tendencies within the governing party itself. In creating "regimes of development," the national revolutionary mass parties typically rely on a network of "mass organizations"—trade unions, peasant leagues, student associations, etc.—representing members with different interests, whose leaders are at the same time influential party officials. Where the ruling party has proclaimed the principle of a single-party regime, it must also prevent the free struggle between these partial interests within its ranks and must thus subject the mass organizations to political directives under centralist discipline (*Gleichschaltung*), as the risk of a factional split in the party cannot be safely eliminated in any other way; but where opposition groups outside the ruling party are admitted in principle, partial interests may also enjoy greater freedom of expression within that party. The evolution of such regimes into true pluralistic democracies may thus take place not only by the growth of the early marginal opposition groups, but also, and perhaps more easily, by the growing differentiation of tendencies and interests within the predominant party.

Much closer in form to the totalitarian regime of the Communists (as well as to that of the National Socialists) are the nationalist *single-party states* proper that have arisen in a number of developing countries. Their ruling groups have the conviction in common that the solution of the problems of development requires a concentration of power to a degree incompatible with the admission of organized opposition or the free representation of partial interests; in such a case, it is of no account whether the formation of other parties is forbidden by law or whether their activity is only gradually paralyzed by persecution, as at first in Ghana— what matters is that the regime regards any form of opposition as "sabotage." But while these single-party states share with the totalitarian regimes proper the decisive rejection of institutional pluralism and of the rule of law for the period of modernization and industrialization, they differ from them by the absence of an ideological program that would transcend the tasks of national liberation from all colonial dependence, whether direct or indirect, and of forcible national development by political means. Accordingly, state compulsion in these countries is directed to the solution of the immediate tasks of development, not to the enforcement of an all-embracing ideological conformity: *They are "development dictatorships," not ideological dictatorships.* . . .

In developing countries that have never been under direct colonial rule, or have been able to produce a native military elite even under colonial rule, the officer corps may form an important sector of the nationalist intelligentsia—particularly if, as is often the case in Islamic countries, a military career is not reserved to the traditional upper classes. In such countries, therefore, the nationalist intelligentsia often wins power by a military *coup d'état;* the resulting regimes, as in Nasser's Egypt, are *plebiscitary military dictatorships,* seeking, just like the nationalist single-party regimes, to concentrate state power for the tasks of development and to suppress any organized opposition while legitimating their rule by an eclectic mixture of nationalist and socialist ideas defining a pragmatically limited program. Frequently, such military regimes attempt to create a "state party" from above, in order to mobilize the masses for active participation in the tasks of development; but where such a party was not the original moving force of the national revolution, it has regularly proved very difficult to organize it after the event.

Finally, there exists in the developing countries a great variety of *mixed types* of authoritarian regimes, intermediate between limited forms of democracy and the "development dictatorships" of a state party or a military junta. Among examples that do not fit into any general formula I should like at least to mention the "guided democracy" of President Sukarno of Indonesia, and the long reign of Perón in Argentina; both regimes rested . . . on the skill of *a leader balancing a plurality of organized forces not by democratic institutions under the rule of law but by his personal authority.* Sukarno, having eliminated a number of Indonesian parties, . . . pledged the remainder—the Nationalists, the Communists, and one section of the Islamic traditionalists—to cooperation under his leadership, but in practice [was] chiefly concerned to hold the balance between the army, the only effective part of the state machine, and the Communists, the best-organized force among the parties; as the balance [was] highly sensitive to any changes in the external or internal situation, the regime must be considered unstable. Perón relied for a long time on a similarly unstable balance between the section of the officer corps loyal to him, a party chiefly based on state trade unions, and the Church, while ruthlessly suppressing all other forces; he achieved considerable results in some fields of development, but was overthrown when he tried to shift the balance decisively in favor of his party and trade-union basis.

All those "regimes of development" which are neither fully grown pluralistic democracies nor totalitarian dictatorships tied to an ideological dogma, from the regimes of one-party hegemony with freedom of criticism through the authoritarian mixed types and the plebiscitary military dictatorships to the regimes of nationalist single-party rule, have a number of features in common. All of them have come to power by the victory of a national revolutionary movement and are primarily supported by nationalist-socialist intelligentsia groups whose main concern are the tasks of development. All are seeking to tackle these tasks by means of a greater concentration of power than is normally possible in pluralistic democracies —by methods that are at least authoritarian and often clearly dictatorial. *All these regimes therefore have, for the sake of the pace of development, rejected the attempt to assure a maximum of freedom from the start.*

But all these regimes, including the outspoken "dictatorships of development," are not tied to an ideological dogma but remain ideologically open-minded. They are open for new ideas and influences reaching them from the outside world, including the old industrial countries of the West, as they do not see themselves as existing in a basically unbridgeable conflict with the outside world. They are, therefore, also open for further evolution of their own political systems as advances are achieved in the political solution of the immediate tasks of modernization. *None of these regimes, then, in contrast to the totalitarian dictatorships, has for the sake of the pace of development renounced an indispensable minimum of freedom*—of freedom of thought and of freedom to determine the direction of its further political evolution. Even when they are dictatorial, they do not erect dictatorship into a principle; and it is certainly no accident that the historically first among these pragmatic, nationalist "dictatorships of development," the Turkish regime founded by the Kemalist revolution, has fulfilled its promise to abandon power in free elections. For though it is in the nature of dictatorial power that its holders will seek to preserve it even when the task that originally justified it has been solved, it is difficult in practice to prolong a dictatorship whose task was defined from the start not by utopian and therefore unlimited goals, but in concrete, pragmatic terms.

. . . I have tried not to judge the various political systems of . . . [the developing] countries by measuring them against the yardstick of our Western democratic values, but to investigate their chances objectively by asking how they can serve the present needs of those countries as conceived by their politically decisive stratum. But inasmuch as we can influence these chances, they depend in part on our own actions. Effective political action, however, is not the same thing as wishful thinking: It cannot consist in simply giving preference to those types of political system which, on the basis of *our* experience, we should prefer in *our* conditions—without regard for the effect in the different conditions of those countries, and particularly for the prospects for the stability of such systems.

The central objective of the decisive stratum in the political life of these countries, of the intelligentsia, is their politically forced development—the overcoming of traditional stagnation by political means. The central objective of Western foreign policy in these countries must be to keep their future evolution open—to avoid the impasse of a totalitarian solution tied to Communist dogma. Experience has shown that the nationalist intelligentsia in those countries will be the less inclined to such a dogmatic solution the earlier it attains power and the more successful it is in tackling the tasks of development by different methods.

If we remain conscious of the dilemma of choice between the pace of development and the degree of freedom, we shall not try in those countries to oppose Communist dogmatism by ultra-liberal dogmatism. Rather, we shall seek to serve the long-term prospects of a liberal-democratic evolution by promoting in each particular case what appears as the most promising alternative to stagnation on one side and to totalitarian dictatorship on the other—whether this alternative turns out to be an imperfect democracy or an undoctrinaire, open-minded "dictatorship of development." For in those countries, maximum approximation to a pluralistic democracy under the rule of law, as we know it in the West, can only be the result of a process of development successfully completed: It can never be its precondition.

Part Four

WHAT PATH TO MODERNIZATION?
THIRD WORLD PERSPECTIVES

THE leaders of the third world are perhaps in the best position to deal with the issues under discussion in these pages. Not only do they have a claim to speak for their people as political leaders, but they also have had direct experience of the pressures to which their societies have been subjected since the advent of modernization. Most of them are relatively well educated and have been exposed to a variety of cosmopolitan influences. Many of them are highly articulate. They often combine a sensitivity for the traditions of their culture with an understanding of the exigencies of modernization. Finally, almost all of them share a sense of humiliation and outraged dignity because of their powerlessness in the face of European encroachments, a feeling heightened by the attitudes of haughty superiority flaunted by officials of colonial regimes. The result has often been a painful ambivalence compounded of hostility towards European politics and governments on the one hand, and a strong attraction towards the products of modern European technology and industry on the other. Such feelings have produced a high degree of frustration. As a result the call to violent revolution has been increasing over the years. These attitudes are well expressed in the selections presented below.

First, Jawaharlal Nehru presents a case for adoption by the third world of a European style of democratic socialism. He argues that such a system is best even for troubled transitional societies such as India. Julius Nyerere, on the other hand, suggests that the classical forms of Western democracy are not appropriate for the radically different social and cultural conditions prevailing in the third world. He argues that, in fact, the one-party system is a truer expression of democracy for these countries than a multiparty competitive system. Lin Piao, Defense Minister of mainland or Communist China, presents the Maoist view that only a violent revolution culminating in seizure of power by the Communist party can bring about the liberation of the countries of the third world.

No study of the developing countries is complete unless it takes account of the feelings that permeate the impassioned writings of the late Frantz Fanon. Fanon's contention that the people of the third world will rise only when they achieve a sense of self-respect and human dignity cannot be denied. His conviction that European colonialists have systematically robbed these people of their humanity through the use of violence, and that only through counterviolence will they be able to regain it is, to say the least, provocative. It is a mark of the volatility of our time that Fanon has found disciples among those who are trying to achieve equality and dignity within the United States itself.

We conclude this section with excerpts from an account of the transformation of a devout Catholic into a determined armed revolutionary, as depicted by Sanche de Gramont. This account clearly illustrates how powerful the personal impact of extreme poverty and misery may be, and how it can drive idealistic young men into complete disillusionment. Where there are signs of the possibility of peaceful change, as for example in Chile, such alienation may yet be prevented. On the other hand, the mere existence of a freely elected parliamentary regime is no guarantee either. Such a regime may also become the victim of violent upheaval if it fails to move toward resolution of basic social and economic problems, or if it does not provide adequate opportunities for its educated younger generation. Thus, India has witnessed the emergence of a fanatical terrorist group known as the Naxalites, which, significantly, seems to appeal especially to university students. But the potential for violence is greatest in a society such as that described by Sanche de Gramont, where corruption and graft abound, and where the social and political systems are highly resistant to change or reform.

17. DEMOCRATIC COLLECTIVISM
AND SOCIALISM

Jawaharlal Nehru

JAWAHARLAL NEHRU (1889–1964) was Prime Minister of India from the achievement of independence until his death, and a leader of the Congress Party for forty years. Son of an aristocratic Brahmin lawyer, he was educated at the prestigious English institutions of Harrow and Cambridge, and studied law in London. As one of the chief founders of Indian independence, he became a leading spokesman for the peoples of underdeveloped countries throughout the world. In addition to a large number of lectures and speeches, he wrote *The Discovery of India* (1944).

DEMOCRATIC COLLECTIVISM

If the spirit of the age demands equality, it must necessarily also demand an economic system which fits in with it and encourages it. The present colonial system in India is the very antithesis of it. Absolutism is not only based on inequality, but must perpetuate it in every sphere of life. It suppresses the creative and regenerative forces of a nation, bottles up talent and capacity, and discourages the spirit of responsibility. Those who have to suffer under it lose their sense of dignity and self-reliance. The problems of India, complicated as they seem, are essentially due to an attempt to advance while preserving the political and economic structure more or less intact. Political advance is made subject to the preservation of this structure and existing vested interests. The two are incompatible.

Political change there must be, but economic change is equally necessary. That change will have to be in the direction of a democratically planned collectivism. "The choice," says R. H. Tawney, "is not between competition and monopoly, but between monopoly which is irresponsible and private and a monopoly which is responsible and public." Public monopolies are growing even in capitalist states, and they will continue to grow. The conflict between the idea underlying them and private monopoly will continue till the latter is liquidated. A democratic collectivism need not mean an abolition of private property, but it will mean the public ownership of the basic and major industries. It will mean the cooperative or collective control of the land. In India especially, it will be necessary to have, in addition to the big industries, cooperatively controlled small and village industries. Such a system of democratic collectivism will need careful and continuous planning and adaptation to the changing needs of the people. The aim should be the expansion of the productive capacity of the nation in every possible way, at the same time absorbing all the labor power of the nation in some activity or other and preventing unemployment. As far as possible, there should be freedom to choose one's occupation. An equalization of income will not result from all this, but there will be far more equitable sharing, and a progressive tendency toward equalization. In any event, the vast differences that exist today will disappear completely, and class distinctions, which are essentially based on differences in income, will begin to fade out.

Such a change would mean an upsetting of the present-day acquisitive society, based primarily on the profit motive. The profit motive may still continue to some extent, but it will not be the dominating urge, nor will it have the same scope as it has today. It would be absurd to say that the profit motive does not appeal to the average Indian, but it is nevertheless true that there is no such admiration for it in India as there is in the West. The possessor of money may be envied, but he is not particularly respected or admired. Respect and admiration still go to the man or woman who is considered good and wise, and especially to those who sacrifice themselves or what they possess for the public good. The Indian outlook, even of the masses, has never approved of the spirit of acquisitiveness. . . .

Behind these problems in India, as in many other countries, lies the real issue—which is not merely the establishment of democracy of the nineteenth-century European type, but also far-reaching social revolution. Democracy has itself become involved in that seemingly inevitable change, and hence among those who disapprove of the latter, doubts and denials arise about the feasibility of democracy, and this leads to fascist tendencies and the continuation of an imperialist outlook. All our present-day problems in India—the communal or minority problem, the Indian princes, vested interest of religious groups and the big landowners, and the entrenched interests of British authority and industry in India—ultimately resolve themselves into opposition to social change. And because any real democracy is likely to lead to such change, therefore democracy itself is objected to and considered unsuited to the peculiar conditions of India. So the problems of India—for all their seeming variety and difference from others—are of the same essential nature as the problems of China, or Spain, or many other countries of Europe and elsewhere. . . . Many of the resistance movements of Europe reflect these conflicts. Everywhere the old equilibrium of social forces has been upset, and till a new equilibrium is established, there will be tension, trouble, and conflict. From these problems of the moment, we are led to one of the central problems of our time: how to combine democracy with socialism, how to maintain individual freedom and initiative and yet have centralized social control and planning of the economic life of the people, on the national as well as the international plane. . . .

INDIAN SOCIALISM

In a country like India—an underdeveloped country—socialism, a real socialist basis of society, can only come gradually. There is no help for it. Take the instance of China: They are very keen on changing their economy, and there are no such difficulties as we have—that is, parliamentary institutions and all kinds of "three readings" and select committees, which take a long time. They can pass a law overnight, if they want to. Even then, they go on saying that it will take them twenty years to lay the socialist basis of their society—to have a socialist economy—in spite of all the speed with which they may work. . . .

If by adopting some method which in theory appeals to us we reduce our production, then we are in effect undermining the growth toward socialism—although that particular step may be called a socialist step. For instance, I am quite clear in my mind that if we start nationalizing the existing institutions, industries, etc., by giving compensation, we reduce our capacity to go ahead. Here you have to be clear about one thing in your minds. Are we going in for possible seizure, expropriation without compensation, or are we not? Generally speaking, if we go in for possible seizure, then we think out its consequences, the consequences of conflict, the consequences of suffering of large numbers. Now, so far as our Constitution is concerned, that is ruled out. Apart from the Constitution, our general policy has been opposed to it. . . .

People do not generally realize how many years it took the Soviet Union to get the machines running. We see Russia today, forty years after the Revolution. It took them years to get the machines moving. Take one simple instance. In their Constitution, they said, in a sense as we say, compulsory free primary education for everybody. As far as I remember, it took them fifteen years to do that, in spite of all the power of the state. These things do take time; you cannot help it, because it involves not only the money factor, but numerous other factors.

I think it is advantageous for the public sector to have a competitive private sector to keep it up to the mark. The public sector will grow. But I feel that, if the private sector is not there, if it is abolished completely, there is a risk of the public sector becoming slow, not having that urge and push behind it. It depends on men, of course. On the whole, it is a good thing to have a private sector, something where the surplus energies of people who are not employed in the public sector may have some play, provided, of course, we control that private sector in the interest of the National Plan. You can control it in a hundred ways. Control it by all means. But where you do not control, give them room to exercise initiative and bring results. That is only a sort of broad approach to this problem. I can understand that a government may gradually take steps which might be said to be in a wrong direction. It may strengthen the existing structure of society rather than weaken it. But in the final analysis, we want to break through the existing structure—the economic as well as the social—because it restricts progress. A country cannot grow if it allows rigid structures. . . . Similarly, we have to break through what might be called a capitalist structure and have something else. But breaking through it has to be in a way so as to replace it for all time, and to begin with—even while it exists—to control it.

18. AFRICAN DEMOCRACY

Julius Nyerere

JULIUS NYERERE is the President of the United Republic of Tanzania. The son of a Tanganyikan tribal chief, he was educated at Makerere College in Uganda and at the University of Edinburgh. As head of the Tanganyikan African National Union (TANU), he won the first general election in 1958 and led the country to independence in 1961. When Tanganyika became a republic in 1962, he was elected President. He retained the post after the union of Tanganyika and Zanzibar formed the present state, and he was re-elected without opposition in 1965. His outstanding contribution has been in his leadership of the drive for African unity and his defense of the one-party political system which has become common in Africa since independence.

DEMOCRACY AND THE PARTY SYSTEM

. . . Democracy, in Africa or anywhere else, is government by the people. Ideally, it is a form of government whereby the people—*all* the people—settle their affairs through free discussion. The appropriate setting for this basic, or pure, democracy is a small community. The city-states of ancient Greece, for example, practiced it. And in African society, the traditional method of conducting affairs is by free discussion. Mr. Guy Clutton-Brock, writing about a typical African village community, puts it neatly: . . . "The Elders sit under the big tree, and talk until they agree." In larger communities, however, government by the people is possible only in a modified form.

After pure democracy, the next best thing is government by the people's representatives. Where it is the affairs of several million people that are to be settled by discussion, it is obviously not possible for all the people to come together and take a direct part in the discussion. So instead, we have a Parliament in which a number of spokesmen, or representatives, conduct the discussion on their behalf. And if these representatives are truly to represent the people, they must be freely chosen by the people from among themselves. So free elections are the essential instruments of representative democracy.

The purpose of a general election, then, is to elect these people's representatives. But, because of the historical circumstances of the countries in which representative democracy has been most highly developed, such elections are usually organized on a party basis. The electorate is offered a choice between contending parties. It could be said that the object is not so much to elect representatives as to elect a representative party.

The countries where this system works most successfully are those which have two major political parties. Now the two-party system requires certain disciplines. I will mention two in particular which are relevant to the case I want to argue. These affect elections and debate—both vital aspects of any form of democracy.

First, where one party is fighting an election against another, it cannot afford to allow more than one of its members to contest the same seat. If it did, it would split the votes of its own supporters and risk handing an easy victory to the rival party. So the first thing such a party must do is select its official candidate, usually by means of some kind of preliminary balloting within its own organization. Once this has been done, *all* party members must support the official candidates only, and fight the public elections as a united group. On this point party discipline is very strict.

Secondly, party candidates who have won the elections and taken their seats in Parliament must remain bound by the rules of party discipline. Once their own leaders have decided on a particular line of policy (even though it may be the purely negative line of opposing the policies of another party), the backbenchers must follow that line, for fear that they might increase the strength or prestige of the rival party by appearing to agree with it.

These disciplines, however, do not apply when each party is conducting what is purely party business. When, for instance, party officials are elected, any member may freely oppose another member, or when the official party candidates for election to national bodies are being selected from within the party organization, fellow members may compete with one another for adoption. The American primary is a typical example of this democratic freedom within a party. Another freedom follows from this: when debate takes place within party circles, it is a free and very often heated debate—each member saying exactly what he feels. The British Labour Party goes as far as allowing this kind of debate to be conducted in public. The Conservatives are more reticent, but it may be presumed that their private debates are just as free and, no doubt, at times as heated.

Those whose political thinking has been molded by the Western parliamentary tradition have now become so used to the two-party system that they cannot imagine democracy without it. It is no good telling them that when a group of a hundred people have sat together as equals and talked until they agreed about where they should dig a well, for example, or whether they should build a new school (and "until they agreed" implies that they will have produced many conflicting arguments before they did eventually agree), they have practiced democracy. No, the Western parliamentarians will want to know whether the talking was properly organized. They will want to know whether there was an organized group whose duty was to talk *for* the motion, and another organized group whose duty was to talk *against* it. They will also want to know whether, at the next debate, the same two groups will remain opposed to each other. In other words, they will be asking whether the opposition is organized and therefore automatic, or whether it is free and therefore spontaneous. Only if it is automatic will they concede that here is democracy! The way they generally put it is: "How can you have democracy with a one-party system?" It may surprise them to know, therefore, that some "heretics" like myself—who also claim to be democrats—are now beginning to ask: "How can you have democracy with a two-party system?"

I must confess that, not so long ago, I would have been content to answer the first of those questions. If I had posed the second it would have been in jest rather than in earnest. Recently, however, I have found myself questioning the democracy of the two-party system very seriously indeed.

Here in Tanganyika, for instance, we have adopted the Westminster type of representative democracy. With it, we took over the whole pattern of parliamentary and local government elections designed for a multi-party system. But it soon became clear to us that however ready we leaders might have been to accept the theory that an official opposition was essential to democratic government, our own people thought otherwise, for the idea did not make sense to them. As a result of the people's choice freely expressed at the polls, we found ourselves with a one-party system.

Now nobody who knew anything about Tanganyika could deny that, in spite of our having only one party, we were very democratic. But we were more democratic within the party than we were outside it. When, for instance, we met to elect our party leaders, nothing could have been more democratic. And our members' freedom of expression during our debates at the party's national executive meetings left nothing to be desired! But since we had adopted the method of election to Parliament and local government bodies which was designed for a contest between parties, we had to apply the party-unity rule. Once we had selected an official TANU candidate, we required all party members to support him. And if any other member disobeyed this rule and stood in opposition to our official candidate, he had to be punished. Invariably his punishment was expulsion from the party. As there is only one party in Tanganyika, the inevitable result of enforcing this rule was to make a contested election a very rare thing indeed. Most TANU candidates for Parliament and for local government councils are returned unopposed, which means, in effect, that they are elected by a party committee. Again, when it came to debates in Parliament we "naturally" (according to the book of rules of the two-party system) had to apply the party-unity rule. . . .

Because of the absence of any rival party, the membership of the TANU Parliamentary Party [TPP] is almost identical with that of the Parliament itself. Yet it is at private meetings of the TPP, and not in the Parliament, that we expect members to speak their minds freely. Here it is that they learn from their leaders what the "party line" is to be, and just how far they may go in criticizing any particular piece of legislation when this comes up for "debate" in Parliament. Fortunately, and I use the word deliberately, this has not so far prevented our members of Parliament (particularly those who are accustomed to the freedom of speech which is characteristic of the national executive) from expressing their own opinions in Parliament from time to time with a most "unparliamentary" independence of the party line! Nevertheless, whenever one of them does this, we leaders are rather disconcerted, and we generally feel obliged to rebuke him severely for his lapse from party discipline.

Now if we can encourage this freedom of expression at national executive meetings, and within the TPP, why do we discourage it in Parliament? There is, of course, a good theoretical reason. At the national-executive level we are deciding in broad terms what the party's policy shall be. This, naturally, requires a free discussion—to which anybody may contribute his suggestions, objections, countersuggestions, and so on. There obviously cannot be a "party line" to conform to at that stage, because the policy has not yet been agreed upon. And this is equally true under a one-party or a two-party system. But when we go into the Parliament we are no longer debating *what* the policy shall be, for by that time it has been settled—at least in outline. Theoretically, then, all that is still open to discussion in Parliament is detail—the question of exactly how, when, in what order of priority, and so on, the agreed policies shall be put into effect. And here we assume that the party leaders know best, and therefore the rest of us must support their decisions. But *why* should we assume this? Why should the question of timing and detail be left entirely to the leaders to decide? In a two-party Parliament there would be, of course, the need to avoid giving accidental support or encouragement to the rival party by any lack of unity between the leaders and their backbench supporters. Where there is only one party, the sole reason—apart from sheer habit—is that the leaders (i.e., the government) are said to have based their decisions on advice made available to them by experts. But this is really nonsense. For there is no valid reason why the relevant information could not also be placed before the people's representatives in the Parliament, so that such decisions were approved after a free and informed discussion had taken place in public. It is not particularly democratic to say, simply, that the details have been decided by the government "in the light of certain knowledge which is available to us but not to you people," and to leave it at that. Nor is it particularly democratic if the people's representatives are given this inside information privately. An intelligent public must know that decisions are only reached after argument. Why, then, should we try to fool them by keeping these arguments out of Parliament? In fact, where there is no opposition party, there is no reason why the debate in Parliament should not be as free as the debate in the national executive.

Given the two-party system, then, some limitation of freedom is essential—both at election time and in debate—in order to enforce party discipline and unity. And we have seen that these restrictions are not necessary where you have only one party. It seems at least open to doubt, therefore, that a system which forces political parties to limit the freedom of their members is a democratic system, and that one which can permit a party to leave its members their freedom is *un*democratic!

I realize that the political theorists are so attached to the pattern of democracy which depends on the existence of opposing parties, that they are likely to have been shocked by my expressing a doubt as to its being so very democratic after all. I am afraid they may be even more shocked by what I am now going to suggest: that where there is *one* party, and that party is identified with the *nation as a whole,* the foundations of democracy are firmer than they can ever be where you have two or more parties, each representing only a section of the community!

After all, we do have it on very reliable authority that a house divided against itself cannot stand! So it is surely up to the advocates of the two-party system to defend their own case more convincingly. It is not enough for them simply to insist that it *is* more democratic than a one-party system, and then be horrified when we presume to disagree with them!

Now my argument is that a two-party system can be justified only when the parties are divided over some fundamental issue; otherwise it merely encourages the growth of factionalism. Or, to put it another way, the only time when a political group can represent the interests of a section of the community, *without* being a faction, is when that group fights to remove a grievous wrong from society. But then the differences between this group and those responsible for the wrong it fights are fundamental; and there can therefore be no question of national unity until the differences have been removed by change. And "change" in that context is a euphemism, because any change in fundamentals is properly termed "revolution." What is more, the reason why the word "revolution" is generally associated with armed insurrection is that the existence of really fundamental differences within any society poses a "civil war" situation, and has often led to bloody revolution. Benjamin Disraeli, who was certainly no advo-

cate of a one-party system, once referred to this situation as tantamount
to "two nations" within a state. . . .

. . . In any country which is divided over fundamental issues you
have the "civil war" situation we have been talking about. If, on the
other hand, you have a two-party system where the differences between
the parties are *not* fundamental, then you immediately reduce politics to
the level of a football match. A football match may, of course, attract
some very able players; it may also be entertaining; but it is still only a
game, and only the most ardent fans (who are not usually the most intelligent) take the game very seriously. This, in fact, is not unlike what has
happened in many of the so-called democratic countries today, where
some of the most intelligent members of society have become disgusted
by the hypocrisy of the party games called politics, and take no interest
in them. They can see no party whose "line" they could support without
reservation and are therefore left with no way of serving their country
in the political field, even should they wish to, except, perhaps, by writing
a book! For the politics of a country governed by the two-party system
are not, and cannot be, *national* politics; they are the politics of *groups*,
whose differences, more often than not, are of small concern to the
majority of the people.

It is hard to avoid the conclusion that people who defend the two-party
system are actually advocating "football politics"; that they really consider
a spirit of purely artificial rivalry, like that which exists between a couple
of soccer teams, is appropriate to the relationship between opposing political parties. . . .

Our critics should understand that, in Africa, we have to take our
politics a little more seriously. And they should also remember the historical difference between parties in Africa and those in Europe or America. The European and American parties came into being as the result of
existing social and economic divisions—the second party being formed to
challenge the monopoly of political power by some aristocratic or capitalist group. Our own parties had a very different origin. They were not
formed to challenge any ruling group of our own people; they were
formed to challenge the *foreigners* who ruled over us. They were not,
therefore, political "parties"—i.e., factions—but nationalist movements.
And from the outset they represented the interests and aspirations of the
whole nation. . . .

Now that the colonialists have gone, there is no remaining division
between rulers and ruled; no monopoly of political power by any sectional group which could give rise to conflicting parties. There can, therefore, be only one reason for the formation of such parties in a country
like ours—the desire to imitate the political structure of a totally dissimilar
society. What is more, the desire to imitate where conditions are not

suitable for imitation can easily lead us into trouble. To try and import the idea of a parliamentary opposition into Africa may very likely lead to violence—because the opposition parties will tend to be regarded as traitors by the majority of our people—or, at best, it will lead to the trivial maneuverings of opposing groups whose time is spent in the inflation of artificial differences into some semblance of reality "for the sake of preserving democracy"! The latter alternative, I repeat, is an over sophisticated pastime which we in Africa cannot afford to indulge in; our time is too short and there is too much serious work to be done. . . .

The parties of our friends in the older parliamentary democracies outside Africa are sectional groups. So, too, are those within Africa which seek to imitate them. Nowadays such parties do not restrict their membership to those who can claim noble birth, or to the wealthy; but there are some which restrict it, instead, to those who belong to an equally exclusive aristocracy of the intellect! And in certain such modern "aristocracies," instead of the blueness of blood which was once the qualification for membership of the ruling class, we now find that it is by the "redness" of his thought that a man is judged worthy of entry into the ranks of the elite. . . . And in all such parties—whether the factional parties of a two-party democracy, or the vanguard aristocracies of an ideological dictatorship—it is the leaders themselves who "elect" each other. The elections, if any, in which the people are permitted to take part, are not for the purpose of choosing their own representatives; they are merely for the purpose of deciding from which sectional group the "people's representatives" shall be selected for them! . . .

. . . Our friends, the Communists, have made their policies a creed, and are finding that dogmatism and freedom of discussion do not easily go together. They are as much afraid of the "other party" as any government in a two-party democracy. In their case the "other party" is only a phantom, but a phantom can be even more frightening than a living rival! And their fear of this phantom has blinded them to the truth that, in a one-party system, party membership must be open to everybody and freedom of expression allowed to every individual. No party which limits its membership to a clique can ever free itself from the fear of overthrow by those it has excluded. It must be constantly on the watch for signs of opposition, and must smother "dangerous" ideas before they have time to spread.

But a national movement which is open to all—which is identified with the whole nation—has nothing to fear from the discontent of any excluded section of society, for there is then no such section. Those forming the government will, of course, be replaced from time to time; but this is what elections are for. The leadership of our movement is constantly changing; there is no reason why the leadership of the nation should not also be constantly changing. This would have nothing to do with the overthrowing of a party government by a rival party. And, since such a national movement leaves no room for the growth of discontented elements excluded from its membership, it has nothing to fear from criticism and the free expression of ideas. On the contrary, both the movement itself and the nation have everything to gain from a constant injection of new ideas from within the nation and from outside. It would be both wrong, and certainly unnecessary, to feel we must wait until the leaders are dead before we begin to criticize them!

Any member of the Movement (which, in this context, means any patriotic citizen since it is a National Movement we are talking about) would be free to stand as a candidate if he so wished. And in each constituency the voters themselves would be able to make their choice freely from among these candidates; they would no longer be obliged to consider the party label rather than the individual. Of such elections it could truly be said that they were for the purpose of letting the people choose their own representatives. If that is not democracy, I do not know the meaning of the word!

19. FOR REVOLUTIONARY DICTATORSHIP

Lin Piao

LIN PIAO has been Minister of National Defense of the People's Republic of China, as well as Deputy Premier and Vice Chairman of the Central Committee of the Communist Party. He has enjoyed the prominence of these positions since the 1950's, and in 1969 was designated heir apparent to Chairman Mao Tse-tung. Trained at the Whampoa Military Academy, he joined the Communist Party as early as 1925 at the age of 17. He helped found the Red Army three years later and became President of the Red Army Academy in 1937. During the Chinese civil war following the Japanese occupation of the 1930's and 1940's, he was the commander of one of the major Communist armies.

THE VICTORY OF THE PEOPLE'S WAR

. . . It was on the basis of the lessons derived from the people's wars in China that Comrade Mao Tse-tung, using the simplest and the most vivid language, advanced the famous thesis that "political power grows out of the barrel of a gun."

He clearly pointed out: The seizure of power by armed force, the settlement of the issue by war, is the central task and the highest form of revolution. This Marxist-Leninist principle of revolution holds good universally, for China and for all other countries.

War is the product of imperialism and the system of exploitation of man by man. Lenin said that "war is always and everywhere begun by the exploiters themselves, by the ruling and oppressing classes." So long as imperialism and the system of exploitation of man by man exist, the imperialists and reactionaries will invariably rely on armed force to maintain their reactionary rule and impose war on the oppressed nations and peoples. This is an objective law independent of man's will. . . .

In the last analysis, whether one dares to wage a tit-for-tat struggle against armed aggression and suppression by the imperialists and their lackeys, whether one dares to fight a people's war against them means whether one dares to embark on revolution. This is the most effective touchstone for distinguishing genuine from fake revolutionaries and Marxist-Leninists.

In view of the fact that some people were afflicted with the fear of the imperialists and reactionaries, Comrade Mao Tse-tung put forward his famous thesis that "the imperialists and all reactionaries are paper tigers. . . . In appearance the reactionaries are terrifying, but in reality they are not so powerful. From a long-term point of view, it is not the reactionaries but the people who are really powerful."

The history of people's war in China and other countries provides conclusive evidence that the growth of the people's revolutionary forces from weak and small beginnings into strong and large forces is a universal law of development of class struggle, a universal law of development of people's war. A people's war inevitably meets with many difficulties, with ups and downs and setbacks in the course of its development, but no force can alter its general trend toward inevitable triumph.

Comrade Mao Tse-tung points out that we must despise the enemy strategically and take full account of him tactically. To despise the enemy strategically is an elementary requirement for a revolutionary. Without the courage to despise the enemy and without daring to win, it will be simply impossible to make revolution and wage a people's war, let alone to achieve victory. . . .

The imperialists are extremely afraid of Comrade Mao Tse-tung's thesis that "imperialism and the reactionaries are paper tigers," and the revisionists are extremely hostile to it. They all oppose and attack this thesis and the Philistines follow suit by ridiculing it. But all this cannot in the least diminish its importance. The light of truth cannot be dimmed by anybody.

Comrade Mao Tse-tung's theory of people's war solves not only the problem of daring to fight a people's war, but also that of how to wage it.

Comrade Mao Tse-tung is a great statesman and military scientist, proficient at directing war in accordance with its laws. By the line and policies, the strategy and tactics he formulated for the people's war, he led the Chinese people in steering the ship of the people's war past all hidden reefs to the shores of victory in most complicated and difficult conditions.

It must be emphasized that Comrade Mao Tse-tung's theory of the establishment of rural revolutionary base areas and the encirclement of the cities from the countryside is of outstanding and universal practical importance for the present revolutionary struggles of all the oppressed nations and peoples in Asia, Africa, and Latin America against imperialism and its lackeys.

Many countries and peoples in Asia, Africa, and Latin America are now being subjected to aggression and enslavement on a serious scale by the imperialists headed by the United States and their lackeys. The basic political and economic conditions in many of these countries have many similarities to those that prevailed in old China. As in China, the peasant question is extremely important in these regions. The peasants constitute the main force of the national-democratic revolution against the imperialists and their lackeys.

In committing aggression against these countries, the imperialists usually begin by seizing the big cities and the main lines of communication, but they are unable to bring the vast countryside completely under their control. The countryside, and the countryside alone, can provide the broad areas in which the revolutionaries can maneuver freely. The countryside, and the countryside alone, can provide the revolutionary bases from which the revolutionaries can go forward to final victory. Precisely for this reason, Comrade Mao Tse-tung's theory of establishing revolutionary base areas in the rural districts and encircling the cities from the countryside is attracting more and more attention among the people in these regions.

Taking the entire globe, if North America and Western Europe can be called "the cities of the world," then Asia, Africa, and Latin America constitute "the rural areas of the world." Since World War II, the proletarian revolutionary movement has for various reasons been temporarily held back in the North American and Western European capitalist countries, while the people's revolutionary movement in Asia, Africa, and Latin America has been growing vigorously. In a sense, the contemporary world revolution also presents a picture of the encirclement of cities by the rural areas. . . .

The October Revolution opened up a new era in the revolution of the oppressed nations. The victory of the October Revolution built a bridge between the socialist revolution of the proletariat of the West and the national-democratic revolution of the colonial and semicolonial countries of the East. The Chinese revolution has successfully solved the problem of how to link up the national-democratic with the socialist revolution in the colonial and semi-colonial countries.

Comrade Mao Tse-tung has pointed out that, in the epoch since the October Revolution, anti-imperialist revolution in any colonial or semi-colonial country is no longer part of the old bourgeois, or capitalist, world revolution, but is part of the new world revolution, the proletarian-socialist world revolution.

Comrade Mao Tse-tung has formulated a complete theory of the new democratic revolution. He indicated that this revolution, which is different from all others, can only be, nay must be, a revolution against imperialism, feudalism, and bureaucratic capitalism waged by the broad masses of the people under the leadership of the proletariat.

This means that the revolution can only be, nay must be, led by the proletariat and the genuinely revolutionary party armed with Marxism-Leninism, and by no other class or party.

This means that the revolution embraces in its ranks not only the workers, peasants, and the urban petty bourgeoisie, but also the national bourgeoisie and other patriotic and anti-imperialist democrats.

This means, finally, that the revolution is directed against imperialism, feudalism, and bureaucratic capitalism.

The new democratic revolution leads to socialism, and not to capitalism.

Comrade Mao Tse-tung's theory of the new democratic revolution is the Marxist-Leninist theory of uninterrupted revolution.

Comrade Mao Tse-tung made a correct distinction between the two revolutionary stages, that is, the national-democratic and the socialist revolutions; at the same time, he correctly and closely linked the two. The national-democratic revolution is the necessary preparation for the socialist revolution, and the socialist revolution is the inevitable sequel to the national-democratic revolution. There is no great wall between the two revolutionary stages. But the socialist revolution is only possible after the completion of the national-democratic revolution. The more thorough the national-democratic revolution, the better the conditions for the socialist revolution.

The experience of the Chinese revolution shows that the tasks of the national-democratic revolution can be fulfilled only through long and tortuous struggles. In this stage of revolution, imperialism and its lackeys are the principal enemy. In the struggle against imperialism and its lackeys, it is necessary to rally all anti-imperialist patriotic forces, including the national bourgeoisie and all patriotic persons. All those patriotic persons from among the bourgeoisie and other exploiting classes who join the anti-imperialist struggle play a progressive historical role: they are not tolerated by imperialism but welcomed by the proletariat.

It is very harmful to confuse the two stages, that is, the national-democratic and the socialist revolutions. Comrade Mao Tse-tung criticized the wrong idea of "accomplishing both at one stroke," and pointed out that this utopian idea could only weaken the struggle against imperialism and its lackeys, the most urgent task at the time. The Kuomintang reactionaries and the Trotskyites they hired during the War of Resistance deliberately confused these two stages of the Chinese revolution, proclaiming the "theory of a single revolution" and preaching so-called socialism without any Communist Party. With this preposterous theory they attempted to swallow up the Communist Party, wipe out any revolution, and prevent the advance of the national-democratic revolution, and they used it as a pretext for their nonresistance and capitulation to imperialism. This reactionary theory was buried long ago by the history of the Chinese revolution.

The Khrushchev revisionists are now actively preaching that socialism can be built without the proletariat and without a genuinely revolutionary party armed with the advanced proletarian ideology, and they have cast the fundamental tenets of Marxism-Leninism to the four winds. The revisionists' purpose is solely to divert the oppressed nations from their struggle against imperialism and to sabotage their national-democratic solution, all in the service of imperialism.

The Chinese revolution provides a successful lesson for making a thoroughgoing national-democratic revolution under the leadership of the proletariat; it likewise provides a successful lesson for the timely transition from the national-democratic revolution to the socialist revolution under the leadership of the proletariat. . . .

Ours is the epoch in which world capitalism and imperialism are heading for their doom, and socialism and Communism are marching to victory. Comrade Mao Tse-tung's theory of people's war is not only a product of the Chinese revolution, but has also characteristics of our epoch. The new experience gained in the people's revolutionary struggles in various countries since World War II has provided continuous evidence that Mao Tse-tung's thought is a common asset of the revolutionary people of the whole world. This is the great international significance of the thought of Mao Tse-tung. . . .

The contradiction between the revolutionary peoples of Asia, Africa, and Latin America and the imperialists headed by the United States is the principal contradiction in the contemporary world. The development of this contradiction is promoting the struggle of the whole world against U.S. imperialism and its lackeys. . . .

The struggles waged by the different peoples against U.S. imperialism reinforce each other and merge into a torrential worldwide tide of opposition to U.S. imperialism. The more successful the development of people's war in a given region, the larger the number of U.S. imperialist forces that can be pinned down and depleted there. When the U.S. aggressors are hard pressed in one place, they have no alternative but to loosen their grip on others. Therefore, the conditions become more favorable for the people elsewhere to wage struggles against U.S. imperialism and its lackeys. . . .

However highly developed modern weapons and technical equipment may be and however complicated the methods of modern warfare, in the final analysis the outcome of a war will be decided by the sustained fighting of the ground forces, by the fighting at close quarters on battle-fields, by the political consciousness of the men, by their courage and spirit of sacrifice. Here the weak points of U.S. imperialism will be completely laid bare, while the superiority of the revolutionary people will be brought into full play. The reactionary troops of U.S. imperialism cannot possibly be endowed with the courage and the spirit of sacrifice possessed by the revolutionary people. The spiritual atom bomb that the revolutionary people possess is a far more powerful and useful weapon than the physical atom bomb. . . .

Ever since Lenin led the great October Revolution to victory, the experience of innumerable revolutionary wars has borne out the truth that a revolutionary people who rise up with only their bare hands at the outset finally succeed in defeating the ruling classes who are armed to the teeth. The poorly armed have defeated the better armed. People's armed forces, beginning with only primitive swords, spears, rifles, hand-grenades, have in the end defeated the imperialist forces armed with modern airplanes, tanks, heavy artillery, and atom bombs. Guerrilla forces have ultimately defeated regular armies. "Amateurs" who were never trained in any military schools have eventually defeated "professionals" graduated from military academies. And so on and so forth. Things stubbornly develop in a way that runs counter to the assertions of the revisionists, and facts are slapping them in the face. . . .

We know that war brings destruction, sacrifice, and suffering on the people. But the destruction, sacrifice, and suffering will be much greater if no resistance is offered to imperialist armed aggression and the people become willing slaves. The sacrifice of a small number of people in revolutionary wars is repaid by security for whole nations, whole countries, and even the whole of mankind; temporary suffering is repaid by lasting or even perpetual peace and happiness. War can temper the people and push history forward. In this sense, war is a great school. . . .

In diametrical opposition to the Khrushchev revisionists, the Marxist-

Leninists and revolutionary people never take a gloomy view of war. Our attitude toward imperialist wars of aggression has always been clear-cut. First, we are against them, and secondly, we are not afraid of them. We will destroy whoever attacks us. As for revolutionary wars waged by the oppressed nations and peoples, so far from opposing them, we invariably give them firm support and active aid. It has been so in the past, it remains so in the present and, when we grow in strength as time goes on, we will give them still more support and aid in the future. . . .

The peoples of the world now have the lessons of the October Revolution, the antifascist war, the Chinese people's war of resistance and war of liberation, the Korean people's war of resistance to U.S. aggression, the Vietnamese people's war of liberation and their war of resistance to U.S. aggression, and the people's revolutionary armed struggles in many other countries. Provided each people studies these lessons well and creatively integrates them with the concrete practice of revolution in their own country, there is no doubt that the revolutionary peoples of the world will stage still more powerful and splendid dramas in the theater of people's war in their countries and that they will wipe off the earth once and for all the common enemy of all the peoples, U.S. imperialism and its lackeys. . . .

20. VIOLENCE WILL BE THE MIDWIFE OF THE NEW WORLD

Frantz Fanon

FRANTZ FANON, born in the French island of Martinique, was a French-trained psychiatrist who practiced in Blida, Algeria. He joined the Algerian National Liberation Front at its founding, and later became Algeria's Ambassador to Ghana. His analysis of the psychological consequences of colonialism and racism, especially in terms of the role of violence, has had a great impact both among intellectuals in the third world and among some of the more militant leaders of the black community in the United States. Fanon died of leukemia in 1961 at the age of thirty-six.

National liberation, national renaissance, the restoration of nationhood to the people, commonwealth: whatever may be the headings used or the new formulas introduced, decolonisation is always a violent phenomenon. At whatever level we study it—relationships between individuals, new names for sports clubs, the human admixture at cocktail parties, in the police, on the directing boards of national or private banks—decolonisation is quite simply the replacing of a certain "species" of men by another "species" of men. Without any period of transition, there is a total, complete and absolute substitution. It is true that we could equally well stress the rise of a new nation, the setting up of a new State, its diplomatic relations, and its economic and political trends. But we have precisely chosen to speak of that kind of *tabula rasa* which characterises at the outset all decolonisation. Its unusual importance is that it constitutes, from the very first day, the minimum demands of the colonised. To tell the truth, the proof of success lies in a whole social structure being changed from the bottom up. The extraordinary importance of this change is that it is willed, called for, demanded. The need for this change exists in its crude state, impetuous and compelling, in the consciousness and in the lives of the men and women who are colonised. But the possibility of this change is equally experienced in the form of a terrifying future in the consciousness of another "species" of men and women: the colonisers.

Decolonisation, which sets out to change the order of the world, is, obviously, a programme of complete disorder. But it cannot come as a result of magical practices, nor of a natural shock, nor of a friendly understanding. Decolonisation, as we know, is a historical process: that is to say that it cannot be understood, it cannot become intelligible nor clear to itself except in the exact measure that we can discern the movements which give it historical form and content. Decolonisation is the meeting of two forces, opposed to each other by their very nature, which in fact owe their originality to that sort of substantification which results from and is nourished by the situation in the colonies. Their first encounter was marked by violence and their existence together—that is to say the exploitation of the native by the settler—was carried on by dint of a great array of bayonets and cannon. The settler and the native are old acquaintances. In fact, the settler is right when he speaks of knowing "them" well. For it is the settler who has brought the native into existence and who perpetuates his existence. The settler owes the fact of his very existence, that is to say his property, to the colonial system.

Decolonisation never takes place un-noticed, for it influences individuals and modifies them fundamentally. It transforms spectators crushed with their inessentiality into privileged actors, with the grandiose glare of history's floodlights upon them. It brings a natural rhythm into existence, introduced by new men, and with it a new language and a new humanity. Decolonisation is the veritable creation of new men. But this creation owes nothing of its legitimacy to any supernatural power; the "thing" which has been colonised becomes man during the same process by which it frees itself.

In decolonisation, there is therefore the need of a complete calling in question of the colonial situation. If we wish to describe it precisely, we might find it in the well-known words: "The last shall be first and the first last." Decolonisation is the putting into practice of this sentence. That is why, if we try to describe it, all decolonisation is successful.

The naked truth of decolonisation evokes for us the searing bullets and bloodstained knives which emanate from it. For if the last shall be first, this will only come to pass after a murderous and decisive struggle between the two protagonists. That affirmed intention to place the last at the head of things, and to make them climb at a pace (too quickly, some say) the well-known steps which characterise an organised society, can only triumph if we use all means to turn the scale, including, of course, that of violence.

You do not turn any society, however primitive it may be, upside-down with such a programme if you are not decided from the very beginning, that is to say from the actual formulation of that programme, to overcome all the obstacles that you will come across in so doing. The native who decides to put the programme into practice, and to become its moving force, is ready for violence at all times. From birth it is clear to him that this narrow world, strewn with prohibitions, can only be called in question by absolute violence.

The colonial world is a world divided into compartments. It is probably unnecessary to recall the existence of native quarters and European quarters, of schools for natives and schools for Europeans; in the same way we need not recall Apartheid in South Africa. Yet, if we examine closely this system of compartments, we will at least be able to reveal the lines of force it implies. This approach to the colonial world, its ordering and its geographical lay-out will allow us to mark out the lines on which a decolonised society will be reorganised.

The colonial world is a world cut in two. The dividing line, the frontiers are shown by barracks and police stations. In the colonies it is the policeman and the soldier who are the official, instituted go-betweens, the spokesmen of the settler and his rule of oppression. In capitalist societies the educational system, whether lay or clerical, the structure of moral reflexes handed down from father to son, the exemplary honesty of workers who are given a medal after fifty years of good and loyal service, and the affection which springs from harmonious relations and good behaviour—all these esthetic expressions of respect for the established order serve to create around the exploited person an atmosphere of submission and of inhibition which lightens the task of policing considerably. In the capitalist countries a multitude of moral teachers, counsellors and "bewilderers" separate the exploited from those in power. In the colonial countries, on the contrary, the policeman and the soldier, by their immediate presence and their frequent and direct action maintain contact with the native and advise him by means of rifle-butts and napalm not to budge. It is obvious here that the agents of government speak the language of pure force. The intermediary does not lighten the oppression, nor seek to hide the domination; he shows them up and puts them into practice with the clear conscience of an upholder of the peace; yet he is the bringer of violence into the home and into the mind of the native.

The zone where the natives live is not complementary to the zone inhabited by the settlers. The two zones are opposed, but not in the service of a higher unity. Obedient to the rules of pure Aristotelian logic, they both follow the principle of reciprocal exclusivity. No conciliation is possible, for of the two terms, one is superfluous. The settlers' town is a strongly-built town, all made of stone and steel. It is a brightly-lit town; the streets are covered with asphalt, and the garbage cans swallow all the leavings, unseen, unknown and hardly thought about. The settler's feet are never visible, except perhaps in the sea; but there you're never close enough to see them. His feet are protected by strong shoes although the streets of his town are clean and even, with no holes or stones. The settler's town is a well-fed town, an easy-going town; its belly is always full of good things. The settler's town is a town of white people, of foreigners.

The town belonging to the colonised people, or at least the native town, the Negro village, the medina, the reservation, is a place of ill fame, peopled by men of evil repute. They are born there, it matters little where or how; they die there, it matters not where, nor how. It is a world without spaciousness; men live there on top of each other, and their huts are built one on top of the other. The native town is a hungry town, starved of bread, of meat, of shoes, of coal, of light. The native town is a crouching village, a town on its knees, a town wallowing in the mire. It is a town of niggers and dirty arabs. The look that the native turns on the settler's town is a look of lust, a look of envy; it expresses his dreams of possession—all manner of possession: to sit at the settler's table, to sleep in the settler's bed, with his wife if possible. The colonised man is an envious man. And this the settler knows very well; when their glances meet he ascertains bitterly, always on the defensive, "They want to take our place." It is true, for there is no native who does not dream at least once a day of setting himself up in the settler's place.

This world divided into compartments, this world cut in two is inhabited by two different species. The originality of the colonial context is that economic reality, inequality and the immense difference of ways of life never come to mask the human realities. When you examine at close quarters the colonial context, it is evident that what parcels out the world is to begin with the fact of belonging to or not belonging to a given race, a given species. In the colonies the economic substructure is also a superstructure. The cause is the consequence; you are rich because you are white, you are white because you are rich. This is why Marxist analysis should always be slightly stretched every time we have to do with the colonial problem.

Everything up to and including the very nature of pre-capitalist society, so well explained by Marx, must here be thought out again. The serf is in essence different from the knight, but a reference to divine right is necessary to legitimise this statutory difference. In the colonies, the foreigner coming from another country imposed his rule by means of guns and machines. In defiance of his successful transplantation, in spite of his appropriation, the settler still remains a foreigner. It is neither the act of owning factories, nor estates, nor a bank balance which distinguishes the governing classes. The governing race is first and foremost those who come from elsewhere, those who are unlike the original inhabitants, "the others."

The violence which has ruled over the ordering of the colonial world, which has ceaselessly drummed the rhythm for the destruction of native social forms and broken up without reserve the systems of reference of the economy, the customs of dress and external life, that same violence will be claimed and taken over by the native at the moment when, deciding to embody history in his own person, he surges into the forbidden quarters. To wreck the colonial world is henceforward a mental picture of action which is very clear, very easy to understand and which may be assumed by each one of the individuals which constitute the colonised people. To break up the colonial world does not mean that after the frontiers have been abolished lines of communication will be set up between the two zones. The destruction of the colonial world is no more and no less than the abolition of one zone, its burial in the depths of the earth or its expulsion from the country.

The natives' challenge to the colonial world is not a rational confrontation of points of view. It is not a treatise on the universal, but the untidy affirmation of an original idea propounded as an absolute. . . .

Nowadays a theoretical problem of prime importance is being set, on the historical plane as well as on the level of political tactics, by the liberation of the colonies: when can one affirm that the situation is ripe for a movement of national liberation? In what form should it first be manifested? . . .

What are the forces which in the colonial period open up new outlets and engender new aims for the violence of colonised peoples? In the first place there are the political parties and the intellectual or commercial *élites*. Now, the characteristic feature of certain political structures is that they proclaim abstract principles but refrain from issuing definite commands. The entire action of these nationalist political parties during the colonial period is action of the electoral type: a string of philosophico-political dissertations on the themes of the rights of peoples to self-determination, the rights of man to freedom from hunger and human dignity, and the unceasing affirmation of the principle: "One man, one vote." The national political parties never lay stress upon the necessity of a trial of armed strength, for the good reason that their objective is not the radical overthrowing of the system. Pacifists and legalists, they are in fact partisans of order, the new order—but to the colonialist bourgeoisie they put bluntly enough the demand which to them is the main one: "Give us more power." On the specific question of violence, the *élite* are ambiguous. They are violent in their words and reformist in their attitudes. When the nationalist political leaders *say* something, they make quite clear that they do not really *think* it.

This characteristic on the part of the nationalist political parties should be interpreted in the light both of the make-up of their leaders and the nature of their followings. The rank-and-file of a nationalist party is urban. The workers, primary school-teachers, artisans and small shop-keepers who have begun to profit—at a discount, to be sure—from the colonial set-up, have special interests at heart. What this sort of following demands is the betterment of their particular lot: increased salaries, for example. The dialogue between these political parties and colonialism is never broken off. Improvements are discussed, such as full electoral representation, the liberty of the press, and liberty of association. Reforms are debated. Thus it need not astonish anyone to notice that a large number of natives are militant members of the branches of political parties which stem from the mother country. These natives fight under an abstract watchword: "Government by the workers," and they forget that in their country it should be *nationalist* watchwords which are first in the field. The native intellectual has clothed his aggressiveness in his barely veiled desire to assimilate himself to the colonial world. He has used his aggressiveness to serve his own individual interests.

Thus there is very easily brought into being a kind of class of affranchised slaves, or slaves who are individually free. What the intellectual demands is the right to multiply the emancipated, and the opportunity to organise a genuine class of emancipated citizens. On the other hand, the mass of the people have no intention of standing by and watching individuals increase their chances of success. What they demand is not the settler's position of status, but the settler's place. The immense majority of natives want the settler's farm. For them, there is no question of entering into competition with the settler. They want to take his place.

The peasantry is systematically disregarded for the most part by the propaganda put out by the nationalist parties. And it is clear that in the colonial countries the peasants alone are revolutionary, for they have nothing to lose and everything to gain. The starving peasant, outside the class system, is the first among the exploited to discover that only violence pays. For him there is no compromise, no possible coming to terms; colonisation and decolonisation are simply a question of relative strength. The exploited man sees that his liberation implies the use of all means, and that of force first and foremost. When in 1956, after the capitulation of Monsieur Guy Mollet to the settlers in Algeria, the *Front de Libération Nationale*, in a famous leaflet, stated that colonialism only loosens its hold when the knife is at its throat, no Algerian really found these terms too violent. The leaflet only expressed what every Algerian felt at heart: colonialism is not a thinking machine, nor a body endowed with reasoning faculties. It is violence in its natural state, and it will only yield when confronted with greater violence. . . .

A colonised people is not alone. In spite of all that colonialism can do, its frontiers remain open to new ideas and echoes from the world outside. It discovers that violence is in the atmosphere, that it here and there bursts out, and here and there sweeps away the colonial regime—that same violence which fulfils for the native a *rôle* that is not simply informatory, but also operative. The great victory of the Vietnamese people at Dien Bien Phu is no longer, strictly speaking, a Vietnamese victory. Since July 1954, the question which the colonised peoples have asked themselves has been "What must be done to bring about another Dien Bien Phu? How can we manage it?" Not a single colonised individual could ever again doubt the possibility of a Dien Bien Phu; the only problem was how best to use the forces at their disposal, how to organise them, and when to bring them into action. This encompassing violence does not work upon the colonised people only; it modifies the attitude of the colonialists who become aware of manifold Dien Bien Phus. This is why a veritable panic takes hold of the colonialist governments in turn. Their purpose is to capture the vanguard, to turn the movement of liberation towards the right, and to disarm the people: quick, quick, let's decolonise. Decolonise the Congo before it turns into another Algeria. Vote the constitutional framework for all Africa, create the French *Communauté*, renovate that same *Communauté*, but for God's sake let's decolonise quick. . . .

What is the real nature of this violence? We have seen that it is the intuition of the colonised masses that their liberation must, and can only, be achieved by force. By what spiritual aberration do these men, without technique, starving and enfeebled, confronted with the military and economic might of the occupation, come to believe that violence alone will free them? How can they hope to triumph?

It is because violence (and this is the disgraceful thing) may constitute, in so far as it forms part of its system, the slogan of a political party. The leaders may call on the people to enter upon an armed struggle. This problematical question has to be thought over. When militarist Germany decides to settle its frontier disputes by force, we are not in the least surprised; but when the people of Angola, for example, decide to take up arms; when the Algerian people reject all means which are not violent, these are proofs that something has happened or is happening at this very moment. The colonised races, those slaves of modern times, are impatient. They know that this apparent folly alone can put them out of reach of colonial oppression. A new type of relations is established in the world. The under-developed peoples try to break their chains, and the extraordinary thing is that they succeed. It could be argued that in these days of sputniks it is ridiculous to die of hunger; but for the colonised masses the argument is more down-to-earth. The truth is that there is no colonial power today which is capable of adopting the only form of contest which has a chance of succeeding, namely, the prolonged establishment of large forces of occupation. . . .

At the level of individuals, violence is a cleansing force. It frees the native from his inferiority complex and from his despair and inaction; it makes him fearless and restores his self-respect. Even if the armed struggle has been symbolic and the nation is demobilised through a rapid movement of decolonisation, the people have the time to see that the liberation has been the business of each and all and that the leader has no special merit. From thence comes that type of aggressive reticence with regard to the machinery of protocol which young governments quickly show. When the people have taken violent part in the national liberation they will allow no one to set themselves up as "liberators." They show themselves to be jealous of the results of their action and take good care not to place their future, their destiny or the fate of their country in the hands of a living god. Yesterday they were completely irresponsible; today they mean to understand everything and make all decisions. Illuminated by violence, the consciousness of the people rebels against any pacification. From now on the demagogues, the opportunists and the magicians have a difficult task. The action which has thrown them into a hand-to-hand struggle confers upon the masses a voracious taste for the concrete. The attempt at mystification becomes, in the long run, practically impossible.

We have pointed out many times . . . that in under-developed regions the political leader is forever calling on his people to fight: to fight against colonialism, to fight against poverty and under-development, and to fight against sterile traditions. The vocabulary which he uses in his appeals is that of a chief of staff: "mass mobilisation"; "agricultural front"; "fight against illiteracy"; "defeats we have undergone"; "victories won." The young independent nation evolves during the first years in an atmosphere of the battlefield, for the political leader of an under-developed country looks fearfully at the huge distance his country will have to cover. He calls to the people and says to them: "Let us gird up our loins and set to work," and the country, possessed by a kind of creative madness, throws itself into a gigantic and disproportionate effort. The programme consists not only of climbing out of the morass but also of catching up with the other nations using the only means at hand. They reason that if the European nations have reached that stage of development, it is on account of their efforts: "Let us therefore" they seem to say, "prove to ourselves and to the whole world that we are capable of the same achievements." This manner of setting out the problem of the evolution of under-developed countries seems to us to be neither correct nor reasonable.

The European states achieved national unity at a moment when the national middle-classes had concentrated most of the wealth in their hands. Shopkeepers and artisans, clerks and bankers monopolised finance, trade and science in the national framework. The middle class was the most dynamic and prosperous of all classes. Its coming to power enabled it to undertake certain very important speculations: industrialisation, the development of communications and soon the search for outlets overseas.

In Europe, apart from certain slight differences (England, for example, was some way ahead) the various states were at a more or less uniform stage economically when they achieved national unity. There was no nation which by reason of the character of its development and evolution caused affront to the others.

Today, national independence and the growth of national feeling in under-developed regions take on totally new aspects. In these regions, with the exception of certain spectacular advances, the different countries show the same absence of infrastructure. The mass of the people struggle against the same poverty, flounder about making the same gestures and with their shrunken bellies outline what has been called the geography of hunger. It is an under-developed world, a world inhuman in its poverty; but also it is a world without doctors, without engineers and without administrators. Confronting this world, the European nations sprawl, ostentatiously opulent. This European opulence is literally scandalous, for it has been founded on slavery, it has been nourished with the blood of slaves and it comes directly from the soil and from the subsoil of that under-developed world. The well-being and the progress of Europe have been built up with the sweat and the dead bodies of Negroes, Arabs, Indians and the yellow races. We have decided not to overlook this any longer. When a colonialist country, embarrassed by the claims for independence made by a colony, proclaims to the nationalist leaders: "If you wish for independence, take it, and go back to the middle ages," the newly-independent people tend to acquiesce and to accept the challenge; in fact you may see colonialism withdrawing its capital and its technicians and setting up around the young State the apparatus of economic pressure. The apotheosis of independence is transformed into the curse of independence, and the colonial power through its immense resources of coercion condemns the young nation to regression. In plain words, the colonial power says: "Since you want independence, take it and starve." The nationalist leaders have no other choice but to turn to their people and ask from them a gigantic effort. A regime of austerity is imposed on these starving men; a disproportionate amount of work is required from their atrophied muscles. An autarkic regime is set up and each state, with the miserable resources it has in hand, tries to find an answer to the nation's great hunger and poverty. We see the mobilisation of a people which toils to exhaustion in front of a suspicious and bloated Europe.

Other countries of the Third World refuse to undergo this ordeal and agree to get over it by accepting the conditions of the former guardian power. These countries use their strategic position—a position which accords them privileged treatment in the struggle between the two *blocs* —to conclude treaties and give undertakings. The former dominated country becomes an economically dependent country. The ex-colonial power, which has kept intact and sometimes even reinforced its colonialist trade channels agrees to provision the budget of the independent nation by small injections. Thus we see that the accession to independence of the colonial countries places an important question before the world, for the national liberation of colonised countries unveils their true economic state and makes it seem even more unendurable. The fundamental duel which seemed to be that between colonialism and anticolonialism, and indeed between capitalism and socialism, is already losing some of its importance. What counts today, the question which is looming on the horizon is the need for a re-distribution of wealth. Humanity must reply to this question, or be shaken to pieces by it. . . .

Come, then, comrades; it would be as well to decide at once to change our ways. We must shake off the heavy darkness in which we were plunged, and leave it behind. The new day which is already at hand must find us firm, prudent and resolute.

We must leave our dreams and abandon our old beliefs and friendships of the time before life began. Let us waste no time in sterile litanies and nauseating mimicry. Leave this Europe where they are never done talking of Man, yet murder men everywhere they find them, at the corner of every one of their own streets, in all the corners of the globe. For centuries they have stifled almost the whole of humanity in the name of a so-called spiritual experience. Look at them today swaying between atomic and spiritual disintegration. . . .

So, my brothers, how is it that we do not understand that we have better things to do than to follow that same Europe?

That same Europe where they were never done talking of Man, and where they never stopped proclaiming that they were only anxious for the welfare of Man: today we know with what sufferings humanity has paid for every one of their triumphs of the mind.

Come, then, comrades, the European game has finally ended; we must find something different. We today can do everything, so long as we do not imitate Europe, so long as we are not obsessed by the desire to catch up with Europe. . . .

Let us decide not to imitate Europe; let us combine our muscles and our brains in a new direction. Let us try to create the whole man, whom Europe has been incapable of bringing to triumphant birth.

Two centuries ago, a former European colony decided to catch up with Europe. It succeeded so well that the United States of America became a monster, in which the taints, the sickness and the inhumanity of Europe have grown to appalling dimensions.

Comrades, have we not other work to do than to create a third Europe? The West saw itself as a spiritual adventure. It is in the name of the spirit, in the name of the spirit of Europe, that Europe has made her encroachments, that she has justified her crimes and legitimised the slavery in which she holds the four-fifths of humanity. . . .

Come, brothers, we have far too much work to do for us to play the game of rear-guard. Europe has done what she set out to do and on the whole she has done it well; let us stop blaming her, but let us say to her firmly that she should not make such a song and dance about it. We have no more to fear; so let us stop envying her.

The Third World today faces Europe like a colossal mass whose aim should be to try to resolve the problems to which Europe has not been able to find the answers.

But let us be clear: what matters is to stop talking about output, and intensification, and the rhythm of work.

No, there is no question of a return to Nature. It is simply a very concrete question of not dragging men towards mutilation, of not imposing upon the brain rhythms which very quickly obliterate it and wreck it. The pretext of catching up must not be used to push man around, to tear him away from himself or from his privacy, to break and kill him.

No, we do not want to catch up with anyone. What we want to do is to go forward all the time, night and day, in the company of Man, in the company of all men. . . .

It is a question of the Third World starting a new history of Man, a history which will have regard to the sometimes prodigious theses which Europe has put forward, but which will also not forget Europe's crimes, of which the most horrible was committed in the heart of man, and consisted of the pathological tearing apart of his functions and the crumbling away of his unity. And in the framework of the collectivity there were the differentiations, the stratification and the bloodthirsty tensions fed by classes; and finally, on the immense scale of humanity, there were racial hatreds, slavery, exploitation and above all the bloodless genocide which consisted in the setting aside of fifteen thousand millions of men.

So, comrades, let us not pay tribute to Europe by creating states, institutions and societies which draw their inspiration from her.

Humanity is waiting for something other from us than such an imitation, which would be almost an obscene caricature.

If we want to turn Africa into a new Europe, and America into a new Europe, then let us leave the destiny of our countries to Europeans. They will know how to do it better than the most gifted among us.

But if we want humanity to advance a step further, if we want to bring it up to a different level than that which Europe has shown it, then we must invent and we must make discoveries.

If we wish to live up to our peoples' expectations, we must seek the response elsewhere than in Europe.

Moreover, if we wish to reply to the expectations of the people of Europe, it is no good sending them back a reflection, even an ideal reflection, of their society and their thought with which from time to time they feel immeasurably sickened.

For Europe, for ourselves and for humanity, comrades, we must turn over a new leaf, we must work out new concepts, and try to set afoot a new man.

21. THE TRANSFORMATION OF MORAL IDEALISM INTO VIOLENT REVOLUTION

Sanche de Gramont

SANCHE DE GRAMONT, a Frenchman who is now living in Tangier, is a distinguished journalist who won a Pulitzer Prize for his reporting on North Africa for the *New York Herald Tribune.* He has written articles that have appeared in magazines both here and abroad. His books include *The Secret War, The Age of Magnificence, Epitaph for Kings, The French,* and a novel, *Lives to Give.*

There had been showers in the afternoon, but winds off the sea blew the clouds away and the evening was cool and pleasant for São Paulo in March, with the reflection of the downtown neon against the sky casting a heavy pink pallor over the city at twilight. Breezes shook the palm fronds on the square where the four men waited, some of them reading newspapers, others gazing at the sky.

The men knew that at 6 o'clock on this evening of March 5, 1970, as on other weekday evenings, a black, chauffeur-driven Oldsmobile belonging to the Japanese consul would slowly turn a corner into the square, carrying the consul home from work. They had been studying the consul's route for several weeks, and it never varied. He was a man of punctual habits.

They had chosen the Japanese consul, a short, dumpy man in his 50's named Nobuo Okuchi, for three reasons. First, Mr. Okuchi is an important man in São Paulo, which boasts a Japanese colony of several hundred thousand. Second, the considerable Japanese investments in Brazilian industry are concentrated in the São Paulo area. Third, a Nisei named Shizuo who belonged to the same organization as the men waiting on the square, the Popular Revolutionary Vanguard (V.P.R.), had been arrested by the political police, and information had reached them that he was being tortured and would probably be executed.

At two minutes past 6, the black Oldsmobile turned slowly into the square. A Simca drove out of a side street to block its passage, and another car moved up behind it, immobilizing the consul's car. Two of the men ran to the second car, pulled a machine gun from the back seat, and set it up on the square so that its field of fire covered the street from which the consul's car had emerged. The two others opened the back door of the Oldsmobile and invited Mr. Okuchi to get out. The chauffeur was nervous. His fingers tapped the steering wheel as if he found it hard to resist blowing the horn. One of the men told him: "Stay quiet. This is a political kidnapping."

"I have no intention of resisting," the consul said. "Is this like what happened to the American Ambassador?" The man nodded. Passers-by strolling on the square quickly changed sidewalks when they saw the three cars in the street. The consul accompanied three of the men to the Simca and drove away with them. The other men put the machine gun back in the second car and drove off in a different direction. The operation had taken roughly five minutes. . . .

The kidnapping of the Japanese consul was not an isolated act, but part of a program of urban guerrilla warfare which has been adopted in the last three years by several Brazilian opposition groups. The 1964 military coup against President João Goulart's reform-minded Government apparently convinced these groups that social change in Brazil could not come about through peaceful means. Constitutional rights were suspended in 1964, and since then Brazil has been ruled by a succession of three generals. Gen. Humberto Castelo Branco died in 1967 and was replaced by Gen. Arturo da Costa e Silva, who died in office and was succeeded by his former secret police chief, Gen. Emilio Garrastazu Medici, who was elected to the office of president by a majority of Brazil's 230 generals.

Today, political opposition to the ruling junta can be divided between those movements that continue to believe in conventional methods like strikes, demonstrations, pamphlets and opposition candidates in national and local elections, and those who argue that since the regime will not tolerate conventional methods of protest, armed action has become the only way.

Perhaps the first opposition leader to decide upon armed action was Carlos Marighella, the veteran militant who joined the Brazilian Communist party at the age of 16, in 1928. The son of a black Brazilian woman and an Italian immigrant, Marighella was dubbed "the ebony giant" by the penny press. He was proud of the fact that his grandmother was a slave. He was first jailed in 1936. After World War II, the Communist party was allowed to surface and he was elected a deputy. He was very active in the Brazilian house of representatives, and made 195 speeches in less than two years.

In 1947, however, Brazil broke off diplomatic relations with the Soviet Union, the Communists were again outlawed, and Marighella again went underground, this time for good. As Communist leader of São Paulo, a sprawling, mushrooming metropolitan area which today has six million inhabitants, his action then consisted largely of organizing the masses: contacts with labor leaders, speeches supporting the demands of the workers, posters and pamphlets.

Under Brazil's last constitutional Government, that of João Goulart, who governed from September, 1961 to April, 1964, Marighella was not actively hunted by the police, for the Communist strategy at that time was to cooperate with the Government and hope eventually to take power through an alliance with the middle class. But just as Goulart was about to embark on a program of reforms, including a law that would have limited to 10 per cent of invested capital the percentage of profits that foreign investors could take out of the country, and an agrarian reform that would have expropriated and redistributed about a million and a half acres (or roughly 3 per cent of the country's privately owned land), he was overthrown by an army putsch backed by a coalition of large land-owners and conservative politicians.

The police began looking for Marighella in earnest and found him one April evening in a Rio de Janeiro movie theater. He resisted arrest and was shot three times in the stomach. He escaped while recovering from his wounds in a prison infirmary. It was then that Marighella began to contest the Communist party's strategy of peaceful resistance. In 1967 he broke with the party and went to Cuba in August to attend the first Conference of Latin-American Solidarity. There, disavowed by the Brazilian Communists, he made his first speech calling for armed action. "The only way to unite Brazilian revolutionaries and to give power to the people is through guerrilla warfare," he said.

Returning clandestinely to Brazil at the end of 1967, Marighella began to form small action groups and outline his new revolutionary program. He formulated two basic principles: first, that the political and military branches of the movement should be one and the same. In this, he was arguing against the so-called *brazo armado* (armed branch) theory according to which revolutionary action can be waged on two complementary fronts, one political and the other military. Marighella had come to believe that only through military action could political results be obtained.

The second basic principle was a refutation of the so-called *foco* (focus) theory of Regis Debray, the French revolutionary who was arrested in Bolivia with Che Guevara, and whose book, "Revolution in the Revolution," has had a wide audience among third-world opposition groups. The *foco* theory gave priority to the rural over the urban guerrilla, and called for guerrilla bands to settle and operate in hard-to-reach rural areas. Their action, supported by the local peasantry, would serve as a focal point of the revolution and as an example for the formation of similar guerrilla centers throughout the country. It was while applying the *foco* theory to the Bolivian hinterland that Debray and Guevara were captured in October 1967. "The trouble with Che Guevara," a Brazilian revolutionary told me, "is that he was known by the wrong people. Everybody all over the world knew him, except the Bolivian peasants."

In the pronunciamento launching his new movement, the A.L.N. (Action for National Liberation), Marighella said: "We are not interested in sending armed men to a certain spot in Brazil and in waiting for other groups to spring up in other parts of the territory. This would be a fatal error." As he began recruiting his first armed groups, he drafted a "Manual for the Urban *Guerrilheiro*," which is a practical handbook of the how-to-do-it variety, full of rather obvious precepts and advice on the order of: "The urban *guerrilheiro* must know how to live amid the people; he must dress in such a manner as not to attract attention; he must use light weapons, which are easy to replace; he must learn to be a good shot; he must attack the enemy by surprise; he must have a strong political motivation and a good technical preparation."

From the fall of 1968, Brazilians were witness to spectacular guerrilla military actions carried out in the heart of their largest cities. More than a hundred banks were robbed by Marighella's A.L.N. and by several smaller, independent groups that formed in his wake. An American Army captain named Charles Chandler was shot and killed as he left his São Paulo apartment building. The *guerrilheiros* said he was a C.I.A. agent. Marighella's men dynamited army barracks and warehouses owned by American companies, they occupied radio stations to broadcast revolutionary proclamations, they freed a group of jailed comrades from a prison in Rio. Another group, the Revolutionary Movement of Oct. 8, kidnapped U.S. Ambassador Charles Burke Elbrick in broad daylight in downtown Rio, and exchanged him for 15 political prisoners.

The large-circulation Brazilian dailies like O Globo called Marighella and his men thieves, bandits and assassins. At the same time they fed the legend of a Brazilian Pimpernel with a charmed life, whom the police were unable to catch. But as Marighella's group grew larger, the risk of capture increased. With the arrests of two Dominican fathers in October, 1969 (Marighella may have been a Marxist-Leninist, but he was hardly sectarian about recruitment), the police were able to dismantle the network. On Nov. 4, 80 policemen laid an ambush for Marighella on a street in São Paulo and killed him in a south-of-the-border version of the shooting of Bonnie and Clyde.

The organization has survived its leader and continues today to carry out armed coups in Brazil's cities. Two other groups that have modeled their action on Marighella's thinking are the M.R.-8, which kidnapped Elbrick, and the V.P.R., whose kidnapping of the Japanese consul has already been described. As Ladislas Dowbor, the 29-year-old economist who became one of the leaders of the V.P.R., explained the process, the decision to deal exclusively in armed actions was not impetuous or improvised, but the result of a careful political analysis.

I met Dowbor . . . in Algiers, where he arrived in June [1970] with 39 other Brazilian political prisoners who had been released in exchange for the kidnapped West German ambassador. The political police had arrested him only seven weeks before his release. But during that time he had been frequently tortured. His ankles were covered with dark blue bruises made by electrodes, and one third-degree burn on his left leg had failed to heal after months of treatment. Despite what he has been through he is already making arrangements to return to Brazil clandestinely and resume his activities.

Algiers, which has earned a reputation as a center for revolutionary exiles, had never received so many all at once. Quarters were found for the 40 Brazilians in a hotel school vacated for the summer holidays, in the suburb of Ben Aknoun. It was in this pleasant compound, with two-room and three-room bungalows scattered around a main building that served as a dining room and lounge, that I found Dowbor, recuperating from his imprisonment. He is a man of middle height with a broad Slavic face (his parents are of Polish origin), large, ingenuous gray eyes, and ash-blonde hair combed straight back from a somewhat bulging forehead. He is scholarly in manner. He never raises his voice. He makes no pretense at toughness or *machismo*. As I saw from his dealings with the other political prisoners, he has the quiet authority of the natural leader. He gives the impression of being a theoretician, who although lacking any aptitude or liking for violent action, has willed himself to participate in the operations of armed groups because they conform with his analysis of the situation in Brazil.

"You cannot build the revolutionary consciousness of a population through political explanations," Dowbor said. "But military actions can create this consciousness. In Brazil, there are deep feelings of discontent. People feel the pressures of the system, but they direct their feelings against their visible enemies—the farm overseer, or the shop foreman, or the landowner who throws squatters off his land. They have not yet reached the stage of holding the system responsible.

"We attack the targets they consciously identify, which provokes a reaction of the system. When we invest a factory and force the manager who is two weeks late with salaries to pay his men, we provoke the army, the police, the press and the clergy into taking positions against us and in support of the visible enemy. It is then that the workers are able to identify the system as an enemy.

"For instance, in Rio de Janeiro, we heard about a machine tool plant where the boss had built a kind of throne where late-comers had to eat their lunch separately from the other workers. We invested the factory with a machine gun-mounted jeep. When the boss arrived in his big red American car, our men burned it, burned the throne and gave him a beating in front of his workers. The result for our group is that it is accepted by the population in that part of Rio.

"The police are caught in a contradiction: if they do nothing, the bourgeoisie says 'you don't protect us.' They have to organize the repression to show they are doing their job. The workers see the police and the army and the press working together and come to recognize that the enemy is not individual but social. And that is already a form of class consciousness.

"Now, this method of creating class consciousness through armed action is very different from the methods that Lenin developed for the creation of a workers' party. If you are mainly concerned with organizing the masses, you address yourself to those classes that are most capable of being organized, like labor, large groups of men with identical interests who are easy to reach. But armed action, which means living in small, clandestine cells, reduces the possibility of contact with the population.

We must rely on the repercussions of our actions. If it is a violent action, it will appeal to those parts of the population that are sensitive to violence—that is, the marginal masses, the unemployed, the *favelados*.

"Tactically, when you perform an armed action, you don't limit yourself to the interests of one class. You are reaching the masses not through political cells or speeches or pamphlets, but through the *fait accompli* of violent action. We are not telling them, look, it's better for you to organize a strike against your oppressors, we are saying, here is what we have done against the system. This makes us a mobilization movement, not an organizational movement.

"Now, these marginal classes, which represent an ever-growing percentage of the Brazilian population, are themselves in a state of permanent violence because of police harassment, the usurpation of their land, the loss of their jobs, and the endemic criminality they are forced into when they move to the cities. Those people are highly sensitive to our form of action.

"Another advantage of small, radical military groups is that it solves the Leninist problem of how to remain in the vanguard, ahead of the masses. Classical Communist parties run the risk of being outflanked by their own rank and file, but we remain far ahead of the masses by the very nature of our struggle. With us, it is not the masses that fight, but the political élite.

"We run the risk of isolating ourselves from the masses, since we are fighting and they are not. That is why we do not attempt political education. We do not lecture on socialism or other theories the masses won't understand. Our attacks against the visible enemy are immediately understood. We start with the hated foreman and his private police. The foreman works for an invisible boss, he is not at the root of the system. But the peasants would not understand if we attacked the boss, whom they never see. So we kill the foreman, and the boss reacts, and the peasant discovers that behind the foreman there is another enemy. Another example: it's not interesting for us to kill a police torturer unless he is widely known as a torturer, because what the population will see is a front-page photograph of the President handing a check to the widow in mourning in front of her weeping children.

"We orient our armed actions in such a way as to make them politically profitable. For instance, the kidnapping of a foreign diplomat creates political problems for the regime. Either the regime agrees with the Minister of Interior not to give in and allows the diplomat to be killed—which creates difficulties with the foreign power the diplomat represents, and with which the regime has economic ties—or the regime meets the demands of the kidnappers and the diplomat is set free; then the army and the police criticize the leniency of the Government, and that creates dissension within the regime. In our case, we only carried out kidnappings when we were fairly sure our demands would be met. We chose diplomats from countries on which Brazil is dependent and we knew the Minister of Interior was not in a position to adopt a tough stance.

"We believe that by spreading armed action we create among the masses a higher level of understanding of the struggle. We will reach our next phase when we are able to recruit enough men under arms so that we can deploy groups in every region of Brazil. Our class analysis is based on the expected growth of the marginal class, those who are outside the system and can expect nothing from it and are its natural enemies.

"The population of Brazil today is estimated at 90 million, but no one knows what the rate of unemployment is. Everyone knows there are two Brazils, an industrial Brazil inside an underdeveloped Brazil. In the south, which includes the industrial triangle of Rio-São Paulo-Belo Horizonte, 60 per cent of the population lives on 20 per cent of the land and earns 80 per cent of the national income.

"You see, capitalism in Brazil did not follow the usual development. It was financed by foreign capital, first mainly English and now mainly American. It superimposed itself on the old structures of a colonial economy based on the culture of sugar and coffee, so that today there are two parallel economies, one modern and the other archaic.

"In the modern sector, you find beautiful, gleaming factories where the investment is so great that it's not productive to underpay the worker. But less workers are needed, and the percentage of salaries in the cost of the product drops. Reasonable salaries are paid to fewer workers.

"The development of this modern sector places traditional industries in a state of crisis. They cannot sustain the competition. They cannot pay workers comparable salaries. They have to modernize or call it quits. Thus, the trend is that part of the working class is gradually expelled from the process of production into the marginal class, leaving a smaller, better-paid, relatively content working class, which is of no use in carrying out the revolution. This is a perfect example of what Lenin called the corruption of the proletariat. Brazil has become a country where it is impossible to evaluate the rate of unemployment, because today a large part of the active population remains outside the system of production. It is commonplace to see one fellow who works and supports his cousins and uncles and brothers-in-law.

"With the latifundia, or big plantations that produce coffee, sugar, cotton and cocoa, and raise cattle, the situation is similar. Hit by the international devaluation of raw materials and various forms of competition (like synthetic fibers for cotton), the landowners have to modernize their methods and expel workers. These expelled workers can either move deeper into the forests where they will find land (only 30 per cent of Brazil's total surface is inhabited), or become migrant workers moving from crop to crop. The mobility of the Brazilian population is fantastic. The third solution, and by far the most popular, is migration to the cities. This creates an imbalance. You have overpopulated cities and a deserted countryside. The marginal masses flock to the cities and create a slum population.

"In Rio and São Paulo, one finds a vast aggregate of unemployed and illiterate people with marginal occupations: they sell oranges, they shine shoes, they wash cars, they become petty thieves and prostitutes and they constitute a social danger to the system. In São Paulo, less than half the population is registered. That means millions of uncontrolled persons, with no documents, no official identity, no address. They live in shacks. You ask someone on the street in São Paulo where he is living, and chances are he will say something like, 'I don't know, last week I was staying at my uncle's, but he threw me out. I'm looking for a place.' An enormous floating population living expediently helps make São Paulo a perfect place for revolutionaries to hide."

I should confess at this point that I have never been to Brazil, I am merely passing along the analysis of a 29-year-old economist who has spent the last three years of his life trying to overthrow the government there, which he considers dictatorial. My own knowledge of Brazil is limited to a small number of elementary and probably erroneous ideas. My Brazil is the land of the Rio carnival, Amazon serpents, alligator hunters, malignant fevers, strong coffee, underfed Indians, and botched revolutions. My Brazil is a tempting but remote El Dorado, beckoning all those with childhood dreams of overnight fortunes, a country of unlimited possibilities and unknown hardships. My Brazil is a former colony founded on slavery, which, miraculously, did not become racist, and where today a white man is a man with a drop of white blood, whereas in some countries a black man is a man with a drop of black blood.

My concern here is less with Brazil, however, than with the mysterious process by which a pleasant, scholarly young man from a middle-class background is transformed into a revolutionary ready to carry out reckless actions such as kidnappings and armed robberies and bombings. I came to realize from my talks with Dowbor that he was dangerous, not because he carried a gun and was willing to use it, but because he is one of those rare persons who carry the notion of moral consistency to its logical outcome.

Most of us are eroded by the practice of compromise. We live in the heart of inconsistency between our beliefs and our behavior. What priest and what doctor can afford to live according to the Gospels or the Hippocratic oath? . . .

Most of us are caught in a web of daily obligations that make it impossible for us to live out our convictions. We inhabit a no man's land between the principles we cherish and the demands that are made upon us to violate or ignore them. We think the war in Vietnam is wrong but we pay taxes to support it. We are against pollution but we use cars and air conditioners that contribute to it. We survive by virtue of arrangements. In this perspective, the man who decides to align his behavior with his beliefs is the truly dangerous one.

Ladislas Dowbor's parents, as we have said, came from Poland. His father is a metallurgical engineer. His mother is a doctor. Fleeing a disintegrating Europe, they reached Brazil in 1940, and he was born in São Paulo. His parents are both practicing Catholics, with the kind of militant faith that once earned the name Belt of High Observance for the part of the world they came from. The four Dowbor children, of whom Ladislas is the youngest, had a very traditional, very morally demanding upbringing, stressing—rather than the small disciplinary matters such as wiping your feet before you come into the house, or how to hold your fork—how to be honest in your ideas and what it means to have a sense of justice.

"My sister is morally conservative," says Dowbor, "but she has the same respect for moral coherence." Moral coherence . . . a phrase few people are in a position to use, and which keeps recurring, with perhaps the slightest touch of smugness, in Dowbor's conversation.

He attended Jesuit schools in São Paulo, and was subjected to their combative brand of Catholicism (the Jesuits still think of themselves, in the light of their founder, Ignatius of Loyola, as soldiers of Christ). He found a Jesuit education propitious for the adoption of extreme viewpoints. "With the Jesuits," he says, "you either become a fascist or a revolutionary. Some of my classmates are in the political police. Their vision of the world is Manichaeistic. There are forces of light and forces of darkness."

When Dowbor graduated from high school, he was not sure he wanted to continue his education. He was more interested in confronting practical economic problems. In 1960, his father gave him the money to buy a share in a chicken farm in the province of Campinas. He found that the individual chicken farmer was totally dependent on the wholesaler, who bought from 30 or 40 small farms.

"The wholesaler signed a contract to buy your chickens at a given price," he says. "But when the time came to pick up the chickens, he couldn't be reached. I had to get rid of the chickens, I had new chickens hatching. I went to see the wholesaler, and he said O.K., we'll come for your chickens, but we can't pay the original price, the market has collapsed. Then I'd get behind in my corn payments—corn is the biggest expense—and I'd have to borrow money at 10 per cent interest. We tried to break the circle by selling directly to restaurants, but we were too small to guarantee them a steady supply, and the wholesaler threatened to cut them off if they bought from us. They couldn't take the risk."

Dowbor sold the chicken farm at a loss after a year and joined his father, who was then working in the northern coastal city of Recife. He found a job on the Journal of Commerce and joined the Movement of Popular Culture, which was devoted to teaching *campesinos* how to read in the backward rural areas of Pernambuco province, where the illiteracy rate reaches 90 per cent. Dowbor had seen poverty, but never like this. "It was about this part of Brazil," he says, "that Josue de Castro wrote 'The Cycle of the Crab.' People settle in the swamps, they are pushed off the good land, and they build their houses on poles. They drop their offal in the mud, and the crabs eat it, and then the people eat the crabs. People find it hard to believe that the average life span in Pernambuco province is 27 years."

As Dowbor continued to teach peasants to read ("For them, it was a matter of dignity, it made them part of society"), he came to understand why they were incapable of revolt. One day he saw a farm overseer tongue-lash a peasant because of work left unfinished. "My baby died yesterday," the peasant said, "and I took the day off." "I realized," Dowbor says, "that the worker felt a sense of guilt at having been absent, rather than a sense of outrage at being reprimanded on a day of great sorrow. I saw that these men are in a psychological and physiological state that precludes political action, they are caught in a cycle of birth, work and death."

Dowbor also found that thanks to his involvement in the literacy program, he had come to the attention of army authorities. He was summoned to an army barracks in Recife for questioning by two officers. The first officer said: "Don't you know the Movement for Popular Culture is financed by the Communists?"

"It was founded by the governor of the province," Dowbor reminded them.

The first officer turned to the second officer and said: "One of these days we are going to get this son of a whore."

"Gradually," Dowbor says, "I began to feel a need to make my life consistent with my ideas. You don't wake up one morning and look into the mirror and announce: I am a revolutionary. You become a revolutionary imperceptibly, by asking yourself questions, by breaking down the structure of power in your head, by a sense of outrage combined with the conviction that certain problems must have solutions. At that point my feelings were still linked to my Catholic upbringing. My reasoning was of the utmost simplicity. My father invited me to a good restaurant and

I refused. As a Catholic, when you see children dying of hunger, either you refuse a meal that could feed five children, or you abandon your Christianity."

In Recife, however, Dowbor's revolutionary aspirations became detached from his notions of Catholic morality. He was living in a beach house that had been loaned to him by a German engineer who was away most of the time. Every two weeks the engineer returned from the bush for a wild weekend with two or three prostitutes in the beach house. In the morning, the prostitutes would chat with Dowbor as they waited for the engineer to rouse from his slumber.

In a typical instance, a girl asked Dowbor: "Can you wake him up? I haven't been paid, and I have to go home and take care of my children."

"How do you manage to do the work you do and take care of your children as well?" Dowbor asked.

"I have to," the girl said. "My husband worked on the docks, but he's been laid off."

"I realized that there was no moral problem for them," Dowbor says. "There was sufficient misery in Recife for morality not to exist. Before, as a result of my Jesuit education, I had divided women into good and bad, and a prostitute was a bad woman. But when I saw a woman who convinced me that she was prostituting herself to feed her children, my values lost their absolute character.

"I worked myself up into a state of moral crisis. I had believed so strongly in the Christian values I had practiced that I now had to replace them with something else equally valid. I could not resolve the contradiction between the morality I had been taught and what I saw around me. It is what the French call *la conscience malheureuse*. I was 20 years old and I will never let anyone tell me it was the happiest time of my life.

"I decided at that time that social change was necessary and that it could only come about through organized group activity. I decided that instead of devoting myself to my own career, to my own life, I would become a social activist. I had wanted to study psychology; I decided economics would be more useful. I put some money aside and went to Switzerland, working as a truck driver during the day, and studying at night at the University of Lausanne, from 1964 until 1967."

Dowbor then found a teaching position in a small American college in the lakeside town of Leysin, near Lausanne. He taught a course in the history and formation of the Common Market. "The students there were the children of diplomats and businessmen," he recalls; "they owned sports cars and patronized the Montreux casino. They had strong feelings about their privileges. They would say things like: 'Peasants live in filth because they don't deserve anything better.' To that I would reply, 'That is not an argument; it is a philosophical position about man.'"

Dowbor decided that he must return to Brazil and take up armed action to overthrow the regime. "I felt it was absurd to hold a pacifist position and encourage the *campesinos* to organize," he says, "for once organized, and at the first test, the army would fire on them. Objectively, by working as a pacifist, one provokes violence. And if one provokes violence, one must assume it. A regime will not leave power by itself. It is hypocrisy to keep your hands clean and say you are a revolutionary but that you are not ready for armed action."

Dowbor left for Paris, where he made contact with several young Brazilians in the process of founding the V.P.R. One of them became his sponsor, and he was assigned to an action group. He returned to Brazil in June, 1968 without telling his family he was back, took a room in a boarding house in São Paulo, and met the leader of the new movement, a black ex-army sergeant named Onofre Pinto. He was given the *nom de guerre* Nelson and told that the first objective of his five-man action group would be to find money to finance its activities.

"We decided to get our money from the banks," Dowbor says. "That seemed normal in that the money in the banks rightly belongs to the workers. We thought we were entering a temporary phase to obtain the means to continue our action. We had not yet grasped the enormous political advantage of conducting armed actions in the large cities."

To hold up banks, they needed cars, and Dowbor became an experienced car thief. He and one of his colleagues would cruise the main boulevards of São Paulo between 5 and 6 in the evening, during the rush hour, pick out a car, and follow it. When the driver parked in front of his home and got out with his keys in his hand, they relieved him of the keys and drove off with the car after telling the owner: "Your car is going to be used in a revolutionary action. Tell the police it was stolen or you will be arrested as an accomplice. In a few days we will call and tell you where you can pick it up."

"We always returned the cars with a tank full of gas," Dowbor says.

Within a month of his return, he was holding up his first bank, the Banco Mercantil, a gleaming, two-story steel and glass structure on Brigadier Luiz Antonio Avenue, in downtown São Paulo. . . .

But . . . in August, 1968, after only two months of revolutionary activity, he found out that it was just as simple to be caught. He was cruising through a residential section at night with two other members of the group, looking for a car to steal. His car was stopped by the police, who found a gun on the back seat. The police were not sure whether they were common thieves or political activists.

Dowbor and his friends were turned over to the State Department of Criminal Investigation (D.E.I.C.) for questioning, which in Brazil has become a euphemism for torture. Dowbor was introduced to the parrot's perch, an iron crossbar hanging from the ceiling, from which a suspect is suspended with his hands tied over his knees. While in this helpless position, electric shocks are applied to various parts of the body. At the end of eight days of beatings and the parrot's perch, Dowbor was in bad shape, with several broken ribs.

"You would hear yelling all day long there [at D.E.I.C. headquarters]," he recalls. "There was always someone being tortured. I realized that the Brazilian police had given up all investigative techniques except torture. A police investigator in Brazil is by definition a torturer. The chief investigator was a police inspector known as Geladeira [refrigerator] because he never betrayed any emotion while doing his work.

"The terrible thing is that they become accustomed to torture. Decent young men from good families who have joined the police from the highest motives are told to torture suspects. The first time they vomit in disgust, and then they get used to it." . . .

Dowbor's lawyer managed to have him visited by a doctor. The lawyer took the doctor's report to a police commissioner, and threatened to have it published. Thanks to this threat and a bribe, the lawyer obtained the release of Dowbor and his two friends, who were never formally charged. Dowbor explains this peculiar turnabout by saying: "You must realize that in an underdeveloped country the repression, too, is undeveloped. The police are underpaid and undermotivated. Once I was stopped in a stolen car. The registration was not in my name. I offered them 50 cruzeiros. They wanted 100. We settled on 70."

Once released, Dowbor became more careful. He rented three separate *cuartos de impregado* (top-floor maid's rooms), using a different name for each, and moved from one to the other, like the mythical king who, fearing assassination, changed bedrooms each night. He continued robbing banks and stealing cars. One day in March, 1969, he saw his own photograph on a wanted poster. The posters were up on street corners, in gas stations and in cafes.

"WANTED," the posters said—"LADISLAS DOWBOR, KNOWN AS NELSON, ONE OF THE HEAVYWEIGHTS OF THE TERRORIST ORGANIZATION, A DANGEROUS COMMUNIST ASSASSIN RESPONSIBLE FOR THE DEATHS OF MANY HEADS OF FAMILIES. HELP US PROTECT YOUR CHILDREN. WARN A POLICEMAN AS SOON AS YOU NOTICE HIS PRESENCE."

"It gives you a funny sensation to see yourself on every city wall," Dowbor says. "I remember buying meat at a butcher's and watching him wrap it up in a newspaper with my photograph on it." In retaliation, the V.P.R. distributed posters with the photograph of the Brazilian President, Costa e Silva, which said: "WANTED BY THE REVOLUTIONARY MOVEMENTS, FOR TORTURE, COLLECTIVE MURDER AND OFFICIAL ROBBERY." . . .

The appearance of the posters, however, was coupled with a police crackdown. At the end of March, 1969, the leader of the V.P.R., Onofre Pinto, was caught. . . .

A month earlier, a respected army officer named Capt. Carlos Lamarca had deserted the Fourth Infantry Regiment with 70 light machine guns and joined the ranks of the V.P.R. Lamarca was known as the best shot in the army, and had been picked by the government to teach bank tellers to fire the guns they were now going to be issued, as a preventive measure to halt the wave of holdups. A widely distributed poster showed the dashing Captain Lamarca instructing a young lady how to fire a revolver. In any case, after Onofre Pinto was caught, Lamarca became the head of the V.P.R., a position he holds to this day. He is also at the head of the Brazilian police's most wanted list.

In April, Dowbor and Lamarca and 10 others attacked a military police barracks in the factory district of São Caetano do Sul. "We wanted their submachine guns and grenades," Dowbor says, "and we also wanted the workers to see the M.P.'s in their gray uniforms and white helmets standing outside their own barracks with their hands up. It may seem strange that we would risk the lives of important leaders in this type of action. But that is proof of total involvement. However important you are, you must do your share of menial jobs like stealing cars or renting hideouts for less experienced companions. People told us they were staying out of our movement because they were political, or that they were going into exile because they were too important to remain in Brazil. That had no meaning for us. Instead of making speeches from foreign countries, we were getting the job done."

On April 21, at 8:30 P.M., Dowbor was on his way to an apartment in the Paraiso section to meet a girl agent when he turned a corner and found himself surrounded by police. The girl had been arrested and had given away the address of the meeting under torture. Dowbor pulled out the Luger he was carrying that day and fired, but it jammed. His only thought as the police slipped handcuffs over his wrists was: Lugers aren't supposed to jam.

He was taken to the interrogation center run by the counterterrorist army squads, who had launched what they called "Operation Bandeirantes," or OBAN, named after the 18th-century adventurers who came to Brazil to hunt for gold and diamonds. The center is a modern, three-story, yellow-and-white house behind a police station on Tutoya Street. Over the door to the room where the torture takes place are the words: *Aqui nao ha Deus nem direitos humanos* (Here there is neither God nor human rights).

Three teams of 10 men commanded by an army captain work eight-hour shifts around the clock in the torture center. . . . The torture room is called the special operations room, or the *sala roxa* (violet room), because the walls are hung with violet cloth.

As soon as he was arrested, Dowbor was taken to the *sala roxa* and questioned for 48 consecutive hours. He tried to talk about things the police already knew, like the bank holdups. One of his interrogators said: "You steal money from the banks; why don't you get it from the crooked politicians instead?"

"Why do you torture prisoners?" Dowbor asked by way of a reply.

"If we don't torture you, you won't talk," the interrogator said. "What can we do?"

"That is up to you. When a regime is forced to stay in power by such means, it has no real validity. For each one of us you torture you create 10 kamikazes and then you will weep about violence in Brazil."

The fatherly, understanding interrogator, who offered coffee and cigarettes, alternated with the ugly interrogator, who applied the electrodes. The nice one said: "We want to talk to you from one soldier to another. You are militants of subversion, we are militants of repression. You are a foolish young idealist. You could help Brazil—instead, you are trying to wreck it. What are you after?"

To gain time, Dowbor explained what his aims were, he talked about Brazil's alienated masses, he discussed the degree of foreign investment in the Brazilian economy. He felt like the concubine in "Thousand and One Nights" whose life was safe as long as she kept talking. The torturers joined in, as though they liked nothing better than a lively political discussion.

"Your methods are wrong," one interrogator said. "Violence will not help. Why are you giving up a comfortable existence for a lost cause?"

At one point, the soldier who was typing Dowbor's statement turned to one of his colleagues and said: "You know, Tiradentes (a famous 18th-century Brazilian hero commonly known as Toothpuller, whose head was shown in a public square in Rio after he was put to death), he fought for independence and had his head cut off and now he's a national hero. Do you suppose someday these people will be the same?"

Dowbor came to the end of his statement by saying: "An honest man who wants to walk with his head up should take up arms nowadays." This was too much for the ugly interrogator, who strapped him to the parrot's perch and applied the electrodes, calling him a "son of a bitch Pole." Later, when Dowbor was in his cell trying to rest his mistreated body, this same interrogator came to apologize, not for having tortured him, but for having made a slurring remark about his national origin.

Dowbor was considered an important catch. He was loaned out by one security organization to the others. "In the following month," he says,

"I was tortured by the São Paulo army, the political police, the Rio de Janeiro army, naval intelligence and the army secret service. It did not matter whether I talked or not. Each new team of interrogators decided the others had not been able to break me because they did not know their job. They made it a point of professional honor to do better."

After several weeks of this treatment, Dowbor had third-degree burns on his legs and sprained back muscles and was unable to walk. He was sent to an ultramodern medical center operated by the DOPS (Department of Order, Political and Social). A team of doctors there is specialized in patching up political prisoners so they can be tortured some more, like ringside attendants who stanch a boxer's cuts so he can keep fighting.

"That was almost worse than being tortured," Dowbor says. Pleasant young doctors in clean white smocks took notes as they asked, with the same impersonal tone as if they were inquiring about a sinus headache: "What was it? Electric shock? What voltage?" They took his temperature, tapped his chest as they listened with a stethoscope, treated his burns, and X-rayed him. "With treatment like that you start to lose your mind," Dowbor says. The doctors pronounced him fit enough to be returned to his interrogators.

"I finally talked," he says. "I had to give away the general aspects of the organization." When he said he did not know where Lamarca was hiding (which was true), one of the interrogators said: "You are lying, but the day will come when you will wish for others to be imprisoned because of you."

Dowbor had been passed along from one security service to the other for roughly six weeks when word filtered down to him that the West German ambassador in Rio de Janeiro had been kidnapped by the V.P.R., which was asking for 40 prisoners in exchange for his release. "I was in my cell in the DOPS," he recalls, "when a policeman whispered to me: 'You're in luck, your people have kidnapped von Holleben [the German ambassador].' That day they stopped torturing me. I could not be sure I was on the list of the 40. The lists are made up according to one's behavior in prison. The next day the names came out and I was on it. The guards started calling me *Senhor.*"

On June 14, Dowbor and others on the list were taken under heavy guard to the military airport in São Paulo. They were flown to Rio de Janeiro, where they were put by twos in cells in the air force prison. The next morning, all the 40 were herded together in the same room. "It was a very joyous scene," says Dowbor. "We found companions whom we thought were dead or whom we had not seen in years." Twenty-seven of the 40 were members of Dowbor's group, the V.P.R., which had carried out the kidnapping. "At midday we boarded the plane for Algiers. We had changed handcuffs three times, because each police organization had its own. The political police had turned us over to the federal police at São Paulo airport. The federal police had turned us over to the air force police in Rio, and on the plane we were back in the hands of the federal police. We remained handcuffed during the flight."

The plane arrived at Maison-Carrée airport in Algiers at 1 A.M. on June 15. A Brazilian policeman stood at the door, at the spot where the smiling air hostess usually wishes passengers farewell, and unsnapped the handcuffs from each disembarking passenger. Dowbor walked down the gangplank, shook his wrists and gazed up at the clear, star-filled North African sky.

Part Five

A NEW PERSPECTIVE: MODERNIZATION AS CONTINUING TRANSFORMATION

THE concluding part of this volume is designed to do two things: to bring together the concepts and perspectives that have been discussed in the preceding parts of the book, and to raise fundamental questions addressed to the future of both the poor and developing, and the rich and modernized nations. The selections presented here approach these questions from two directions.

First, Robert L. Heilbroner analyzes the position of the developing nations from the perspective of American foreign policy. His analysis confirms the potential for instability and revolution which has been stressed throughout this volume. Heilbroner raises a basic question: must the United States oppose every revolutionary outbreak in the third world? The fundamentally humane impulses of the American people suggest that the answer should be negative. Yet the specific history of American foreign policy since the end of World War II points in the opposite direction. As Heilbroner says, because of preoccupation with the cold war, American policy-makers have all too readily identified nationalist revolution in the third world with communism. The result has been a grave misallocation of resources and an overemphasis on military power in dealing with the essentially political and social problems of modernization. Episodes like the Dominican intervention of 1965 and the agony of the Vietnam war indicate that persistence in the pursuit of such a policy will not only brand America as a counterrevolutionary force in the world, but will contribute to acute social and political crisis within the United States itself.

This brings us to our final selection. Manfred Halpern here sets forth a new way of thinking not only about modernization but about the general condition of the contemporary age. He suggests that the end product of the process of modernization is not any predetermined or static social system, but rather a continuous transformation of social and personal interrelationships. He sees two possible outcomes of the burgeoning domestic and international crisis of our day. On the one hand, we may learn how to manage this continuous transformation and thus achieve a new level of stability and social order. Alternatively, we may miss the opportunity for reasoned control and management and instead witness an inexorable disintegration of social interactions at all levels. In that event, social order and tranquility will be replaced by violent chaos and incoherence.

The stakes are indeed high—higher perhaps than at any time in history. The detached observer—if there are any left in these troubled times—might conclude that the time for decision may well be at hand before the decade of the 1970's has run its course.

22. MUST AMERICA BE COUNTERREVOLUTIONARY?

Robert L. Heilbroner

ROBERT LOUIS HEILBRONER, well-known economist and historian, teaches at the Graduate Faculty of the New School for Social Research in New York City, and has lectured at numerous universities. His many books include *The Worldly Philosophers* (1953), *The Future as History* (1960), *Limits of American Capitalism* (1966), and *Between Capitalism and Socialism* (1970).

Is the United States fundamentally opposed to economic development? The question is outrageous. Did we not coin the phrase, "the revolution of rising expectations"? Have we not supported the cause of development more generously than any nation on earth, spent our intellectual energy on the problems of development, offered our expertise freely to the backward nations of the world? How can it possibly be suggested that the United States might be opposed to economic development?

The answer is that we are not at all opposed to what we conceive economic development to be. The process depicted by the "revolution of rising expectations" is a deeply attractive one. It conjures up the image of a peasant in some primitive land, leaning on his crude plow and looking to the horizon, where he sees dimly, but for the *first time* (and that is what is so revolutionary about it), the vision of a better life. From this electrifying vision comes the necessary catalysis to change an old and stagnant way of life. The pace of work quickens. Innovations, formerly feared and resisted, are now eagerly accepted. The obstacles are admittedly very great—whence the need for foreign assistance—but under the impetus of new hopes the economic mechanism begins to turn faster, to gain traction against the environment. Slowly, but surely, the Great Ascent begins.

There is much that is admirable about this well-intentioned popular view of "the revolution of rising expectations." Unfortunately, there is more that is delusive about it. For the buoyant appeal of its rhetoric conceals or passes in silence over by far the larger part of the spectrum of realities of the development process. One of these is the certainty that the revolutionary aspect of development will not be limited to the realm of ideas, but will vent its fury on institutions, social classes, and innocent men and women. Another is the great likelihood that the ideas needed to guide the revolution will not only be affirmative and reasonable, but also destructive and fanatic. A third is the realization that revolutionary efforts cannot be made, and certainly cannot be sustained, by voluntary effort alone, but require an iron hand, in the spheres both of economic direction and political control. And the fourth and most difficult of these realities to face is the probability that the political force most likely to succeed in carrying through the gigantic historical transformation of development is some form of extreme national collectivism or Communism.

In a word, what our rhetoric fails to bring to our attention is the likelihood that development will require policies and programs repugnant to our "way of life," that it will bring to the fore governments hostile to our international objectives, and that its regnant ideology will bitterly oppose capitalism as a system of world economic power. If that is the case, we would have to think twice before denying that the United States was fundamentally opposed to economic development.

But is it the case? Must development lead in directions that go counter to the present American political philosophy? Let me try to indicate, albeit much too briefly and summarily, the reasons that lead me to answer that question as I do.

I begin with the cardinal point, often noted but still insufficiently appreciated, that the process called "economic development" is not primarily economic at all. We think of development as a campaign of production to be fought with budgets and monetary policies and measured with indices of output and income. But the development process is much wider and deeper than can be indicated by such statistics. To be sure, in the end what is hoped for is a tremendous rise in output. But this will not come to pass until a series of tasks, at once cruder and more delicate, simpler and infinitely more difficult, has been commenced and carried along a certain distance.

In most of the new nations of Africa, these tasks consist in establishing the very underpinnings of nationhood itself—in determining national borders, establishing national languages, arousing a basic national (as distinguished from tribal) self-consciousness. Before these steps have been taken, the African states will remain no more than names insecurely affixed to the map, not social entities capable of undertaking an enormous collective venture in economic change. In Asia, nationhood is generally much further advanced than in Africa, but here the main impediment to development is the miasma of apathy and fatalism, superstition and distrust that vitiates every attempt to improve hopelessly inefficient modes of work and patterns of resource use: while India starves, a quarter of the world's cow population devours Indian crops, exempt either from effective employment or slaughter because of sacred taboos. In still other areas, mainly Latin America, the principal handicap to development is not an absence of national identity or the presence of suffocating cultures (although the latter certainly plays its part), but the cramping and crippling inhibitions of obsolete social institutions and reactionary social classes. Where landholding rather than industrial activity is still the basis for social and economic power, and where land is held essentially in fiefdoms rather than as productive real estate, it is not surprising that so much of society retains a medieval cast.

Thus, development is much more than a matter of encouraging economic growth within a given social structure. It is rather the *modernization* of that structure, a process of ideational, social, economic, and political change that requires the remaking of society in its most intimate as well as its most public attributes. When we speak of the revolutionary nature of economic development, it is this kind of deeply penetrative change that we mean—change that reorganizes "normal" ways of thought, established patterns of family life, and structures of village authority as well as class and caste privilege.

What is so egregiously lacking in the great majority of the societies that are now attempting to make the Great Ascent is precisely this pervasive modernization. The trouble with India and Pakistan, with Brazil and Ecuador, with the Philippines and Ethiopia, is not merely that economic growth lags, or proceeds at some pitiable pace. This is only a symptom of deeper-lying ills. The trouble is that the social physiology of these nations remains so depressingly unchanged despite the flurry of economic planning on top. The all-encompassing ignorance and poverty of the rural regions, the unbridgeable gulf between the peasant and the urban elites, the resistive conservatism of the village elders, the unyielding traditionalism of family life—all these remain obdurately, maddeningly, disastrously unchanged. In the cities, a few modern buildings, sometimes brilliantly executed, give a deceptive patina of modernity, but once one journeys into the immense countryside, the terrible stasis overwhelms all.

To this vast landscape of apathy and ignorance one must now make an exception of the very greatest importance. It is the fact that a very few nations, all of them Communist, have succeeded in reaching into the lives and stirring the minds of precisely that body of the peasantry which constitutes the insuperable problem elsewhere. In our concentration on the politics, the betrayals, the successes and failures of the Russian, Chinese, and Cuban revolutions, we forget that their central motivation has been just such a war *à l'outrance* against the arch-enemy of backwardness—not alone the backwardness of outmoded social superstructures but even more critically that of private inertia and traditionalism.

That the present is irreversibly and unqualifiedly freed from the dead hand of the past is, I think, beyond argument in the case of Russia. By this I do not only mean that Russia has made enormous economic strides. I refer rather to the gradual emancipation of its people from the "idiocy of rural life," their gradual entrance upon the stage of contemporary existence. This is not to hide in the smallest degree the continuing backwardness of the Russian countryside where now almost fifty—*and formerly perhaps eighty*—per cent of the population lives. But even at its worst I do not think that life could now be described in the despairing terms that run through the Russian literature of our grandfathers' time. Here is Chekhov:

> During the summer and the winter there had been hours and days when it seemed as if these people [the peasants] lived worse than cattle, and it was terrible to be with them. They were coarse, dishonest, dirty, and drunken; they did not live at peace with one another but quarreled continually, because they feared, suspected, and despised one another. . . . Crushing labor that made the whole body ache at night, cruel winters, scanty crops, overcrowding, and no help, and nowhere to look for help.

It is less certain that the vise of the past has been loosened in China or Cuba. It may well be that Cuba has suffered a considerable economic decline, in part due to absurd planning, in part to our refusal to buy her main crop. The economic record of China is nearly as inscrutable as its political turmoil, and we may not know for many years whether the Chinese peasant is today better or worse off than before the revolution. Yet what strikes me as significant in both countries is something else. In Cuba it is the educational effort that, according to the New York *Times,* has constituted a major effort of the Castro regime. In China it is the unmistakable evidence—and here I lean not alone on the sympathetic account of Edgar Snow but on the most horrified description of the rampages of the Red Guards—that the younger generation is no longer fettered by the traditional view of things. The very fact that the Red Guards now revile their elders, an unthinkable defiance of age-old Chinese custom, is testimony of how deeply change has penetrated into the texture of Chinese life.

It is this herculean effort to reach and rally the great anonymous mass of the population that is *the* great accomplishment of Communism—even though it is an accomplishment that is still only partially accomplished. For if the areas of the world afflicted with the self-perpetuating disease of backwardness are ever to rid themselves of its debilitating effects, I think it is likely to be not merely because antiquated social structures have been dismantled (although this is an essential precondition), but because some shock treatment like that of Communism has been administered to them.

By way of contrast to this all-out effort, however short it may have fallen of its goal, we must place the timidity of the effort to bring modernization to the peoples of the non-Communist world. Here again I do not merely speak of lagging rates of growth. I refer to the fact that illiteracy in the non-Communist countries of Asia and Central America is increasing (by some 200 million in the last decade) because it has been "impossible" to mount an educational effort that will keep pace with population growth. I refer to the absence of substantial land reform in Latin America, despite how many years of promises. I refer to the indifference or incompetence or corruption of governing elites: the incredible sheiks with their oildoms; the vague, well-meaning leaders of India unable to break the caste system, kill the cows, control the birthrate, reach the villages, house or employ the labor rotting on the streets; the cynical governments of South America, not one of which, according to Lleras Camargo, former president of Colombia, has ever prosecuted a single politician or industrialist for evasion of taxes. And not least, I refer to the fact that every movement that arises to correct these conditions is instantly identified as "Communist" and put down with every means at hand, while the United States clucks or nods approval.

To be sure, even in the most petrified societies, the modernization process is at work. If there were time, the solvent acids of the 20th century would work their way on the ideas and institutions of the most inert or resistant countries. But what lacks in the 20th century is time. The multitudes of the underdeveloped world have only in the past two decades been summoned to their reveille. The one thing that is certain about the revolution of rising expectations is that it is only in its inception, and that its pressures for justice and action will steadily mount as the voice of the 20th century penetrates to villages and slums where it is still almost inaudible. It is not surprising that Princeton historian C. E. Black, surveying this labile world, estimates that we must anticipate "ten to fifteen revolutions a year for the foreseeable future in the less developed societies."

In itself, this prospect of mounting political restiveness enjoins the speediest possible time schedule for development. But this political urgency is many times compounded by that of the population problem. Like an immense river in flood, the number of human beings rises each year to wash away the levees of the preceding year's labors and to pose future requirements of monstrous proportions. To provide shelter for the three billion human beings who will arrive on earth in the next forty years will require as many dwellings as have been constructed since recorded history began. To feed them will take double the world's present output of food. To cope with the mass exodus from the overcrowded countryside will necessitate cities of grotesque size—Calcutta, now a cesspool of three to five millions, threatens us by the year 2000 with a prospective population of from thirty to sixty millions.

These horrific figures spell one importunate message: haste. That is the *mene mene, tekel upharsin* written on the walls of government planning offices around the world. Even if the miracle of the loop is realized—the new contraceptive device that promises the first real breakthrough in population control—we must set ourselves for at least another generation of rampant increase.

But how to achieve haste? How to convince the silent and disbelieving men, how to break through the distrustful glances of women in black shawls, how to overcome the overt hostility of landlords, the opposition of the Church, the petty bickerings of military cliques, the black-marketeering of commercial dealers? I suspect there is only one way. The conditions of backwardness must be attacked with the passion, the ruthlessness, and the messianic fury of a jehad, a Holy War. Only a campaign of an intensity and singlemindedness that must approach the ludicrous and the unbearable offers the chance to ride roughshod over the resistance of the rich and the poor alike and to open the way for the forcible implantation of those modern attitudes and techniques without which there will be no escape from the misery of underdevelopment.

I need hardly add that the cost of this modernization process has been and will be horrendous. If Communism is the great modernizer, it is certainly not a benign agent of change. Stalin may well have exceeded Hitler as a mass executioner. Free inquiry in China has been supplanted by dogma and catechism; even in Russia nothing like freedom of criticism or of personal expression is allowed. Furthermore, the economic cost of industrialization in both countries has been at least as severe as that imposed by primitive capitalism.

Yet one must count the gains as well as the losses. Hundreds of millions who would have been confined to the narrow cells of changeless lives have been liberated from prisons they did not even know existed. Class structures that elevated the flighty or irresponsible have been supplanted by others that have promoted the ambitious and the dedicated. Economic systems that gave rise to luxury and poverty have given way to systems that provide a rough distributional justice. Above all, the prospect of a new future has been opened. It is this that lifts the current ordeal in China above the level of pure horror. The number of human beings in that country who have perished over the past centuries from hunger or neglect, is beyond computation. The present revolution may add its dreadful increment to this number. But it also holds out the hope that China may finally have been galvanized into social, political, and economic attitudes that for the first time make its modernization a possibility.

Two questions must be answered when we dare to risk so favorable a verdict on Communism as a modernizing agency. The first is whether the result is worth the cost, whether the possible—by no means assured—escape from underdevelopment is worth the lives that will be squandered to achieve it.

I do not know how one measures the moral price of historical victories or how one can ever decide that a diffuse gain is worth a sharp and particular loss. I only know that the way in which we ordinarily keep the books of history is wrong. No one is now toting up the balance of the wretches who starve in India, or the peasants of Northeastern Brazil who live in the swamps on crabs, or the undernourished and permanently stunted children of Hong Kong or Honduras. Their sufferings go unrecorded, and are not present to counterbalance the scales when the furies of revolution strike down their victims. Barrington Moore has made a nice calculation that bears on this problem. Taking as the weight in one pan the 35,000 to 40,000 persons who lost their lives—mainly for no fault of theirs—as a result of the Terror during the French Revolution, he asks what would have been the death rate from preventable starvation and injustice under the *ancien regime* to balance the scales. "Offhand," he writes, "it seems unlikely that this would be very much below the proportion of .0010 which [the] figure of 40,000 yields when set against an estimated population of 24 million." [1]

Is it unjust to charge the *ancien regime* in Russia with ten million preventable deaths? I think it not unreasonable. To charge the authorities in pre-revolutionary China with equally vast and preventable degradations?

[1] *Social Origins of Dictatorship and Democracy*, p. 104.

Theodore White, writing in 1946, had this to say: . . . ."some scholars think that China is perhaps the only country in the world where the people eat less, live more bitterly, and are clothed worse than they were five hundred years ago." [2]

I do not recommend such a calculus of corpses—indeed, I am aware of the license it gives to the unscrupulous—but I raise it to show the one-sidedness of our protestations against the brutality and violence of revolutions. In this regard, it is chastening to recall the multitudes who have been killed or mutilated by the Church which is now the first to protest against the excesses of Communism.

But there is an even more terrible second question to be asked. It is clear beyond doubt, however awkward it may be for our moralizing pro-pensities, that historians excuse horror that succeeds; and that we write our comfortable books of moral philosophy, seated atop a mound of victims—slaves, serfs, laboring men and women, heretics, dissenters—who were crushed in the course of preparing the way for our triumphal entry into existence. But at least we are here to vindicate the carnage. What if we were not? What if the revolutions grind flesh and blood and produce nothing, if the end of the convulsion is not exhilaration but exhaustion, not triumph but defeat?

Before this possibility—which has been realized more than once in history—one stands mute. Mute, but not paralyzed. For there is the necessity of calculating what is likely to happen in the absence of the revolution whose prospective excesses hold us back. Here one must weigh what has been done to remedy underdevelopment—and what has not been done—in the past twenty years; how much time there remains before the population flood enforces its own ultimate solution; what is the likelihood of bringing modernization without the frenzied assault that Communism seems most capable of mounting. As I make this mental calculation I arrive at an answer which is even more painful than that of revolution. I see the alternative as the continuation, without substantial relief—and indeed with a substantial chance of deterioration—of the misery and meanness of life as it is now lived in the sinkhole of the world's backward regions.

I have put the case for the necessity of revolution as strongly as possi-ble, but I must now widen the options beyond the stark alternatives I have posed. To begin with, there are areas of the world where the imme-diate tasks are so far-reaching that little more can be expected for some decades than the primary missions of national identification and unifica-tion. Most of the new African states fall into this category. These states may suffer capitalist, Communist, Fascist, or other kinds of regimes dur-

[2] *Thunder Out of China,* p. 32.

ing the remainder of this century, but whatever the nominal ideology in the saddle, the job at hand will be that of military and political nation-making.

There is another group of nations, less easy to identify, but much more important in the scale of events, where my analysis also does not apply. These are countries where the pressures of population growth seem sufficiently mild, or the existing political and social framework sufficiently adaptable, to allow for the hope of considerable progress without resort to violence. Greece, Turkey, Chile, Argentina, Mexico may be representatives of nations in this precarious but enviable situation. Some of them,ⁱ incidentally, have already had revolutions of modernizing intent—fortunately for them in a day when the United States was not so frightened or so powerful as to be able to repress them.

In other words, the great arena of desperation to which the revolutionizing impetus of Communism seems most applicable is primarily the crowded land masses and archipelagoes of Southeast Asia and the impoverished areas of Central and South America. But even here, there is the possibility that the task of modernization may be undertaken by non-Communist elites. There is always the example of indigenous, independent leaders who rise up out of nowhere to overturn the established framework and to galvanize the masses—a Gandhi, a Marti, a pre-1958 Castro. Or there is that fertile ground for the breeding of national leaders—the army, as witness Ataturk or Nasser, among many.

Thus there is certainly no inherent necessity that the revolutions of modernization be led by Communists. But it is well to bear two thoughts in mind when we consider the likely course of non-Communist revolutionary sweeps. The first is the nature of the mobilizing appeal of any successful revolutionary elite. Is it the austere banner of saving and investment that waves over the heads of the shouting marchers in Jakarta and Bombay, Cairo and Havana? It most certainly is not. The banner of economic development is that of nationalism, with its promise of personal immortality and collective majesty. It seems beyond question that a feverish nationalism will charge the atmosphere of any nation, Communist or not, that tries to make the Great Ascent—and as a result we must expect the symptoms of nationalism along with the disease: exaggerated xenophobia, a thin-skinned national sensitivity, a search for enemies as well as a glorification of the state.

These symptoms, which we have already seen in every quarter of the globe, make it impossible to expect easy and amicable relations between the developing states and the colossi of the developed world. No conceivable response on the part of America or Europe or, for that matter, Russia, will be able to play up to the vanities or salve the irritations of the emerging nations, much less satisfy their demands for help. Thus, we must anticipate an anti-American, or anti-Western, possibly even anti-white animus from any nation in the throes of modernization, even if it is not parroting Communist dogma.

Then there is a second caution as to the prospects for non-Communist revolutions. This is the question of what ideas and policies will guide their revolutionary efforts. Revolutions, especially if their whole orientation is to the future, require philosophy equally as much as force. It is here, of course, that Communism finds its special strength. The vocabulary in which it speaks—a vocabulary of class domination, of domestic and international exploitation—is rich in meaning to the backward nations. The view of history it espouses provides the support of historical inevitability to the fallible efforts of struggling leaders. Not least, the very dogmatic certitude and ritualistic repetition that stick in the craw of the Western observer offer the psychological assurances on which an unquestioning faith can be maintained.

If a non-Communist elite is to persevere in tasks that will prove Sisyphean in difficulty, it will also have to offer a philosophical interpretation of its role as convincing and elevating, and a diagnosis of social and economic requirements as sharp and simplistic, as that of Communism. Further, its will to succeed at whatever cost must be as firm as that of the Marxists. It is not impossible that such a philosophy can be developed, more or less independent of formal Marxian conceptions. It is likely, however, to resemble the creed of Communism far more than that of the West. Political liberty, economic freedom, and constitutional law may be the great achievements and the great issues of the most advanced nations, but to the least developed lands they are only dim abstractions, or worse, rationalizations behind which the great powers play their imperialist tricks or protect the privileges of their monied classes.

Thus, even if for many reasons we should prefer the advent of non-Communist modernizing elites, we must realize that they too will present the United States with programs and policies antipathetic to much that America "believes in" and hostile to America as a world power. The leadership needed to mount a jehad against backwardness—and it is my main premise that only a Holy War will begin modernization in our time—will be forced to expound a philosophy that approves authoritarian and collectivist measures at home and that utilizes as the target for its national resentment abroad the towering villains of the world, of which the United States is now Number One.

All this confronts American policymakers and public opinion with a dilemma of a totally unforeseen kind. On the one hand we are eager to assist in the rescue of the great majority of mankind from conditions that we recognize as dreadful and ultimately dangerous. On the other hand, we seem to be committed, especially in the underdeveloped areas, to a policy of defeating Communism wherever it is within our military capacity to do so, and of repressing movements that might become Communist if they were allowed to follow their internal dynamics. Thus, we have on the one side the record of Point Four, the Peace Corps, and foreign aid generally; and on the other, Guatemala, Cuba, the Dominican Republic, and now Vietnam.

That these two policies might be in any way mutually incompatible, that economic development might contain revolutionary implications infinitely more far-reaching than those we have so blandly endorsed in the name of rising expectations, that Communism or a radical national collectivism might be the only vehicles for modernization in many key areas of the world—these are dilemmas we have never faced. Now I suggest that we do face them, and that we begin to examine in a serious way ideas that have hitherto been considered blasphemous, if not near-traitorous.

Suppose that most of Southeast Asia and much of Latin America were to go Communist, or to become controlled by revolutionary governments that espoused collectivist ideologies and vented extreme anti-American sentiments. Would this constitute a mortal threat to the United States?

I think it fair to claim that the purely *military* danger posed by such an eventuality would be slight. Given the present and prospective capabilities of the backward world, the addition of hundreds of millions of citizens to the potential armies of Communism would mean nothing when there was no way of deploying them against us. The prospect of an invasion by Communist hordes—the specter that frightened Europe after World War II with some (although retrospectively, not too much) realism—would be no more than a phantasm when applied to Asia or South America or Africa.

More important, the nuclear or conventional military power of Communism would not be materially increased by the armaments capacities of these areas for many years. By way of indication, the total consumption of energy of all kinds (in terms of coal equivalent) for Afghanistan, Bolivia, Brazil, Burma, Ceylon, Colombia, Costa Rica, Dominican Republic, Ecuador, El Salvador, Ethiopia, Guatemala, Haiti, Honduras, India, Indonesia, Iran, Iraq, Korea, Lebanon, Nicaragua, Pakistan, Paraguay, Peru, Philippines, U.A.R., Uruguay, and Venezuela is less than that annually consumed by West Germany alone. The total steel output of these countries is one-tenth of U.S. annual production. Thus, even the total communization of the backward world would not effectively alter the present balance of military strength in the world.

However small the military threat, it is undeniably true that a Communist or radical collectivist engulfment of these countries would cost us the loss of billions of dollars of capital invested there. Of our roughly

$50 billions in overseas investment, some $10 billions are in mining, oil, utility, and manufacturing facilities in Latin America, some $4 billions in Asia including the Near East, and about $2 billions in Africa. To lose these assets would deal a heavy blow to a number of large corporations, particularly in oil, and would cost the nation as a whole the loss of some $3 to $4 billions a year in earnings from those areas.

A Marxist might conclude that the economic interests of a capitalist nation would find such a prospective loss insupportable, and that it would be "forced" to go to war. I do not think this is a warranted assumption, although it is undoubtedly a risk. Against a Gross National Product that is approaching $\frac{3}{4}$ of a trillion dollars and with total corporate assets over $1.3 trillions, the loss of even the whole $16 billions in the vulnerable areas should be manageable economically. Whether such a takeover could be resisted politically—that is, whether the red flag of Communism could be successfully waved by the corporate interests—is another question. I do not myself believe that the corporate elite is particularly war-minded—not nearly so much so as the military or the congressional—or that corporate seizures would be a suitable issue for purposes of drumming up interventionist sentiment.

By these remarks I do not wish airily to dismiss the dangers of a Communist avalanche in the backward nations. There would be dangers, not least those of an American hysteria. Rather, I want only to assert that the threats of a military or economic kind would not be insuperable, as they might well be if Europe were to succumb to a hostile regime.

But is that not the very point?, it will be asked. Would not a Communist success in a few backward nations lead to successes in others, and thus by degrees engulf the entire world, until the United States and perhaps Europe were fortresses besieged on a hostile planet?

I think the answer to this fear is twofold. First, as many beside myself have argued, it is now clear that Communism, far from constituting a single unified movement with a common aim and dove-tailing interests, is a movement in which similarities of economic and political structure and ideology are more than outweighed by divergencies of national interest and character. Two bloody wars have demonstrated that in the case of capitalism, structural similarities between nations do not prevent mortal combat. As with capitalism, so with Communism. Russian Communists have already been engaged in skirmishes with Polish and Hungarian Communists, have nearly come to blows with Yugoslavia, and now stand poised at the threshold of open fighting with China. Only in the mind of the *Daily News* (and perhaps still the State Department) does it seem possible, in the face of this spectacle, to refer to the unified machinations of "international Communism" or the "Sino-Soviet bloc."

The realities, I believe, point in a very different direction. A world in which Communist governments were engaged in the enormous task of trying to modernize the worst areas of Asia, Latin America, and Africa would be a world in which sharp differences of national interest were certain to arise within these continental areas. The outlook would be for frictions and conflicts to develop among Communist nations with equal frequency as they developed between those nations and their non-Communist neighbors. A long period of jockeying for power and command over resources, rather than anything like a unified sharing of power and resources, seems unavoidable in the developing continents. This would not preclude a continuous barrage of anti-American propaganda, but it would certainly impede a movement to exert a coordinated Communist influence over these areas.

Second, it seems essential to distinguish among the causes of dangerous national and international behavior those that can be traced to the tenets of Communism and those that must be located elsewhere. "Do not talk to me about Communism and capitalism," said a Hungarian economist with whom I had lunch this winter. "Talk to me about rich nations and poor ones."

I think it *is* wealth and poverty, and not Communism or capitalism, that establishes much of the tone and tension of international relations. For that reason I would expect Communism in the backward nations (or national collectivism, if that emerges in the place of Communism) to be strident, belligerent, and insecure. If these regimes fail—as they may—their rhetoric may become hysterical and their behavior uncontrolled, although of small consequence. But if they succeed, which I believe they can, many of these traits should recede. Russia, Yugoslavia, or Poland are simply not to be compared, either by way of internal pronouncement or external behavior, with China, or, on a smaller scale, Cuba. Modernization brings, among other things, a waning of the stereotypes, commandments, and flagellations so characteristic of (and so necessary to) a nation engaged in the effort to alter itself from top to bottom. The idiom of ceaseless revolution becomes less relevant—even faintly embarrassing —to a nation that begins to be pleased with itself. Then, too, it seems reasonable to suppose that the vituperative quality of Communist invective would show some signs of abating were the United States to modify its own dogmatic attitude and to forego its own wearisome clichés about the nature of Communism.

I doubt there are many who will find these arguments wholly reassuring. They are not. It would be folly to imagine that the next generation or two, when Communism or national collectivism in the underdeveloped areas passes through its jehad stage, will be a time of international safety. But as always in these matters, it is only by a comparison with the alternatives that one can choose the preferable course. The prospect that I have offered as a plausible scenario of the future must be placed against that which results from a pursuit of our present course. And here I see two dangers of even greater magnitude: (1) the prospect of many more Vietnams, as radical movements assert themselves in other areas of the world; and (2) a continuation of the present inability of the most impoverished areas to modernize, with the prospect of an eventual human catastrophe on an unimaginable scale.

Nevertheless, there *is* a threat in the specter of a Communist or near-Communist supremacy in the underdeveloped world. It is that the rise of Communism would signal the end of capitalism as the dominant world order, and would force the acknowledgement that America no longer constituted the model on which the future of world civilization would be mainly based. In this way, as I have written before, the existence of Communism frightens American capitalism as the rise of Protestantism frightened the Catholic Church, or the French Revolution the English aristocracy.

It is, I think, the fear of losing our place in the sun, of finding ourselves at bay, that motivates a great deal of the anti-Communism on which so much of American foreign policy seems to be founded. In this regard I note that the nations of Europe, most of them profoundly more conservative than America in their social and economic dispositions, have made their peace with Communism far more intelligently and easily than we, and I conclude that this is in no small part due to their admission that they are no longer the leaders of the world.

The great question in our own nation is whether we can accept a similar scaling-down of our position in history. This would entail many profound changes in outlook and policy. It would mean the recognition that Communism, which may indeed represent a retrogressive movement in the West, where it should continue to be resisted with full energies, may nonetheless represent a progressive movement in the backward areas, where its advent may be the only chance these areas have of escaping misery. Collaterally, it means the recognition that "our side" has neither the political will, nor the ideological wish, nor the stomach for directing those changes that the backward world must make if it is ever to cease being backward. It would undoubtedly entail a more isolationist policy for the United States *vis-à-vis* the developing continents, and a greater willingness to permit revolutions there to work their way without our interference. It would mean in our daily political life the admission that the ideological battle of capitalism and Communism had passed its point of usefulness or relevance, and that religious diatribe must give way to the pragmatic dialogue of the age of science and technology.

I do not know how to estimate the chances of affecting such deep-seated changes in the American outlook. It may be that the pull of vested interests, the inertia of bureaucracy, plus a certain lurking fundamentalism that regards Communism as an evil which admits of no discussion—the antichrist—will maintain America on its present course, with consequences that I find frightening to contemplate. But I believe that our attitudes are not hopelessly frozen. I detect, both above and below, signs that our present view of Communism is no longer wholly tenable and that it must be replaced with a new assessment if we are to remain maneuverable in action and cogent in discourse.

Two actions may help speed along this long overdue modernization of our own thought. The first is a continuation of the gradual thawing and convergence of American and Russian views and interests—a rapprochement that is proceeding slowly and hesitantly, but with a discernible momentum. Here the initiative must come from Russia as well as from ourselves.

The other action is for us alone to take. It is the public airing of the consequences of our blind anti-Communism for the underdeveloped world. It must be said aloud that our present policy prefers the absence of development to the chance for Communism—which is to say, that we prefer hunger and want and the existing inadequate assaults against the causes of hunger and want to any regime that declares its hostility to capitalism. There are strong American currents of humanitarianism that can be directed as a counterforce to this profoundly anti-humanitarian view. But for this counterforce to become mobilized it will be necessary to put fearlessly the outrageous question with which I began: is the United States fundamentally opposed to economic development?

23. A REDEFINITION OF THE REVOLUTIONARY SITUATION

Manfred Halpern

TRANSFORMING OUR CONSCIOUSNESS

. . . Never before have we lived in an age marked in every society in the world by the continuous breaking of connections—connections between generations, between established ideas and their intended consequences, between talking and the possibility of being heard, between felt pain and perceived remedy. Our best artists and critics have dramatized both the threat and the freedom of our dissolving connections.

Surely this persistent incoherence in all systems by which man has organized his life constitutes the fundamental revolution of our times.

The world is being molded neither by a conspiracy of world revolutionaries nor by counterrevolutionary forces (as both these terms are conventionally defined), but primarily by unintended, incoherent change. This kind of incoherent transformation turns encounters into chaos, renders dialogue impossible, and obscures (and so also deepens) injustice. Political and intellectual traditions have focused our attention primarily on stability and those famous and particular revolutions of modern history that, thanks to their victory or defeat, seemed to return us to stability. What we do not understand is incoherent revolutionary change. What we are least able to achieve is the transformation of such change into coherent change conducive to justice. . . .

. . . [The] underlying revolution we have neglected—the revolution of modernization—is not a peculiar burden carried temporarily by the underdeveloped, but rather history's first common, world-wide revolution. The main lines of my argument may be summarized in a single paragraph:

Change in the modern age is historically unique in its quality. For the first time, man and all the political, social, economic, religious, intellectual, aesthetic, and psychological systems by which he has so far organized his life are persistently being rendered incoherent. Elements are being destroyed, and the linkages between them disconnected. Specifically, the connections being broken are those inherited, concrete links between individuals, groups, and concepts that give men the capacity to cope simultaneously with continuity and change, collaboration and conflict, and with justice. My hypothesis is that this breaking of connections, and therefore the destruction of the capacity to deal with the most basic issues of social life, is the persistent and permanent challenge of the modern age. Since our perceptions and actions have not yet caught up with this new quality of change, most of the breaking is unintended and uncontrolled. If this be the nature of the modern age, we have two alternatives. We can live with incoherence—and with the apathy, repression, and normless violence that usually accompany it. (I expect most of the world in the foreseeable future will either choose this alternative or lack the will or ability to avoid such incoherence.) Or else, we can seek to create an enduring capacity to overcome persistent incoherence and to take creative advantage of the opportunities that arise from the breaking of established connections. Such a capacity is constituted of four components to which economic development or education contribute only if they are deliberately designed for that purpose and not otherwise. The four required components that together constitute an enduring capacity to generate and absorb persistent transformation are new forms of consciousness, creativity, institutionalized power, and justice. . . .

To perceive connections breaking, one must first have perceived the connections that count in history and society. Such connections are those links between individuals, groups, and concepts that create and shape human capacity to deal with the five central issues of all human relationships. How do men bind each other in *collaboration*,[1] yet free each other for *conflict* from opposing positions; assure *continuity* in their relationship with each other, yet allow for *change* in the balance of costs and benefits in their relationship; and thus produce *justice?* . . .

I must begin with patterns and processes of society in order to be able to move on to a more interesting hypothesis regarding history— namely, that the modern age is an age of permanent revolution in two specific ways: (1) in the constant breaking of precisely those inherited, concrete connections between self and other that give us the capacity to deal with these five central issues, and (2) in the creative opportunities to fashion new linkages capable of producing coherent change. . . .

CAUSES OF INCOHERENT CHANGE

The modern age begins for any society when its network of [encounters] . . . can no longer serve to deal simultaneously with the five central issues—thus, when incoherence takes their place. Incoherence is the absence of any shared forms of tension-management between individuals and groups who stand, nonetheless, in conscious encounter with each other. Incoherence is more than tension. Tension is the experience by individuals and groups of changing balances of costs and benefits as men relate to each other in opposing positions. Tension, in this sense, is the normal accompaniment of human relationships. Incoherence is more than strain. Strain is the experience of great imbalance of costs and benefits in the relationship between poles. Such imbalances can presumably be remedied by changes possible within the prevailing polarity. Incoherence, I repeat, is the absence of that connection between individuals, groups, and ideas that gives capacity to maintain a shared form of tension-management between them. . . .

If it can be empirically demonstrated that incoherence will continuously arise in the modern age, . . . then it follows that incoherence arises be-

---

[1] By collaboration I do not mean harmony. Two medieval knights who have agreed to fight each other, even unto death, collaborate with each other throughout their conflict. They do not start until the trumpet sounds; they do not end until the trumpet sounds again. They collaborate in agreeing not to use any illegitimate moves or weapons. I know of no form of conflict, except incoherent conflict, that is possible without collaboration, and of no collaboration, not even love, that is possible without taking account of that conflict-ridden fact that the other is not the self.

cause the quality of change with which individuals and groups must come to terms has itself now changed, and no inherited type of . . . [encounter] can cope with it.[2] If change in the modern age were novel only in its quantity, we would continue to find its essence familiar and its rate would decelerate after a while. There is a limit to man's material production and consumption, however far we may now be from that point. But we do not yet know, and cannot even imagine, the limits of the quality of consciousness and creativity, or the limits of the quality of institutionalized power in terms of links between individuals, groups, and concepts, or the limits of the quality of justice.

The causes of incoherence in the modern age may be the intended result of destruction or innovation. Most of the time, however, incoherence is the unintended result of unconscious or conscious attempts to conserve existing connections—to maintain coherence through polarities that possess no capacity to generate and absorb persistent transformation. . . . *Modern societies* are therefore to be critically differentiated into two categories: *transient societies,* which are being moved primarily by incoherent change because they possess only polarities capable of dealing with changes within relationships, and *modernizing societies,* which are capable of transforming relationships in the face of persistently breaking connections.

THE CAPACITY FOR TRANSFORMATION

What are the components of the capacity for transforming any relationship between self and other?

The first component is a new form of consciousness, rather than knowledge. Although the modern age has witnessed a knowledge explosion that has contributed to a new form of consciousness, knowing is still different from knowing that you know, and from knowing the limits and potentialities of what you know. The heart of the matter is not scientific thinking or its fruits in technology, though obviously these have helped to create a new form of consciousness. It is this consciousness itself that we must try to define and see how it differs from that of any previous age. Modern consciousness in relation to society and history is constituted of an awareness that there are patterns in the encounter of individuals, groups, and concepts; that these patterns have been developed by man; that these patterns are breaking; and that they can be transformed by man. This statement has in essence been made by men many times before

[2] Incoherence need not be total throughout society before it becomes critical. The Algerian nationalist of the mid-1950s often continued to work on the French landowner's farm while fighting to destroy the political, economic, social, and moral relationships that allowed that landowner to monopolize political power, assert his individual superiority, and keep that land. For the same reason, it is seldom necessary to fight "the whole system" all at once in order to begin its transformation.

in our age. My only contribution here is, perhaps, to systematize its context.

This kind of consciousness, though it seems to me irreversible, can be expressed in two radically different forms. In relation to society and history, one form expresses an inability or unwillingness to move beyond incoherence. I call this form transient because it involves constantly shifting patterns of unintended, uncontrolled change, or else repression of consciousness by self or others, or normless violence. For the moment I want to concentrate on the alternative road, namely toward a modernizing capacity. This capacity for transformation also cannot be achieved without incoherence, without a breaking with earlier patterns. The genesis of the capacity for modernization therefore begins with what has conventionally been called polarization—the emergence of a new and distinct self that refuses to abide by ongoing patterns for dealing with continuity, change, collaboration, conflict, and justice. If the new self remains merely polarized, it will remain locked in incoherence.

The next required component of the capacity to modernize, therefore, is creativity. Over two thousand years ago, it was possible for the Chinese to write in *I Ching* (or *Book of Changes*) that "transformation is the creation of creativity." What, then, is new about creativity in the modern age? In the past, creative transformation centered above all upon man's inner life. Transformation of social relations or of man's relation to the material world took place only rarely, at great intervals, and produced either prolonged incoherence, or else new closed systems that endured with their new networks of polarity for centuries. Now individuals, society, concepts, nature, and their linkage to each other have all become subject to persistent breaking and reshaping. Transformation still includes the creation of creativity, but the power and context of creativity have changed, and therefore so has even the meaning of inner transformation.

For the capacity to deal with modernization, minimum creativity is the ability to formulate questions relevant to fundamentally new situations. Maximum creativity is the ability, paraphrasing Henry James, to woo new combinations into being. Creativity, as I have defined it, is therefore not only the rare capacity of genius, or the professional aspiration of scientists, artists, statesmen, and saints. Creativity is achieving or maintaining coherence—that is, wholeness through connection with self and others—in the midst of system-transforming change.

Such creativity is also needed to achieve institutionalized power—the third of the four components of a modernizing capacity. Institutionalized power in any age represents linked consciousness and pooled creativity. Institutionalized power does not mean bureaucracy. Modern bureaucracy is one of the most valuable social inventions of mankind. Its relevance for modernization is tested, however, not by any of the attributes usually associated with it, including its rational-legal character, but by whether any particular bureaucracy is capable of employing its collective power for structuring change. "Most organizations in the United States," said John W. Gardner recently, "have a structure that was designed to solve problems that no longer exist." The reason for this failure is that most modern bureaucracies are organized [with a] . . . style and capacity [which] . . . have given [them] . . . an unusual strength—a combination of autonomous responsibility, rationality, legality, uniformity, efficiency, and productivity. However, if the transformation of Europe in the modern age has been achieved at the cost of extraordinarily violent politics both at home and abroad, it is in part because . . . [this] autonomy and stability . . . can only be achieved if men and groups are in fact prepared to defend boundaries, and if they restrict innovations to those that help to support or expand existing claims of jurisdiction. The consciousness, creativity, and institutionalized power necessary to deal with persistent incoherence do not lie in [this mode of encounter which is domination in westernization, but not modernization]. . . .

The primary function of institutionalized power in modernization is not the protection of authority or the boundaries of its jurisdiction. It is to achieve and maintain coherent change conducive to justice. . . . For example, leaders may indeed present themselves as models of the modernizing man, and . . . seek to inspire others to embody this same model. Subjection may be used by a single party to overcome barriers to change and install a cadre of modernizing men. However, the achievement of the capacity for persistent transformation by society must be measured by the willingness of the leader to yield to those who have attained the capacity to create coherent change on their own. The success of the modernizing single party must be measured by its own transformation into evermore freely, more widely, and more creatively linked power.

Institutionalized power that serves to maintain an enduring capacity to generate and absorb persistent transformation may take the form of procedures linking individuals in community, as among scientists, or as between government and opposition in a legislative assembly. Individuals may be linked by commitments to common tasks of individual, social, or political therapy; by intellectual collegiality; by love—always by shared consciousness and creativity for collaborating in the world-wide task of transforming unintended, uncontrolled change into justice.

Justice as the final component of the capacity to modernize means participating in the production, and sharing in the products of increased consciousness, creativity, and linked power—a harvest that is itself constituted of concrete manifestations of growing consciousness, creativity, and linked power. This conception of productive and distributive justice reflects the fact that each of the four components of the capacity for modernization constitutes at the same time process and goal, means and end. To possess this capacity to deal with the problems of society and history, to participate fully and freely in the transformation of encounters between individuals, groups, and concepts in the modern age—this is justice in the Polarity of Transformation.

If the hypothesis that this is an age of persistent incoherence is correct, then it is not utopianism based on imaginative idealism, but historical and social analysis that leads to the conclusion that such a capacity with its four components is required for generating and absorbing persistent transformation. In the creation of such a capacity, each component is a prerequisite for the next component, and all four are required for the maintenance of transformation. I have emphasized consciousness of the patterns of relationship in society and history as the first prerequisite component. Without such consciousness, men will continue to think of "revolution" as large-scale, violent change, without becoming aware that the breaking of connections between individuals, groups, and concepts is a precondition to, but different from, transforming connections, and that violence may or may not be necessary for achieving incoherence or transformation.[3] Without such consciousness, ideology becomes a political dogma of change, freezing a particular moment of partial insight; or else it turns into the misleading rationalization of the right of established elites to rule. Ideology as an instrument of modernization must be based upon a theory that can explain the breaking and transforming of relationships in society and history. Ideology can then be fashioned into an explicit framework of political means and ends capable of stimulating policy-oriented analysis, inspiring new patterns of encounter, and constituting the normative and practical touchstone of accomplishments. Such an ideology develops and changes as theory and practice develop and change.

Seizing power is much easier than attaining capacity for transformation. Power is ability to deal with only one of the five issues at a time—most often the ability to conflict with others. It is a highly unstable ability possessed by children as well as the United States of America. Power must be turned into capacity. The power of the self must be linked to the power of others through consciously and creatively structured encounters, if there is to be ability in the modern age to deal simultaneously with collaboration, continuity, change, and justice, as well as with conflict. Achieving this capacity constitutes the cost and the benefit—the essence—

[3] *The Dialectics of Transformation in Politics, Personality, and Society* (Princeton, N.J.: Princeton University Press, 1972) explores how these three variables in "revolution"—incoherence, transformation, and violence—can in fact vary with each other.

of the revolution of modernization. It is a more difficult but also a more rewarding challenge than is posed by most current theories and ideologies of modernization. . . .

Transformation, by its nature, must not predetermine its final form: that is why my analysis has stressed process and capacity, not final models or utopias of the future. Still, we have barely begun to think about linkages and methods that make for transformation. The nineteenth century, Whitehead tells us, saw the invention of the methods of invention. The twentieth century saw the planning of the process. The past two centuries have also witnessed the first efforts at the social institutionalization of methods of transformation in psychiatry, politics, art, and economics. We have scarcely begun; to develop linkages and methods that make for conscious, creative transformation remains one of the greatest unfinished tasks of our practical imagination.

For the first time in history there is the possibility for genuine collaboration between ourselves and all other people of the world. It remains true that the United States still possesses a more penetrating scientific enterprise, a more powerful civilian and military technology, a more advanced economy than most of the world. But when it comes to the five central issues, we are all now entering an Age of Incoherence. We must all learn afresh how to fashion new connections between individuals, groups, and concepts that give us capacity to deal with continuity, change, collaboration, conflict, and justice. Not power to affect the subjection, bargaining, or boundaries of ourselves and others, but capacity to affect the quality and direction of life has now become the most strategic problem for all peoples. In this task of transformation, all peoples of the world can truly collaborate as equals—in combining research, analysis, resources, and action. In the task of developing therapies of transformation, we all now possess a common concern.[4]

Most individuals and societies are, however, as yet unwilling or unable to accept this challenge. They will therefore suffer the costs of increasing incoherence: repression of self and others; deprivation in failing to seize the creative opportunities of the modern age; normless violence by officials and antiofficials. Perhaps all I have done is give an advance report of much greater misery ahead, and explanation of why the world is moving toward uncontrolled devolution—toward uncontrolled unwinding —rather than conscious and creative revolution. We remain free to pay the increasingly familiar costs of incoherence. As long as we neglect the underlying meaning of the revolution of our times, we will be able to

---

[4] The new theory of continuity, change, collaboration, conflict, and justice in human relations that underlies this essay is elaborated in greater detail and applied to violence, racism, and strategies of transformation in *The Dialectics of Transformation in Politics, Personality, and Society* (see note 3).

respond only to its always unanticipated crises, which allow only for yea-or-nay decisions, thus reinforcing (even in American society) the tendency toward hierarchy, secrecy, and unrestrained power. The world's wars of liberation reflect deeper issues than any current ideologies can explain. These issues cannot be successfully countered by war, but only by liberation—liberation that requires the deliberate transformation of man and society.

SUGGESTIONS FOR FURTHER READING

THE emergence of the countries of the third world onto the stage of world politics has had a great impact on scholarship in the social sciences, particularly in the United States and especially in the field of political science. Since the early 1950's there has been an outpouring of books and articles offering new insights and new approaches to the subject. The result has been a shift in attention away from the traditional descriptive analyses of the institutional makeup of the governments of Western Europe which characterized earlier scholarship in the field of comparative politics.

In the vanguard of the new approach has been Gabriel Almond, who set forth his structural-functional approach in the Introduction to *The Politics of the Developing Areas* (jointly edited with James S. Coleman; Princeton University Press, 1960). A refinement and elaboration of this approach is embodied in Almond and G. Bingham Powell, Jr.'s *Comparative Politics: A Developmental Approach* (Boston: Little, Brown, 1967). Shorter statements may be found in numerous articles published by Professor Almond, such as "Political Systems and Political Change," *American Behavioral Scientist*, VI (June 1963), and "A Developmental Approach to Political Systems," in *World Politics*, XVII, No. 2 (January 1965). Professor Almond was instrumental in establishing a committee of leading political scientists under the auspices of the Social Science Research Council. Known as the Committee on Comparative Politics, this group has organized a number of conferences to examine various aspects of political development. The papers presented at these conferences have been published by the Princeton University Press in a series of valuable books, a number of which are represented in this reader. They are *Communications and Political Development*, edited by L. W. Pye (1963); *Bureaucracy and Political Development*, edited by Joseph LaPalombara (1963); *Political Modernization in Japan and Turkey*, edited by Robert E. Ward and Dankwart A. Rustow (1964), which examines in a comparative manner the nature of traditional culture and society and their transformation in these two countries; *Education and Political Development*, edited by James S. Coleman (1965); *Political Culture and Political Development*, edited by Lucian W. Pye and Sidney Verba (1965); *Political Parties and Political Development*, edited by Joseph La-Palombara and Myron Weiner (1966); and *Crises and Sequences in Political*

Development, edited by Leonard Binder, James S. Coleman, Joseph LaPalombara, Lucian W. Pye, and Myron Weiner (1971). Individual members of the committee have also set forth their observations, notably Lucian W. Pye in *Aspects of Political Development* (Boston: Little, Brown, 1966), and Dankwart A. Rustow, *A World of Nations* (Washington: Brookings Institution, 1967).

Other contributions to our understanding of the social, economic, and political transformation of third world countries include S. N. Eisenstadt's *Modernization: Protest and Change* (Englewood Cliffs, N.J.: Prentice-Hall, 1966) and his *The Political Systems of Empires* (New York: The Free Press, 1963), a voluminous study of the bureaucratic empire as a transitional phase of political development. Daniel Lerner elaborates a highly interesting theory of modernization based on the concept of *empathy;* see especially Chapters I and II of *The Passing of Traditional Society* (New York: The Free Press, 1958). David E. Apter's version of modernization hinges on the concept of *free choice;* it is elaborated in *The Politics of Modernization* (Chicago: University of Chicago Press, 1965). Samuel P. Huntington has suggested that the process of political development is not necessarily a one-way street, as indicated by the title of his provocative article "Political Development and Political Decay," in *World Politics,* XVII, No. 3 (April 1965). A more complete statement is his *Political Order in Changing Societies* (Yale University Press, 1968). Most recently, Huntington has comprehensively reviewed the treatment of the concepts of modernization and development by contemporary social scientists; see his "The Change to Change: Modernization, Development, and Politics," *Comparative Politics,* III, No. 3 (April 1971). Karl W. Deutsch's works emphasize the idea of political mobilization, which he defines as the breakdown of traditional patterns of social interactions and relationships and their replacement by new social ties; see his "Social Mobilization and Political Development," *American Political Science Review,* LV, No. 3 (September 1961). For an attempt to apply quantitative measures to the analysis of modernization and political stability, see Ronald D. Brunner and Garry D. Brewer, *Organized Complexity: Empirical Theories of Political Development* (New York: Free Press, 1971). Other basic theoretical statements may be found in E. E. Hagen, *On the Theory of Social Change* (Homewood, Ill.: Dorsey Press, 1962), published in condensed form in "How Economic Growth Begins: A Theory of Social Change," *Journal of Social Issues,* Vol. 19 (January 1963), pp. 20–34; and in David C. McClelland, *The Achieving Society* (Princeton, N.J.: Van Nostrand, 1961), summarized in "The Achievement Motive in Economic Growth," in B. F. Hoselitz and W. E. Moore, eds., *Industrialization and Society* (The Hague: UNESCO and Mouton, 1963), pp. 74–96.

One of the main themes of this collection of readings has been the universality of the transformation of modernization. As has been pointed out, this transformation has been running its course in Western Europe, North America, and the Soviet orbit for some years. An exceptionally fine analysis which takes account of the full sweep of history is Cyril E. Black's *The Dynamics of Modernization* (New York: Harper and Row, 1966), also represented here, in selection two. A shorter account written with the hand of an expert but on a high level of generalization is E. A. Shils's *Political Development in the New States* (S'Gravenhage: Mouton, 1962). Marion J. Levy's two-volume *Modernization and the Structure of Societies* (Princeton, N.J.: Princeton University Press, 1966) is an exhaustive treatment. Volume 358 of the *Annals of the American Academy of Political and Social Science* (March 1965), entitled *New Nations: The Problem of Political Development*, embodies a number of significant articles, including Myron Weiner's analysis of political integration (selection five above).

On the specific topics covered in this book, the reader should consult the original texts of the excerpted selections for full statements of each of the arguments. In addition, the following books and articles are well worth consulting:

On *integration:* Claude Ake's *A Theory of Political Integration* (Homewood, Ill.: Dorsey, 1967) is a concise but well-argued work. A shorter statement is his "Political Integration and Political Stability: A Hypothesis," in *World Politics*, XIX, No. 3 (April 1967). Clifford Geertz presents a basic statement of the concept in his chapter, "The Integrative Revolution," in *Old Societies and New States* (Glencoe, Ill.: Free Press of Glencoe, 1963), which he edited on behalf of the Committee for the Comparative Study of New Nations of the University of Chicago. More specific studies include Ronald Cohen and John Middleton, eds., *From Tribe to Nation in Africa* (Scranton, Pa.: Chandler, 1970); and S. N. Eisenstadt, *Integration and Development in Israel* (New York: Praeger, 1970).

On *nationalism:* Rupert Emerson's *From Empire to Nation* (Cambridge: Harvard University, 1960) is the best account currently available with specific reference to the underdeveloped countries. A shorter statement by Emerson appears in "Nationalism and Political Development," in *Journal of Politics*, XXII (February 1960). On nationalism in general, Hans Kohn's *The Idea of Nationalism* (New York: Macmillan, 1944; republished in paperbound form, 1961) and C. J. H. Hayes, *The Historical Evolution of Modern Nationalism* (New York: 1931), are classics. Beyond these general works, the best accounts of nationalism in the third world are to be found in books dealing with specific countries or regions, such as *Arab Nationalism: An Anthology*, edited by Sylvia G. Haim, including her own insightful introduction (Berkeley: University of California Press, 1962); Henry Siegman, "Arab Unity and Disunity," *The Middle East Journal*, XVI, No. 1 (Winter 1962); Charles Cremeans, *The Arabs and the World* (New York: Frederick A. Praeger, 1963); Richard Cottam, *Nationalism in Iran* (Pittsburgh: University of Pittsburgh Press, 1964); F. Tachau, "The Face of Turkish Nationalism," *Middle East Journal*, XIII, No. 3 (Summer 1959); J. S. Coleman, *Nigeria: Background to Nationalism* (Berkeley: University of California Press, 1958); and others.

On *elites:* E. A. Shils's article, "The Intellectuals in the Political Development of New States," *World Politics*, XII, No. 3 (April 1960), has often been reprinted or excerpted. It is a definitive statement. There has also been much interest in the phenomenon of charismatic leadership, first delineated by Max Weber in the early twentieth century. See *Max Weber on Charisma and Institution Building: Selected Papers* edited and with an introduction by S. N.

Eisenstadt (Chicago: University of Chicago Press, 1968). Many observers feel that the frequent appearance of this type of leadership in the third world is no accident. Ann Ruth and Dorothy Willner attempt to explain why in "The Rise and Role of Charismatic Leaders," in *The Annals*, CCCLVIII (March 1965). For a fuller statement, see A. R. Willner, *Charismatic Political Leadership: A Theory* (Princeton, N.J.: Center for International Studies, Research Monograph No. 32, 1968). An interesting and interpretive account is Jean Lacouture's *The Demigods: Charismatic Leadership in the Third World.* (New York: Alfred A. Knopf, 1970).

On the *military:* the frequent appearance of military regimes in the third world has given rise to a spate of books and articles that seek to explain the phenomenon. John J. Johnson has edited a book of essays detailing the experience of specific regions and countries in *The Role of the Military in the Underdeveloped Countries* (Princeton, N.J.: Princeton University Press, 1962). A more general and also more succinct account is Morris Janowitz's *The Military in the Political Development of New Nations* (Chicago: University of Chicago Press, 1964). An interesting analysis covering both underdeveloped and developed nations is S. E. Finer's *The Man on Horseback* (New York: Frederick A. Praeger, 1962). W. C. McWilliams has edited a collection of essays under the title *Garrisons and Government* (Scranton, Pa.: Chandler, 1967).

On *education:* the Social Science Research Council's volume on *Education and Political Development*, edited by James S. Coleman (cited above), concentrates on the political ramifications of education. Of a more general nature is Don Adams and Robert M. Bjork, *Education in Developing Areas* (New York: David McKay, 1969).

On *political parties:* the Social Science Research Council series includes a volume edited by Myron Weiner and Joseph LaPalombara (*Political Parties and Political Development*), which includes chapters on both developed and underdeveloped countries and a comprehensive bibliography. Most studies on this subject, however, concentrate on specific cases. Examples are Myron Weiner's *Party Building in a New Nation: The Indian National Congress* (Chicago: University of Chicago, 1967) on India; Ruth Schachter Morgenthau's *Political Parties in French-Speaking West Africa* (London: Oxford University Press, 1964); Thomas Hodgkin's *African Political Parties* (Hammondsworth: Penguin Books, 1961); A. R. Zolberg's *Creating Political Order* (Chicago: Rand McNally, 1966); and Michael Suleiman's *Political Parties in Lebanon* (Ithaca: Cornell University Press, 1967).

On *economic development:* one of the most influential books has been W. W. Rostow's *The Stages of Economic Growth: A Non-Communist Manifesto* (Cambridge: Cambridge University Press, 1960). Rostow divides the process of economic development into five stages, the most crucial of which is the "take-off" stage, during which self-sustaining economic growth begins. Contrariwise, Albert O. Hirschman in *The Strategy of Economic Development* (New Haven: Yale University Press, 1958) argues that the economic development of the countries of the third world will not necessarily follow any predetermined pattern, but is more likely to take place in an inefficient and even haphazard manner, the advice of economic planners and international investment bankers to the contrary notwithstanding. A more popular account may be found in Robert L. Heilbroner's *The Great Ascent* (New York: Harper and Row, 1963), while those interested in the theoretical aspects of the subject may consult W. Arthur Lewis, *Theory of Economic Growth* (London: Allen and Unwin, 1955); *Theories of Economic Growth*, edited by B. F. Hoselitz (New York: The Free Press, 1960); or B. Higgins, *Economic Development* (New York: W. W. Norton, 1959).

Many third world leaders have recorded their own observations and theories over the past twenty years. They include Nehru, Nasser, Ho Chi Minh, and of course, Mao Tse-tung. A useful sampling of these writings is *The Ideologies of the Developing Nations*, edited by Paul Sigmund, rev. ed. (New York: Praeger, 1967).

In the late 1960s, a new body of literature appeared. Initially it took the form of a challenge to conventional ideas on American foreign policy which had evolved during the Cold War. Ultimately, however, even the notions of political development and modernization presented in this volume were subjected to fundamental criticism. The selections by Manfred Halpern and Robert L. Heilbroner reflect this new critical approach. Halpern is developing his ideas more fully in a work to be published in 1972. Among representative titles in this genre are the following: Gar Alperovitz, *Cold War Essays* (New York: Doubleday Anchor, 1970), especially Chapter VI, "The United States, the Revolutions and the Cold War: Perspective and Prospect"; Norman Miller and Roderick Aya, *National Liberation: Revolution in the Third World* (New York: The Free Press, 1971), which includes Halpern's essay; Stuart Hall, Raymond Williams, and Edward Thompson, "From *The May Day Manifesto*," in Carl Oglesby, ed., *The New Left Reader* (New York: Grove Press, 1969); Eqbal Ahmad, *Revolution and Reaction in the Third World* (forthcoming); and Eric R. Wolf, *Peasant Wars of the Twentieth Century* (New York: Harper and Row, 1969).